Cannibalism, Headhunting and Human Sacrifice in North America

Cannibalism, Headhunting and Human Sacrifice in North America

A HISTORY FORGOTTEN

George Franklin Feldman

Alan C. Hood & Co., Inc.
Chambersburg, Pennsylvania

Published by:

Alan C. Hood & Co., Inc.
P. O. Box 775
Chambersburg, PA 17201
www.hoodbooks.com

ISBN-10: 0-911469-33-8

ISBN-13: 978-0-911469-33-2

Manufactured in the United States of America

Interior design by Sans Serif, Inc., Saline Michigan

Cover design by James F. Brisson

Library of Congress Cataloging-in-Publication Data

Feldman, George Franklin, 1930-
   Cannibalism, headhunting and human sacrifice in North America : a history forgotten / George Franklin Feldman
         p.   cm.
   Includes bibliographical references and index.
   ISBN 978-0-911469-33-2
      1.   Indians of North America--Warfare. 2.   Indians of North America--Rites and Ceremonies. 3.   Cannibalism--North America. 4.   Headhunters--North America. 5. Human sacrifice--North America. 6.   Violence--North America. 7.   North America-- History. I. Title
   E98.W2F45 2008
   970.004'97—dc22
                                                          2007049463

This work is dedicated to Ernest Scott, a very patient and talented editor who for over five years erased commas, indented quotations and corrected my grammar and focus when I wandered astray.

And to James Hiller, friend, publisher and entrepreneur, who pursued this project from idea to manuscript to first printing.

Most of all, I dedicate this work to my beloved daughter Eva.

Contents

Basketmaker rock art at Butler Wash in the San Juan River Basin in Utah. Photo by George F. Feldman.

Must we forever continue to accept the
wild and impracticable theories of parlor
readers on Indian character?

JOHN CREMONY
1868

But, after all, the final moral estimate of a
tribe or nation is a thing that no other tribe
or nation is competent to undertake. It will be
made by different individuals differently,
depending on the standards, environment, and
prejudices, or, on the other hand, the sympathetic
appreciation of the person acting as judge.

JOHN R. SWANTON
1911

Preface

When I was a young country boy living in Southern Indiana near the Angel Mounds site, one day, a tall, very impressive man gave me a teaspoon and allowed me to move dirt around a dark spot in the soil. He told me the stain was what remained of a post implanted five hundred or more years ago. He was Dr. Glenn Black. When my spooning became hazardous to the site, I was allowed to hang around and watch the field archaeology students from Indiana University find wonderful things in the yellow clay. It was my favorite place to go in those pre-teen years.

My contacts with Glenn Black gave me a hero, and an all-consuming desire to become an archaeologist, even though I couldn't spell the word. Had those boyhood years been spent elsewhere, I am certain that I would not have had the interest in early American history necessary to prod along for years on this project.

I've been greatly influenced by two other prominent archaeologists: Dr. Stuart Streuver and Dr. William D. Lipe. Stuart invented avocational archaeology, first in Illinois and later as the founder of the Crow Canyon Archaeology Center in Cortez, Colorado. Bill Lipe is professor emeritus at Washington State University, and a leading authority on Southwestern archaeology.

A persistent problem facing any writer or student of Indian and early American history is the correct spelling of Indian tribal, proper, and place names. I have used John R. Swanton's *The Indian Tribes of North America*, published by the Bureau of American Ethnology, as my spelling guide. Swanton, however, does not always use the same spelling as contemporary Indians, so in a few cases of proper names, I have deviated from Swanton and used the current Indian spelling.

In the effort to respect blocks of American citizenry, ethnic and racial nomenclature is constantly being revised, often from racial designations to multi-geographical names, i.e., Negro to African-American. The nomenclature used by non-native Americans is frequently criticized, particularly when American indigenous peoples are called "American Indians," a phrase many Indian activists do not believe is appropriate, since it literally designates Americans who originated in India. Issue is also taken with the anthropological terms "tribes and tribelets," since the words have a primitive connotation. Here the word "nation" is preferred, but that, too can be inaccurate, since it implicitly infers political organization. In this text, "tribes" are culture-sharing units, which may or may not be politically organized.

In the pages that follow, clarity is given preference over sensitivity. Native Americans are called Indians, American Indians, American aboriginals, American indigenous peoples and by pluralized tribal names—Pawnees, Navajos, etc.—as they are appropriate to the text and to the comprehension of the reader.

I have borrowed heavily from the encyclopedic knowledge of historian John Upton Terrell and in several instances used his excellent book *American Indian Almanac* to guide my research. I also used Utley and Washburn's *Indian Wars* as a primary source document for the Pequot wars.

The work of George Foster and Walter Goldschmidt, heavily quoted in the chapter on the Yuki and Kato Indians of California, was published by the American Folklore Society and is reprinted by permission of the society from the *Journal of American Folklore* 52:204, 1939, and is not for further reproduction.

Librarians throughout North America provided invaluable aid and direction in finding those obscure, out-of-print books and publications I sought. The Indianapolis-Marion County Central Librarians gave me access to rare volumes of *Jesuit Relations*, the source of much of the content of the chapter on the Iroquois Indians. My thanks to the staff of the Library of Rhode Island History, a treasure trove of early colonial history, for assistance on material on King Phillip's war. Patricia Capone of the Peabody Museum of Archaeology and Ethnology at Harvard University was very helpful in providing information about Anasazi Basketmaker human remains from early expeditions.

I am heavily indebted to the groundbreaking work of Lawrence H. Keeley, Professor of Anthropology at the University of Illinois. Keeley wrote *War Before Civilization, The Myth of the Peaceful Savage* (Oxford University Press, 1996), which I discovered half way through the writing of this book. His scholarly approach to the *Myth of the Peaceful Savage* provided the encouragement and affirmation I required to dig deeper and deeper into the real history of North America.

GEORGE FRANKLIN FELDMAN

Introduction

During a rock art expedition in the San Juan River basin, I offered a young lady an unsolicited explanation of what seemed to be a head grasped in the hand of a huge anthropomorphic figure pecked out of the soft stone of a cliff face. I casually said, "The Basketmakers were headhunters, you know." The young lady looked at me with incredulity and said, "Not true. American Indians were not headhunters." She was quite emphatic, and since I had to be with her and the other members of the expedition for another five days, I let the matter rest. Nothing would have happened, I suppose, if she had not written me several months later to say that she had discussed my claim with a history professor. The history professor had reassured her that the practice of head hunting did not exist at any time in North America.

The history professor was spewing sanitized history, a bane of modern education. We neglect true history when we hide the uniqueness of the varied cultures that evolved during the thousands of years before Europeans invaded North America. We further compound the negligence and abandon truth when we gloss over the clashes between Native Americans and Europeans, encounters of parties equally matched in barbarity.

I began to compile a list of cultural anomalies and conflicts specific to North America, which have been hidden from the history-reading public. After paring the list to thirteen topics, I began a search of contemporary and early American journals, books, and letters, a research project that took me from ocean to ocean.

As I delved into ritualistic practices that were extensively recorded by early explorers and missionaries (though little known), I became extremely cautious. I was familiar with the old etchings and woodcuts circulated in Europe after Columbus, showing Indians as ape-like monsters, tearing apart and devouring their enemies. I knew, too, the prevalent belief of the period that natural man, the primitive who was not Christian, was little more than a beast of the forest. The ironies of North American culture clashes were all around me. Though aboriginal Americans practiced headhunting, human sacrifice, and cannibalism, they did not advance as far culturally and scientifically as their tormentors, after all they hadn't slaughtered the Moors in the

Crusades, or invented the guillotine or the rack or eye gouging, and they had no Inquisition.

I began to synthesize the research, ever questioning whether the subject matter was too strong, too violent, too disturbing for even the most avid history buff. I decided early that the most gruesome of the violent incidents should be presented in the same words I found them, to give the questioning reader both the source and the verbatim account. Sources I have used and sources quoted I believe are true accounts of real events.

Slowly, as I began to write, I realized that this book related incidents, horribly violent incidents, of a very long, continuous, continental war, a war that began sometime before 100 B.C. and did not slow down until the "red men" were forcibly placed in concentration camps, inappropriately called "reservations," under the Indian Removal Act of 1830. The last major battle of this war resulted in the surrender of the Apache Geronimo in 1886, ten years after Custer's defeat at Little Big Horn. The Great War lasted two thousand years.

A dictionary definition of war as open armed conflict between two countries or factions within a country is overly simplistic. Wars are events, and even though it is often difficult to determine when they actually started, there is always an end date. When an entire continent consisting of hundreds of tribal and sub-tribal groups with disparate religions, languages and customs are in open hostility, fighting, forming alliances, invading and retreating from territories, all at a tremendous cost in human lives, does the fact that there are many more than two or three opposing sides at any one time, make it less a war? If one group fights to satisfy a hereditary hate, while another group thousands of miles away is invading a new territory for food and fighting to stay alive, it is still a war, a war with fluid, ever changing enemies, rolling this way and that over a confused continent. It actually lasted longer than two thousand years, but finding a start date is impossible.

Recognizing that the giant battles and small skirmishes of two thousand years was but a single war fought by generations of warriors, first intra and intertribal, and near its end, interracial, allows a better understanding of the aggressive and vicious take-no-prisoners policy demanded by the conflicting cultures of the participants.

The prehistoric battles of North America have never made it to the history books.

There is a popular belief that Native Americans never fought among themselves before the time of the white man. It is an understandable misconception. I tested it in a library. A computer search of books with the subject content "Indians" and "War" in a respected public library produced 246 titles—fully one-third were about Custer, the remaining books covered the battles between the French and the Indians, the Spanish and the Indians, the British and the Indians, and, of course, the Euro Americans and the Indians. Terrible conflicts all—but the most devastating of Indian hostilities were between Indians and Indians and this Boolean search did not kick out a single book on the subject.

Long before the white Europeans knew a North American continent existed, Indians of the Northern Plains were massacring entire villages. One of the worst such massacres, and one of the most investigated (recorded in over twenty-six books and articles), dates to around A.D. 1325 and happened on what is now the Crow Creek Sioux Reservation in central South Dakota near the Missouri River. It is called the Crow Creek site. The people who were slaughtered were probably ancestors of the Arikara tribe. Who was responsible for the massacre is unknown. Archaeologists call the dwellers of the Crow Creek village "initial coalescent" peoples, because the era was a time when cultures in the northern plains seemed to be mixing. It is possible that as many as eight thousand people were living up and down the banks of the Missouri at the time, in numerous villages. The attackers could have been neighbors seeking food, or a group of Indians from the north, ancestors of the Mandan.

Whoever the attackers were, there is archaeological evidence that the village expected them. A huge fortification ditch, 1,250 feet long, had just been completed, or was in the process of completion, when the attackers struck. At least five hundred men, women and children were killed—and not just killed, but mutilated. Hands and feet were cut off, each body's head was scalped; the remains were left scattered around the village, which was burned.

Wild animals fed on the villagers until sometime later when they were all dumped into the fortification ditch and covered with clay brought up from the nearby Missouri River bottom. War was not new to these unknown people. At least two of them had been scalped before and survived; others had projectile points embedded in their bones, which had healed over. Other excavations at a site north of Crow Creek, Whistling Elk Village, also indicate that warfare in the plains was a way of life in the pre-history era of Middle America.

Crow Creek and Whistling Elk Village were not anomalous incidents. Twenty per cent of the burial remains found in the Channel Islands off the California coast show skulls that have been fractured or crushed during the period 1400 B.C. to A.D. 300, prior to the introduction of the bow and arrow. In the Santa Barbara channel region, the burial population of the Calleguas Creek site had ten percent of the population with evidence of death from arrows sometime after A.D. 500 when the bow and arrow was introduced to these populations. Thirty habitation excavations in the Northern San Juan River region, which includes the Four Corners area where the borders of Arizona, New Mexico, Colorado and Utah meet, show unquestioned evidence of warfare and violent death dating from before 500 B.C. to late A.D. 1200s.

Investigators searching for reasons for early tribal mass murders universally link warfare with weather. It is true that during the same period of the droughts in the Southwest, heat and lack of rain in the Plains must have put pressure on food resources. Examination of the skeletons found at Crow Creek show evidence of the lack of important vitamins and minerals.

Warfare intensified when the Europeans invaded the Americas and deceived, bought, fought and otherwise took land from the Indians. In the forty-five years after the Pilgrims landed at Plymouth Rock, the white population of New England grew to forty-thousand—double the population of the Indians. The Indians had difficult decisions to make; they could try to adapt to the new settlers' ways, they could fight for their lands and way of life, or they could pack up and move to areas they believed would be free from interference from the white man, his weapons and his intolerance. The same tribes used all three options, often. History tells us that none of these methods of survival worked very well.

It is difficult for us to imagine now, but population pressures became major factors around 1675 in many parts of the New World, and Indians began to migrate away from the dangers brought by the new invaders. Estimates on Indian population vary greatly; the painter George Catlin, who spent eight years among the Western and Southern Tribes in the early 1800s, thought there were about fourteen million Indians in North America at the time of the first white settlements. It is not difficult to find estimates as high as twenty million or as low as two, but most ethnologists today believe that Catlin was pretty close. While Catlin's number was a guess, scholarly analysis by Henry F. Dobyns in 1983 put the pre-Columbian Native American population at eighteen million in the lands north of the Rio Grande River. Kirkpatrick Sale in *Conquest of Paradise* estimated fifteen million. (Chapter 14 deals with population issues and genocide.)

These numbers are small by our skyscraper lifestyle, but just about the right density for the hunting, gathering and farming existence of the American aboriginal. Except for a few tribes in the Northwest, individual Indians did not own land; tribes had "territories" in which they were dominant and which they either gave permission or not to migrating groups to settle as they were pushed ever westward. Intertribal conflict caused by movements into claimed territories intensified. Indian fought Indian, and it was the white man's fault.

Yet, long before any white explorers came, the Calusa Indians of southern Florida extended their territories from the Keys to Tampa Bay through warfare. The tribes of the plains were known to muster up to five hundred warriors for intertribal strife. The Crow Creek site is just one example of their destruction. And the major massacres discovered in the ruins of prehistoric Basketmaker habitats mean that from 100 to 150 warriors went on rampages of killing and scalping, an extremely large number for what had to be a very small total area population. Another misconception that wormed its way into popular history was created when early white settlers, traders and adventurers assumed that the different Indian tribes with their differing style dwellings, clothing, ornaments, customs and languages were met where they had always lived. Early reporters of Indian life did not realize that the populations around them were always shifting, tribes merging one into another, tribes pushing others away as they migrated into previously settled territory. Almost every tribe's oral history has it coming from somewhere else at some early time before the Europeans arrived. Many of these migrations were the cause of warfare, for they were invasions.

While it is easy to claim that population migrations caused wars, it is far more difficult to posit a reason for the migrations before the European invasion. One reason must have been population explosions resulting from technological innovation—better ways to store and preserve food, more efficient weapons and hunting techniques, the introduction of new crops. Or population growth could come from an unusually long span of years with perfect growing conditions. In short, good times. Good times mean more people, and more people create a desire for more territory. The opposite must also be true. Deprived, starving societies left drought-dry lands in search of more food and a better life.

On top of this, however, one must add a history and tradition of war. War for fun. The pioneering anthropologist George Bird Grinnell, writing about the Cheyenne, explained, "the chief motive [for war] was the love of fighting, which was instilled . . . from early youth. From their earliest days boys were taught to long for the approbation of their elders, and this approbation was most readily to be earned by success in war. The applause of their public was the highest reward they knew."

If population growth (European and Indian), deprivation and starvation, and an instilled aggressiveness combined with love of fighting are root causes of territorial invasions—migrations—the conflicts they produced evolved to a repetitious pattern of vengeance between the two or more enemies long after territorial ambitions had been satisfied. Each death, each injury, each insult was avenged, so the war never ended.

Large bands of screaming Indians with tomahawks, lances, bows and arrows charging down a hill to confront the enemy, their feather bonnets flying in the wind, while the chief, mounted on his pinto pony, watched from above, is the stuff of Hollywood. There were large battles, but they were exceptions.

What really happened during those two thousand years can be deduced from a little known archaeological site in Illinois, called Norris Farms # 36.

In the late prehistoric period around the year 1300, a small group of Oneota Indians moved from their central group to establish a small village in what is now west-central Illinois in the Illinois River valley. They were sedentary villagers, farmers, and hunters who also gathered wild plants and nuts. They settled, it appears, in a no man's land, adjacent to, or actually in the territory of a tribe of the Mississippian culture. As with most villages in the plains, the Oneotas had a well-planned, large cemetery, which was used for several decades. Archaeologists from the Illinois State Museum excavated the site. What they found has been found in hundreds of sites in North America that date to the pre-European contact period. One-third of the 246 burials in this cemetery were the remains of men and women who died violently. Some had broken arms and collapsed faces indicating an attempt at defense from a frontal attack, others had huge holes in the rear of their heads where they were struck with stone axes, and some skeletal remains had no heads at all. This is not a massacre site where the dead were thrown into a mass grave. The Norris Farms #36 graves of those who violently died are spaced randomly near the remains of other villagers who died natural deaths, leading to a conclusion that those killed were not the victims of a single or even several battles, and were not buried at the same time.

This was chronic warfare, two or three villagers planting corn or harvesting a crop, cut off from the protection of the village population, suddenly attacked, killed, and left to the preying animals of the forest. A victim may have been a hunter, wandering away from the village, stalking deer or smaller animals.

The fear of attack and the serious loss of men and women who provided much of the food for the Oneota group had a significant deleterious effect on the health of the population. Examination of the skeletal remains of those who died from natural causes indicates nutritional deficiencies, infectious diseases and possibly tuberculosis. The Oneotas probably remained in the Illinois River basin as long as they could; it was the richest land around.

Insidious endemic warfare over long periods in thousands of small settlements across North America defined tribal enemies and fed the fire of hostility that flared when Europeans began pushing the aboriginal Americans further west.

Head hunting, cannibalism and human sacrifice were the institutionalized by-products of this long conflict.

Most American school and popular history books have no mention of human sacrifice or headhunting, and the only reference to cannibalism concerns a stranded wagon train of California-bound starving settlers. It is understandable. For when the subject goes beyond the usual horrors of war to human sacrifice, cannibalism and headhunting in North America—not the occasional aberrant incident by deranged individuals, but the institutionalized, socially acceptable practices of cultural groups—the records are hidden in the journals of archaeology, the letters and reports of early missionaries, and in the storage bins of museums. The material is not easy to find, but it is there for those who seek it.

The most difficult subject to treat in these pages has been cannibalism. The practice is so repugnant to modern man that one anthropologist—William Arens—has written a book titled *The Man Eating Myth* questioning the existence of human cannibalism as it is popularly understood. There are only a few examples of starvation cannibalism included here, and as gruesome as they are, most modern men and women understand, if not sympathize, with the conditions that created the act. Cannibalism practiced as the highest form of hate and vengeance is more difficult to comprehend. Yet, you will find it often in the real history of North America. In any study of cannibalism real or feared, one must remember "Cannibalism was *supposedly* the trait that characterized those parts of the world into which the torch of civilization had not yet shown"[1] and was often used as an excuse to exploit the "savages."

Even the suggestion of cannibalism in historic or prehistoric North America raises the ire of many American Indians, historians and anthropologists, and the inclusion of the subject in this work was not done without considerable research. It became obvious that many charges of cannibalism were made from ignorance or fear—two chapters mention cannibalism when the subject group has been accused of the practice: the chapter on the Nootka (Mowachaht), and the chapter on the Kato and Yuki of California are good examples. The evidence against these tribes is slight indeed, certainly controversial and highly questionable.

Two chapters in this book are about Euro Americans. Although much has been written of late about the cruelty and injustice inflicted on Native Americans, little attention has been focused on the subjects of these chapters: Puritans cutting off the heads of Indians and publicly displaying them for years as they rotted, and the shame of the Southwest, when bounty hunters—large gangs of thugs—collected the scalps of Indian men, women and children, all redeemable for cash from local governments. These events have been glossed over as an embarrassment to the American story. I must admit that I have never believed the Pilgrim story of mutual aid and friendship with the Indians; that these pious pioneers collected the heads of Indians came as no revelation to me.

Readers may not be surprised at the cruelty of the Puritans nor of the scalp hunters, but they may be surprised and outraged to discover that the early American Indian was not quite the Indian depicted in Disney movies. The prehistoric Native American was no different than early warring peoples everywhere. He fought and killed without mercy, took heads from his enemies and proudly displayed them, ate the young children of his enemies as he fled, captured young maidens and sacrificed them, stripped the flesh from tortured captives for feasts, and threw babies into sacrificial fires to mollify his gods. Of course, no single tribe was responsible for all of these cruelties, yet they happened—regularly.

For me, discovering the underside of our history has banished the mythic and fictive illusions portrayed by guilt-ridden idealists and erased the compulsion to go easy on my subjects simply because there have been no people in recorded history so badly treated by invaders. (Had there been war crime tribunals during the first four hundred years after Columbus, more than half of the American presidents, all of the early colonial authorities, and every general would have been tried and probably convicted of crimes against humanity for what they did to the American Indian.)

Even the on-scene, eye-witness reports of the good Jesuit Fathers who lived with the Indians are tinged with the prevalent beliefs of sixteenth and seventeenth century philosophers who considered Indians just a short step up the staircase of evolution from a dangerous, raging, irrational animal. The Spanish explorers thought nothing of cutting off the heads of neck-chained Indian prisoners if they fainted or were ill, because it was easier than shearing off the locks, and the prisoners were not "human," after all. Immanuel Kant claimed that the basic ground for inhumanity is the treatment of people as "objects." The Spanish believed non-Christian peoples *were* objects. Not very many years earlier in their own country, the Spanish were given permission by the Church to take the heads of the Moors and display them on their wagons and spears during the campaign to oust the African invaders from the Iberian Peninsula. Yet these are the people who wrote the history of first contact with Native Americans. They wrote, I suggest, more or less accurately about the events they reported, but they were hardly innocent themselves, and the events they reported were those that reinforced their ethnocentric racial bias.

In the history of North America, greed, ignorance, and racial prejudice have been intrinsic elements of what has been called "the progress of civilization." War was an integral part of the culture of primitive society, and the wholesale slaughter of men, women and children of all ages is recorded in the graveyards of history. Rising above these aggressive behaviors, we abhor them and codify our laws to forbid them, but in so doing, we have also implicitly forbidden recognition that they ever happened. Anthropologist Lawrence Keeley calls it "the pacification of the past."

GEORGE FRANKLIN FELDMAN
Naples, Florida

1

Temples of the Sun —
The Taensa and Natchez

The French explorer La Salle—René Robert Cavelier, sieur de, to give him his due—had explored the Great Lakes region from his base in Montreal since 1669. In 1682, he descended the Mississippi River to the Gulf of Mexico, claiming the whole Mississippi Valley for Louis XIV and naming it Louisiana for his patron. Close to the end of his 1682 expedition to the lower Mississippi, he fell ill north of present day St. Joseph, Louisiana. So the first Europeans to visit the Taensa were his close associates: Henri de Tonti, second in command, and a Roman Catholic missionary, Friar Zenobius Membre.

Emissaries of the great chief of the Taensa led the party on foot and by canoe to a village of permanent structures that amazed the French explorers. The walls of the chief's house, a foot thick, were topped by a dome rising fifteen feet. Tonti later wrote that the house was located near a similar building decorated with wood carvings of eagles facing east, a holy place to the Indians called the Temple of the Sun. The temple was enclosed in a mud brick wall with sharpened wood spikes that bore the decaying heads of enemies who had been sacrificed to the Sun God. Outside the temple there was a large shell surrounded by scalps with braided hair, which Tonti believed to be the last remains of other sacrifices.

Tonti and Membre were seasoned explorers familiar with the atrocities of the Iroquois and the Huron in the north, so their writings of this event express little surprise or astonishment over the evidence of human sacrifice. What appears to have impressed them most was the workmanship, size and permanence of the buildings and the discovery of guns, breastplates, knives and sabers in the temple. The Taensa claimed that they had found these things, and that they came from an army that had crossed the Mississippi and disappeared into the sky, but at a time so long ago that not even the oldest member of the tribe could recall it.[1] The only European group that history records in the lower Mississippi valley prior to La Salle was the ill-fated army commanded by Hernando De Soto, who died near the river in 1542, 140 years before the Frenchmen discovered the rusty remnants of the Spaniards' destructive journey across the southeastern North American continent.

Both the Taensa and their linguistic cousins, the Natchez, told early explorers how large and great their peoples had been, and explained that their small population in the 1600s was caused by a great plague which they believed was punishment for once allowing the eternal log fire in their temple to go out. It is far more probable that they had contact with other tribes who carried the smallpox virus introduced by De Soto's army 140 years earlier.

When the chief of the Taensa learned that LaSalle was ill and could not travel, he decided to visit the white man's camp on the river. Friar Membre later wrote of this:

> The chieftains have much greater power and authority than among any of our Indians. They command and are obeyed. They have valets to wait on them at table. Food is brought to them from the outside. Their drink is served to them in a cup that has been rinsed, and no one drinks from it except themselves.[2]

Describing the procession to the French camp, Membre wrote that

> The Chief sent his master of ceremonies with five or six servants who swept with their hands the path by which he was to come, prepared a place for him, and spread a carpet over it in the form of a reed mat, very delicately and artistically woven. This chief was dressed in a very beautiful white cloth. Two men preceded him ceremoniously carrying feather fans. No man has ever carried himself with such gravity as this chief during this visit.[3]

1758 sketch by early French explorer DuPratz of the Sun God (chief) of the Natchez Tribe transported on a litter.

LaSalle and his men met most of the tribes of the Lower Mississippi, but his references to the Natchez are scant, and are often confused with the Taensa. The Natchez were a much larger tribe whose principal village was on the eastern side of the river along St. Catherine's Creek, just east of the present Mississippi city that bears their name. Tonti, who lived until 1704, estimated that the tribe had fifteen hundred warriors in 1668, and no more than a thousand in 1698.[4]

This shrinking population occupied nine or ten villages strung out along the creek; the Great Village, or principal village, was probably the one known as Naches, from which we derive their tribal name. Pierre Le Moyne d'Iberville, who later explored the Mississippi delta for the French and finally discovered the mouth of the river at the Gulf of Mexico, knew the Natchez well. In 1700 he wrote: [Their] "chief is a man 5 feet 3 or 4 inches tall, rather thin, with an intelligent face. He appeared to me the most absolute savage I had seen, as beggarly as others, as well as his subjects, all of whom were large, well-formed men, very idle, but showing much friendship toward us." [5]

During a visit to the Taensa the same year, Iberville happened to arrive when the temple was burning from a lightning strike. He saw five infants thrown into the fire to appease the Sun God.[6] Infant sacrifice was common among the tribes living along the Gulf Coast. The Natchez had a particularly cruel practice that was based on their strict caste system. Members of the ruling family were called Suns. Below them were the Nobles, and below the

Nobles were the Honored People, who in turn, were above the common people, the Stinkards. (Stinkard is a literal English translation of the Natchez word for the common class.)

Movement upward in this system was accomplished through marriage or notable and heroic action. Confusing the hierarchal structure even further, Suns, Nobles and Honored People could only marry Stinkards, and titles and privileges descended from the mothers, never the fathers. The Great Chief of all of the Natchez was the son of a Sun mother and Stinkard father. He, too, could only marry a Stinkard wife, and none of their children could inherit the Sun title or the kingship because the next-in-line had to have a Sun mother. The next ruler could be the son of the past ruler's sister.

A climb from Stinkard to the Honored People level could be achieved during the death ceremonies of a ruling Sun. At least four early French clerics and explorers describe this practice. This is how Dumont de Montigny, who lived among the Natchez for eight years, put it:

> Here is still another means by which a Stinkard, provided he is married, may attain to the rank of the Honored. If this Stinkard, at the death of the great chief of the nation, has a child at the breast, or at any rate of very tender years, he repairs with his wife and his child to the cabin where this chief is laid out. As soon as they have arrived there the father and mother wring the neck of their infant, which they throw at the feet of the body, as a victim which they immolate to the manes of their chief. After this barbarous sacrifice they roll between their hands some twists of Spanish beard [Spanish moss], which they put under their feet, as if they would signify by that they are not worthy to walk on the earth, and in this condition they both remain standing before the corpse of the great chief without changing their positions or taking nourishment all day.
>
> During that time the cabin is visited by all kinds of persons who come, some from curiosity, others to see one time more the one who had governed them and to desire him a good passage. Finally, when the sun has set, the man and the woman come out of the cabin and receive the compliments of all the warriors and Honored men, to the number of whom they have been added by the strange and cruel ceremony.[7]

It is noted in other literature of the period that the man and wife who sacrifice a child for the funeral rites of a Sun eliminate themselves as potential victims in future sacrificial ceremonies.

Jean Babtiste Le Moyne, sieur de Bienville, sometimes referred to as Jean Bienville, was Iberville's younger brother who spent several years exploring the lower Mississippi after Iberville left the territory, and who eventually became the first governor of French Louisiana. He had in his company a carpenter—who today would be titled "engineer" or "architect"—by the name of Andre Penicaut. Penicaut spent time among the tribes visited by Bienville and became a serious recorder of their customs and history. Sometime around 1704 he wrote a firsthand account of the funeral ceremonies of the Great Female Sun. Pierre Margry included the Penicaut narrative in his history of Louisiana:

> . . . we saw the burial ceremony, which is indeed the most horrible tragedy that one can witness. It made myself and all my comrades tremble with horror. She was a chieftainess, noble in her own right. Her husband, who was not at all noble, was immediately strangled by the first boy she had had by him, to accompany his wife into the great village, where they believe that they go. After such a fine beginning they put outside of the cabin of the great chief all that was there. As is customary they made a kind of triumphal car in the cabin, where they placed the dead woman and her strangled husband. A moment later they brought 12 little dead infants, who had been strangled, and whom they placed around the dead woman. It was their fathers and mothers who brought them there, by order of the eldest of the dead chieftainess' children, and who then, as grand chief, commands to have die to honor the funeral rites of his mother as many persons as he wishes. They had 14 scaffolds prepared in the public square, which they ornamented with branches of trees and with cloth covered with pictures." [8]

The practice of servants and followers of kings and queens following their leaders in death probably predates the pharaohs of ancient Egypt; it is not uncommon in strict hierarchical primitive cultures. With the Natchez, self-sacrifice during the burial ceremony of a king or queen was the fulfillment of a pledge made to the leader, and a high honor. Penicaut wrote that some of the men to be strangled in the burial ceremony of the queen or chieftainess knew of their fate ten years or more before they died. Each of the condemned plaited their own cords with which they would be strangled. Dressed in their best clothing, each holding a large shell and with their faces painted red, they stood on scaffolds with their nearest relatives, the relatives who would kill them so that they might follow the Sun to the village of the dead. The anointed relative, often the eldest son, carried a club and the strangulation cord. When the fourteen men who were to follow their leader in death moved from the platform to the temple and the house of the dead Sun Queen, their relatives walked behind them chanting a death song. Penicaut describes the ceremonial "march of the bodies," which began after four days of mourning:

> The fathers and mothers who had brought their dead children took them and held them in their hands; the oldest of these children did not appear to be more than three years old. They placed them to the right and left of the entrance to the cabin of the dead female chief. The 14 victims destined to be strangled repaired there in the same order; the chiefs and relatives of the dead woman appeared there all in mourning—that is to say, with their hair cut. . . . The unfortunate persons destined to death danced and the relatives of the dead woman sang.
>
> When the march of this fine convoy was begun by two and two, the dead woman was brought out of her cabin on the shoulders of four savages as on a stretcher. As soon as she had been taken out, they set fire to the cabin (it is the usual custom with the Nobles). The fathers who carried their dead children in their hands, marched in front, four paces distant from each other, and after marching 10 steps they let them fall to the ground. Those who bore the dead woman passed [walked] over [the bodies] and went around these children three times. The fathers then gathered them up and reassumed their places in the ranks, and at every 10 paces they recommenced this frightful ceremony, until they reached the temple, so that these children were in pieces when this fine convoy arrived. While they interred the female Noble in the temple the victims were stripped before the door, and, after they had been made to sit on the

ground, a savage seated himself on the knees of each of them while another behind held his arms. They then passed a cord around his neck and put the skin of a deer over his head; they made each of these poor unfortunates swallow three pills of tobacco, and gave him a draught of water to drink, in order that the pills should dissolve in his stomach, which made him lose consciousness; then the relatives of the deceased ranged themselves at their sides, to the right and left, and each, as he sang, drew an end of a cord, which was passed around the neck with a running knot until they were dead after which they buried them.[9]

During these funeral ceremonies twenty-five men, women and children were killed. Penicaut alleged that "the death of a chief sometimes costs the lives of more than 100 persons," a statement which later historians have questioned.

Their eagerness to join their chiefs in afterlife obviously contributed to the eventual extinction of the Natchez and Taensa. According to their own myths, when the ceremonial eternal fire in the temple was allowed to go out, and was secretly re-lit with "profane" fire, immediately sickness took hold of the Suns. In a few days, they were seen to die in rapid succession, and it was necessary to send after them into the world of spirits many people to serve them. This mortality lasted four years, without anyone being able to guess what had occasioned it. Nine Great Suns who succeeded each other died in this interval, and a multitude of people with them.[10]

When the guardian of the temple who re-lit the fire to hide his great error in allowing it to go out became sick himself, he confessed to the Great Sun:

> I am going to die, so it makes no difference to me whether
> the sickness or a man kills me. I know that I am a bad man
> for having for so long a time concealed, in order to preserve
> my life, what I am going to tell you. I am the cause of the
> death of my nation, therefore I merit death, but let me not
> be eaten by the dogs.[11]

After this confession, the Great Sun gathered the elders about him and to-gether they resolved to get sacred fire from another temple. "That was exe-cuted and the Suns ceased dying." The speaker was a guardian of the temple who explained to Le Page Du Pratz, a Frenchman who lived among the

Natchez, why the fires were so important. The disease that killed so many and caused so many others to be killed to go with them was probably the white man's smallpox.

Du Pratz wrote:

> I wished to know first of the guardian of the temple what he and his fellow countrymen thought of God . . . he . . . told me that God was so powerful that all things were nothing before him, that he had made all that we see, and that we are able to see; that he was so good that he was not able to do harm to anyone even if he wished it; that he thought that God had made all things by his will; that nevertheless the little spirits who were servants of God might, indeed, at his order have made in the universe the beautiful works which we admire, but that God himself had formed man with his own hands.[12]

He told Du Pratz that God had formed man out of clay and breathed on him and he received life. Given a God, there must be a son, a brother, or a prophet of that God who descends to the earth to teach men and women how to live. For the Natchez, life revolved around the story of the first Sun, the myth of the beginning of the ruling family, and faithful adherence to the caste system.

Du Pratz's rendering of the guardian's explanation continues:

> A very great number of years ago there appeared among us a man and his wife who had descended from the Sun. It is not that we thought that he was the son of the Sun or that the Sun had a wife by who he begot children, but when both of them were seen they were still so brilliant that it was not difficult to believe that they had come from the sun. This man told us that having seen from above that we did not govern ourselves well, that we did not have a master, that each one of us believed that he had sufficient intelligence to govern others while he was not able to guide himself, he had taken the determination to descend in order to teach us how to live better.
>
> He then told us that in order to be in condition to govern others it was necessary to know how to guide one's self, and that in order to live in peace among ourselves and

please the Supreme Spirit it was necessary to observe these points: To kill no one except in defense of one's own life, never to know another woman than one's own, to take nothing that belongs to another, never to lie or become drunk, and not to be avaricious, but to give freely and with joy that which one has, and to share food generously with those who lack it.[13]

It appears that the elders met and decided that this man must be their king. When he agreed, he set the conditions that structured their society. There is another myth, though, that seems to have credence. This story says that a relative of the Great Spirit came to earth to be the chief of all people, but he became so powerful that he made men die just by looking at them. To spare his subjects, he turned himself into stone and asked to be always in the temple. All Suns who came after him were spirits descended from the stone image in the temple. Several early French visitors were allowed into the temple, but were not allowed to look into the baskets and boxes strewn around one side of the building. It is reasonable to assume that the idol was stored before any but the chiefs or guardians were allowed to enter. In 1925, specialists from the Bureau of Ethnology of the Smithsonian Institution interviewed four Indians who were then living with the Cherokees in Oklahoma and who spoke the Natchez language. They told the interviewers that their fathers had told them that they were the only tribe in the United States that worshiped a stone idol.[14]

If the Natchez believed "to kill no one except in defense of one's own life," it was not reflected in their methods of warfare. Like many of the woodland tribes to the north of them, they warred by stealth, gathering a band of from twenty to thirty warriors that timed its marches to be at the edge of the enemy village before sunrise. They chose one or two cabins to attack while the inhabitants were asleep. Du Pratz again:

They enter it at daybreak and with the assistance of the fire which burns there all night. The warriors who attack knock down the men as fast as they awake and endeavor to carry one away living. They pull off the scalps of the dead, take the women and children, who do not dare to cry for fear of being killed, tie them all, and retire with as much rapidity as secrecy. Near this cabin they leave the hieroglyphic tablet [15]

leaning against a tree, and in front of this tablet they plant
two red arrows in the form of a St. Andrew's Cross. They
then pass back through the wood with great rapidity and
make many turns to conceal their route.

If they are able to carry away any of the enemies of
their nation they are received honorably. If these are women
or children they are enslaved. They serve in this capacity
after their hair has been cut extremely short. But if it is a
man that they have made prisoner the joy is general and
their glory is at its height. On arriving near their nation
they make the war cry three times repeated, and in this case,
however wearied the warriors may be, they go at once to
hunt for the three poles which are necessary for the construction of the fatal instrument on which they are going to
make the enemy they have taken die. I mean the frame
which they cruelly immolate the unfortunate victim of their
vengeance.

Du Pratz goes on to describe the pole structure, the two uprights and two
crossbars that became the standard sacrificial altar for warring tribes throughout North America. The victim was tied, upright and spread-eagled, totally
helpless and at the mercy of his captors. He knew he was about to die, and
sang what is often called "the death song," but which some observers have
described as the piercing screams and yowls of a frightened warrior. He knew
he not only would die, but that he would die in great pain.

First, his scalp was taken. Then, if conscious and able to eat, he was allowed his last meal. The warriors also ate before the torture-to-the-death ceremonies began.

When the warriors have finished their meal they come to
the place where the frame is planted to which the victim is
tied. They make him advance a little and turn his entire
body around in order that the people may see him. The one
who has taken him gives a blow of his wooden war-club
below the back part of his head, making the death cry. Having thus stunned him he cuts the skin around his hair, puts
his knees on his forehead, takes his hair in both hands, pulls
it from the skull, and makes the death cry while removing
the scalp in the best manner he is able without tearing it.

After the scalp has been taken from the victim, they tie a cord to each of his wrists, throw the ends of the cords over the upper crosspiece, which many take and draw in order to pull him up while others lift him, placing his feet on the crosspiece below and tying him to the corners of the square. They do the same to his hands at the upper corners of the square in such a manner that the victim in this position has his body free and entirely bare, and the four limbs form a St. Andrew's cross.

Most of the Natchez tribe lived near the present day city in Mississippi that bears their name, and it was here that many of the tortures occurred. It was a place of hills and lowlands, heavily forested then as today. Near the streams and bayous, canes and reeds grew in abundance, a valuable resource to mix with mud to construct their homes and temples. When a prisoner was to be punished, the canes and reeds served another more painful purpose.

They were bound together to make torches—firebrands to jab selectively and hold to the victim. When his scalp was ripped from his skull, the act signaled the tribe to gather material for more firebrands.

Du Pratz continues:

The one who took him is the first one to take a single crushed cane, light it, and burn the place he may choose. But he devotes himself especially to burn the arm with which he [the prisoner] had best defended himself. Another comes and burns another place. These, with their pipes filled with dried and burning tobacco, burn him about the foot. Those heat a nail red hot, with which they pierce his foot. All, in fact, one after the other, revenge themselves as best they are able on this victim, who, so long as strength remains to him, employs it in singing the death song. Some have been seen to suffer and sing continually during three days and three nights without anyone giving them a glass of water to quench their thirst, and it is not permitted to anyone to give it to them, even should they ask for it, which they never do, without doubt, because they know that the hearts of their enemies are inflexible. In fact, it must be admitted that if the natives are good friends during peace, they are in war irreconcilable enemies.

> It sometimes happens that a young woman who may
> have lost her husband in war, seeing the victim when he ar-
> rives entirely naked and without means of concealing his
> defects, if he has any, demands him for her husband, and he
> is granted to her on the spot. It also happens that when he
> suffers too long a pitying woman lights a cane torch, and
> when it is burning well makes him die in an instant by put-
> ting this torch to the most sensitive place, and the tragic
> scene is in this way ended.[16]

As cruel as the torture-to-death practice of the Natchez appears, it only differs in small detail from that of most of the tribes of the eastern half of the
North American continent. In fact, the death of prisoners by firebrands is one
of the few characteristics the Natchez shared with other tribes.

Early French visitors among the Natchez and the Taensa noted an absence
of deformed or seriously handicapped individuals. In many tribal groups as
early as the Neanderthals in Europe and Asia, seriously wounded, hunchbacked
or crippled individuals appear to have been taken care of by their relatives or
the entire tribe. This was not so among the Natchez and many other tribes in
the Lower Mississippi valley. Writing of a Yazoo warrior in extreme pain, possibly from arthritis, who loaded a musket and killed himself, Dumont de Montigny explained the lack of handicapped individuals this way:

> . . . when one among them has had the misfortune to have a
> leg or an arm broken, as they are very sure that their alexis
> [medicine men] have not the art of resetting it, and besides
> they have among them neither hunchbacks nor crooked
> people, they made a feast to the one who is thus crippled,
> and after some days of amusement they strangle him. [17]

Strangling their own also is reported by these early writers in their descriptions of the sex life of unmarried girls. John R. Swanton, the famous ethnologist, summed up the early literature on the subject this way:

> Chastity in unmarried girls was not valued and was nearly
> nonexistent. Looseness on the part of Natchez and Taensa
> women was particularly noted and commented upon by the
> first missionaries, and there was little in their dealing with
> the Frenchmen to improve them in this respect. Far from

being held in contempt, a girl was esteemed in proportion
to the dowry she could amass by the loan of her person. [18]

The French officer Dumont was incensed to see the young women rent themselves "as slaves and mistresses" to the French soldiers and traders. He claimed
that they lived with their masters for a month for a bolt of cloth worth about
sixteen pounds in the currency of the day. He decried the lack of religion or
laws that permitted "this libertinism . . . without shame and without scruple."
[19] That they would give themselves to one Frenchman and then another to
amass a large dowry was incomprehensible to Dumont.

Penicaut agreed. He watched the seductive dances of the unmarried girls
and blamed their "licentious" life on their parents. He wrote that their fathers
and mothers taught the girls that they would enter their heaven by walking
across a plank to the other world, and only the girls who have "disported
themselves" well with boys would make it.

He added:

> One sees the consequences of these detestable lessons,
> which are Instilled into them from their earliest years, sup-
> ported by the liberty and idleness in which they are kept,
> since a girl up to the age of 20 or 25 does nothing else, the
> father and mother being obliged to have her food provided,
> and yet in accordance with her taste and what she asks for,
> until she is married. If through these infamous prostitutions
> one becomes pregnant and is delivered of a child, her
> mother and father ask her if she wishes to have children; if
> she replies no, and they are unable to nourish it, they imme-
> diately strangle this poor little new-born child outside of
> the cabin and inter it, without its making the least impres-
> sion on them, but if the girl wishes to keep her child, they
> give It to her and she nourishes it. [20]

The Natchez did not know divorce. Once a couple married, they stayed so,
and even though there are reports of warriors lending their wives to visitors
and friends, it does not appear to have been a widespread practice.

Eventually, of course, this tribe and most of the others in the Lower Mississippi Valley came into conflict with the white invaders, and the French almost exterminated the Natchez in a series of wars. The survivors fled to other

tribes, many making it as far as Oklahoma where in the 1800s they were gradually absorbed into the Cherokee tribe.

Du Pratz made this point: "I am convinced that those who would see the true portrait of them. . .will be convinced with me that it is very wrong to call men savages who know how to make such very good use of their reason, who think justly, who have prudence, good faith, generosity much more than certain civilized nations who will not suffer themselves to be placed in comparison with them for want of knowing or wishing to give things the value they deserve."[21]

Du Pratz was a very understanding and charitable Frenchman. The Taensa and the Natchez were just two tribes of the death-cult group that ranged all along the lower Mississippi and around the Gulf Coast. Because North American Indians generally had great love for children and always tried to keep them out of harm's way, it is often speculated that the infanticide of the death cults came in some way from Mexico, where it was widely practiced. That theory is also used to explain the unusual culture of the Calusa.

2

"I Shall Receive You with Love and Charity"—The Calusa and Timucua

In the calm waters of Estero Bay near Fort Myers, Florida, there stands a small island that rises thirty-two feet above the water. This veritable mountain in a flat, swampy land is overgrown with black mangrove trees. It is accessible only by boat; a few tourists roam the mound on the island and listen to professional guides tell abbreviated tales of the people who once lived there: the Calusa.

The island is Mound Key, and it is generally acknowledged as the site of historical Calos, a royal city of over one thousand people, the capital city of the Calusa Indians.

The mounds on the island are shell middens, the trash heaps of millions of oyster shells, the garbage of centuries, redolent of the seafood diet of the Calusa. The mounds were built during the great religious revival of all of the tribes of the Gulf Coast—ranging from Texas to Florida—that began about A.D. 700. Archaeologists believe that on top of one mound the cacique's (chief, ruler) house and a temple were built. The cacique ruled an empire that included the area from slightly south of Tampa to around Lake Okeechobee and all the way to the Florida Keys. The capital was not always on Mound Key; there are shell mounds in Pine Island Sound, at Sarasota, on some of the Ten Thousand Islands, and throughout the Florida Keys. Some were ceremonial only, but others, particularly one of the mounds on Pine Island, probably served as the capital of the Calusa empire at some point in history. Today the mounds are hard to find because many have been leveled by the bulldozers of

A Calusa shell mound in the Ten Thousand Islands area of the Everglades in south Florida. Photo by George F. Feldman.

progress, but in the 1530s they were so prominent along the southwestern coast of Florida that one Spanish map demarcated the area "La Costa de Caracoles," The Coast of Shells.

Archaeologists trace a small population of Florida Indians back to the Paleo-Indian period, 12,000 years ago, when mastodons, mammoth, bison, giant ground sloths, saber-toothed cats, and giant armadillos—labeled megafauna—ranged across the peninsula. Large projectile points, called "clovis points," after those first found in 1932 around Clovis, New Mexico, have been discovered in the rivers of Florida. These two to three-inch shaped cert points are fluted to be affixed to a staff to make a spear or jabbing weapon, and they have been found with the bones of giant mammoth. These early big-game hunters were the ancestors of the tribes the Spanish encountered and fought in the early 1500s—conquistadors like Ponce de León, Alonzo de Pineda, and Panfilo de Narváez—men whose names now grace streets and parks in modern Florida.

Throughout great periods of climatic change in Florida one thing remained constant: there was always an abundance of food for the small nomadic population. As waters rose and temperatures changed, sand dunes became islands and plains became swamps. Food sources became more fixed as diets changed from big mammals to seafood. The nomadic populations eventually settled down and built small fishing villages on the riverbanks and islands. This process probably began as early as nine thousand years ago and continued sporadically through the archaic to the modern period as Florida developed into an estuarine environment. The number of Native Floridians gradually increased on the Gulf Coast, culminating with the population explosions of the Mississippian-mound and village-building era.

Among all of the early Spanish reports about the mounds, there is only one detailed description of a temple. The Indians called it the House of Mahoma. It was described as very tall and wide, and filled with mats on latticework seats. The interior walls were completely covered with masks that represented the gods of the Calusa. Every third night, the Calusa gathered in the Mahoma to dance and worship their deities. There were three principal gods: the god of nature, a god of rule and government, and a god of war.

There is an isolated place on Mound Key called the "water court," a low basin that the Calusa flooded by digging canals to it from the bay, thereby creating a calm spot to beach their canoes. One author described it as " . . . a magical place. The quiet is so intense that only occasional bird calls or insects making humming or clicking sounds break the stillness."[1] Some five hundred years ago, slim poles supporting bloody heads decorated the water court, a public showing of the punishment meted to those who opposed the will of the cacique, whose power was absolute. His power was so obvious to the early Spanish explorers and soldier-missionaries that they often referred to the ruler of the Calusa as the king. He wore a gold ornament on his forehead, and beads around his legs. To approach the king, the subject knelt and held out his outstretched hands palms up. The king then placed his hands on

Calusa Spirit Mask. Photo courtesy National Museum of Natural History—Smithsonian.

the subject's hands. Whether he was called king, chief, or cacique, there was no doubt that he was *the* ruler, a man of enormous power and prestige.

It was such a king who first chased Ponce de León from the western shores of Florida in 1513, just twenty-one years after Columbus's first voyage. Both Spaniards and Calusa were killed during these skirmishes between canoes and Spanish ships.[2]

Undaunted, Ponce returned in 1521 with two hundred men, horses, seed and livestock to establish a garrison and mission on what is now Pine Island in Charlotte Harbor.[3] He never completed the task. Attacked and routed by Calusa warriors, Ponce was wounded in the thigh by an arrow. During his return to Havana, the wound became gangrene infected, and he died shortly after going ashore. He was one of the first of many European victims of the religious and territorial ferocity of the Calusa.

Although there were other tribal groups in Southern Florida—the Ais, Matecumbe, Tequesta, Hobe, and Santaluces—historians claim that they were subjects of the Calusa, or at the very least, political and warfaring allies. Tempestuous Florida weather periodically sent Spanish ships into the shallows shortly after they began their voyages to Spain with their holds stuffed with loot from the Caribbean and Central and South America. When the ships wrecked, the Calusa and their allies relieved the Spanish of their tools, gold, silver, and slaves, and took captive the crew and passengers who survived. One of the few captives who later was freed, Hernano d'Escalante Fontaneda, wrote of how the Calusa cacique divided and distributed salvage to chiefs of vassal tribes.

"These things Carlos[4] [ruler of the Calusa] divided with the caciques of Ais, Jeaga, Guacata, Mayajuaco, and Mayaca, and he took what pleased him, or the best part."[5]

A memoir by Fontaneda, written in Spain about nine years after his release, provides the earliest glimpse into the ways of the Calusa. He was captured from a shipwreck around 1545 and spent twenty years with the tribe before he was freed in 1566. Fontaneda was only ten years old[6] when he was captured, and he learned the now-lost language of the tribe. In later years, he claimed, in fact, to speak four different Indian languages. He described the Calusa this way: ". . . the people are great anglers, and at no time lack fresh fish. They are great bowmen, and very faithless. I hold it certain they never will be at peace, and less will they become Christians."[7] He was the first to explain that their name in their own language meant "fierce people," and clearly he regarded the appellation as apt. In his description of their diet, he lists almost everything that swims or lives in the Gulf of Mexico and in the fresh and brackish water of the bays and rivers. He included alligators, and surprisingly, seals, which were found on the southeast coast of Florida until the nineteenth century.[8]

Fontaneda and the Cacique Carlos were about the same age, and in Fontaneda's *Memoir* he quotes Carlos as saying to him " . . . you well know that I like you much."

Fontaneda explained why shipwrecked Spanish were often executed soon after capture. The Indians ordered the captives to sing and dance. Not understanding the Calusa language, the frightened, uncomprehending prisoners could only stare back, which their captors interpreted as defiance. The Spanish were slaughtered on the spot.

Spending his youth and young adulthood with the Calusa, Fontaneda witnessed the murder and sacrifice of at least two hundred Spanish captives. He saw the annual sacrifice ceremony to the "God Who Eats Eyes," the beheading of the victim, and the frenzied dance that followed, wherein the shaman held the bloody head high for all to see. It is not unreasonable to assume that he participated in some of these ceremonies, including the sacrifice of babies and young children at the death of a child of the cacique or other leader. Yet nowhere in his *Memoir* did he provide details of these ceremonies; perhaps when he wrote, the details were considered common knowledge and he did not think them worth repeating, or, more ominously, the adopted young Spaniard was a participant, and in his later years, did not wish to divulge his intimate knowledge of the practices.

When archaeologist Clarence B. Moore excavated a burial mound on Pine Island in 1904, he found the complete remains of 41 individuals and 177 skulls. In 1928, 70 more skulls were found in a previously looted mound on Captiva Island. Both of these mounds appear to have been built before the Europeans arrived because no trade goods were found in either of them. Beheading and sacrifice were an important and ancient religious ritual of the Calusa. "On one occasion, more than fifty sacrificial heads lay at the base of a tree in the town of Carlos."[9]

Nothing is known of the activities of the Calusa from 1521 to around 1545, and the only information after 1545 to the mid-1560s comes from Fontaneda, who was released in a good will gesture by the Cacique Carlos to Pedro Menéndez de Avilés, the Spanish governor or "adelantado" of Florida at that time. Fontaneda became Menéndez's interpreter. Impressed by Spanish weapons and armor, and looking for allies to fight the Tocobaga, Carlos made Menéndez de Avilés his "big brother," and gave his sister to the Spanish governor to be his wife as a further demonstration of "friendship." Most of the history books that record this incident call it a mock wedding, and a few relate how Menéndez de Avilés sent Carlo's sister, who was renamed Dona Antonia, to Havana with an entourage of servants to be educated and converted to Christianity.

An interesting account of the events surrounding Menéndez de Avilés and Carlos's sister appears in a little known biography of Menéndez written by his brother-in-law, Gonzalo Solís de Meras, around 1567, a work that was translated and published by the Florida Historical Society in 1923.

After Carlos gave Menéndez his sister, the cacique suggested that the newlyweds retire to a private room and consummate the marriage. "The Adelantadeo showed a little perturbation, and said to him through the interpreter that Christian men could not sleep with women who were not Christians."

Carlos insisted, saying that if he were to take her and make her a Christian, she could return and help him become a Christian. "The Adelantado showed much desire to try some other expedient, but as none could be found, it was decided that thus it should be done . . . Then the Christian women who were there bathed and clothed her, and she appeared much better than before, when she was naked."

After a party of "music and merriment" in tents provided by Menéndez, "her Indian women and the Christian women danced with the soldiers, and when that was ended, they conducted her to rest on a bed which the Adelantado ordered to be made, and he followed her; and in the morning she arose very joyful and the Christian women who spoke to her said that she was *very much pleased.*"[10]

Menéndez had visited the Calusa to free the Christian prisoners he had heard were living there and to find his son who was missing from a shipwreck. Carlos agreed to give up the prisoners—nine Spanish men and women who had been living with the Calusa for almost twenty years after being captured from shipwrecks in the Florida Keys. But just before the ship sailed, two of the women turned back to the village, preferring to stay with their Indian husbands and children rather than go to Havana or Spain. The Christians who escaped said that Carlos and his father had sacrificed over two hundred Christian prisoners "to the devil, [with] their feasts and dances on those occasions; and that they were all people from shipwrecked vessels of the Carrera of Indies, because even though they were lost one hundred leagues from there, they were brought to him, as he was the cacique of much of the sea coast near Los Martires [Florida Keys] and the Bahamian Channel."[11]

Menéndez sent a small force of Spanish soldiers to establish a fort at the Calusa capital on Mound Key. When he returned and attempted to convince the Calusa to make peace with their traditional enemies, the Tocobaga, the new friendship chilled. Eventually, the Spanish moved their base to a nearby island. They had planned to have the Indians do it for them, but changed their minds and used their own boats because they feared the angered Calusa would drown them.

According to Francisco de Reinoso, the captain that Menéndez left in charge of the fort, Carlos made plans to kill the Spanish contingent after Menéndez departed in March, 1567.

Into this tense atmosphere stepped Father Juan Rogel, a Jesuit charged with the task of teaching and converting the heathen Indians to Christianity.

By this time, the Calusa were only tolerating the Spanish, and taking what food and gifts they could get from the invaders.

When Rogel condemned their religious idols, Carlos became furious. Rogel later wrote that, Carlos . . . "had a great hate for me especially because I discredited and spoke evil about his idols." Carlos was the son of the shaman or high priest of the tribe, and as cacique, was the interpreter of the will of their gods, and wanted no interference from a Spaniard. Whether it was because of his plots to kill the Spanish or his resistance to the evangelism of the Jesuit, we will never know, but for whatever reason, the captain of the Spanish garrison, Francisco de Reinoso, murdered Carlos. Carlos was invited to visit the captain, and when he paid the visit, he and the two aides who accompanied him were killed.

Carlos had been strong and unbending, controlling not only the Calusa, but most of the tribes whose land abutted Calusa territory. The new cacique, who had led a faction opposed to Carlos, was the son of the cacique who preceded Carlos; his name according to Spanish sources was Filipe, and he was installed with the backing of the Spanish garrison.

This new cacique was not well liked among the Calusa. Almost immediately, two village chiefs transferred allegiance to the hated Tocobaga. Rogel alleged that "were it not for the favor and support that he enjoys among the Christians, they would have killed him quite a while ago." [12]

It was Felipe who decorated the slender posts of the water court and the temple on Mound Key with freshly severed heads. More than fifteen minor Calusa village chiefs and headmen were beheaded because of Felipe's suspicions that they were making plots against him. Rogel saw one of the festivals where the celebrants danced around four newly severed heads.

Rogel worked hard to convert Felipe to Christianity in the belief that if he were to be successful with the cacique, all of the Calusa would follow. Felipe repeatedly promised to become a Christian, but only when Menéndez de Avilés returned. On one occasion, Felipe objected to Rogel's insistence that he have only one wife, and to Rogel's outrage over a Calusa custom that permitted Felipe to marry his own sister.

Rogel related the conversation in a report to his superiors:

> . . . and, consequently, he replied to me . . . my wanting to strip old men and men of adult age of all their customs and make them perfect Christians was not possible of

achievement . . . . I should content myself with his [prom-
ise of] forsaking and burning his idols and all the witchcraft that he has practiced up to now; that he would totally
remove the sodomites; that they would not kill children
even when his sons or he himself die or something he
likes very much . . . [13]

The Calusa practice of human sacrifice is well documented. In the archives of
the Indies in Seville, Spain, there are notes recorded by cosmographer Juan
López de Velasco in 1575, that he entitled *Memorial.*

About what happens in Florida concerning the Indians of
the same land. Those of Carlos firstly have as a custom each
time a son of the cacique dies each inhabitant sacrifices his
sons or daughters, who go in company of the death of the
cacique's son; the second sacrifice is that when the chief
himself or the chieftainess dies, they kill his or her own servants, and this is the second sacrifice.

   The third sacrifice is that each year they kill a Christian
captive so that they may feed their idol, which they adore in
[doing] it. That they say their idol eats human men's eyes.
And they dance with his head each year. They have this as a
custom.

   And the fourth sacrifice is that after the summer some
shamans come in the guise of the devil with some horns on
their head. And they come howling like wolves and many
other different idols, which make noises like animals from
the woods. And these idols are four months that they never
rest neither day nor night that they go running about with
great fury. That the great bestiality that they do is a thing to
tell about.[14]

Felipe was no more anxious to be converted from these old ways than Carlos
had been. He continued to lead his people in the old religion of human sacrifice to the colorfully decorated wooden masks that represented the gods of
his people. And then Felipe too was murdered by the Spanish. His successor
was the heir and first cousin of the murdered Carlos, a member of the ruling
family the Spanish called Pedro or Don Pedro. When it became obvious to
Menéndez that the strong-willed Calusa would not bow to Spanish authority

or religion, Menéndez proposed to Spain that he be allowed to take them as slaves and sell them to plantation owners in the Caribbean. The request was refused.

Velasco, writing about abandoned settlements and forts, told the story this way:

> The year of 1566 the adelantado Pedro Menéndez put a settlement in the Bay of Carlos on an islet that is in the middle [of the bay], with thirty-six houses encircled with brushwood faggots and lumber. This settlement lasted until the year of 1571. That, the Indians have rebelled against the Spaniards and having created problems for them, Pedro Meléndez Marqués, by order of the adelantado, beheaded the cacique along with twenty-two other leading Indians and abandoned the said fort.[15]

After the murder of two of their chiefs, the Calusa wanted no more of the Spanish invaders. The Indians burned their villages near the Spanish fort and fled to the interior of Florida and to islands further south. With no heathens to convert, the Spanish returned to Havana, and the Jesuits in Florida were transferred to Mexico. From that time to around 1612, the Calusa immediately killed any Spaniards or the survivors of any ship that wrecked in Calusa territory.

There is a record of a ship that sailed near Tequesta in 1574 where the captain and four men were killed with many other sailors wounded. [16]

A proposal by a Spanish official to build a fort in the Florida Keys in 1600 reflects the fear the Spanish had of the Calusa: "And the shipwrecked people who survive are killed by the Indians with terrible torments. And it is said even that they eat human flesh." [17] One historian agrees: "In warfare [the Calusa] habitually scalped and dismembered the bodies of wounded enemies, and sometimes ate human flesh." [18]

In the early 1600s, a new Carlos rose from the ghosts of Mound Key to rule over the Calusa, and the tribe was again as strong and as big as the days when it first faced off against Ponce de León. The tribe managed to remain isolated from the Spanish for over fifty years. When one Spanish expedition with Indian guides, porters, and warriors started out from settlements in the north in an attempt to find Cacique Carlos and ransom Spanish prisoners, they were warned by the chiefs in four separate villages that if they allowed the Spanish to continue, they—the chiefs—would be killed. Indians who accompanied the Spanish fled, and the expedition turned back. The Calusa never abandoned their old ways, but the religious zealots from Spain would not give up, either.

In October 1697, when five catholic priests came from Havana with "provisions and ornaments" for the Calusa, they placed their gifts in the cacique's hut. But he was seriously ill, near death. The dying Carlos allowed the friars to baptize him when they gave him provisions and gifts. As he lay dying, and after the missionaries had removed the gifts from the hut, they urged Carlos to take confession and "extreme unction" to be sure he died a Christian. The cacique summoned the strength to reply that he was not a Christian and that if he was a Christian because of four old rags that they had given him, he did not want his body to be lost, but to be buried where his ancestors were. According to Fray Feliciano López, "He died in obstinacy." [19]

The friars' troubles began in earnest when they went to the Mahoma in an attempt to interrupt the Indians' religious ceremonies. On their first trip to the building, the Indians scattered, but several days later, when the evangelists tried again, the Indians forcefully pushed the friars back, lifting and carrying one persistent robed Christian back to his hut. During this confrontation, an Indian smeared human feces on the face of one of the religious intruders.

Days later, as Fray Miguel Carrillo was preaching from the door of his hut, Indians threw mud in his face and ran. Other Indians created a first in American history when they turned their backs on the friar, bent over and showed him their buttocks—performing the earliest recorded incident of "mooning" in North America.[20]

The new young cacique, yet another Carlos, insisted that the Spaniards leave, and promised canoes and guides to the Key of Bones (Key West) where they would be able to hail a Spanish ship and return to Cuba. The voyage was one of total humiliation for the friars. They were dumped in the water, deserted, picked up again, and all the while the Indians took everything they had. In the end, they even lost their clothes and would have become just one more assortment of bones on the Key of Bones, had not a wandering Spanish fisherman found the naked friars.

The period from 500 A.D. to around 1500 in Florida is called the "Mississippian." The art, rituals and customs of the aboriginal Floridians were analogous to the Indians of Cahokia in Illinois and Etowah in Georgia. They were different, however from the other mound builders, as they were different as well from the Southern Cult, sometimes called the Southern Death

Cult, that existed from the northeastern coast of Mexico through the coasts of Texas, Louisiana, Mississippi, Alabama and Florida. Their art and craftsmanship was among the finest in North America. They were extraordinarily skilled painters and woodcarvers; Calusa creations of turtles, birds, fish, and even a cat grace museums from South Florida to the Smithsonian in Washington. As warriors, they invented ingenious weapons, including a sword made from hardwood embedded with shark's teeth.

There is marked similarity between the sacrificial practices of the Calusa and the Taensa and Natchez tribes described in Chapter 1. Evidence of similar rituals and sacrifice also exist in the Huastec region of Mexico, an area that came under the influence of the Aztecs. The pottery styles of the Huastec are easily recognized in Mississipian wares from the Cahokia mound sites in Illinois to the panhandle of northern Florida. Painted figures and breastplates of hammered copper illustrating a "hawk man or bird man" with a weapon in one hand and a severed head in the other, along with masks of long, pointed-nosed faces, are characteristic of the cult, and they too, have been found in Florida. A nineteenth century excavation of a Calusa site on Marco Island produced a long-nosed "birdman" mask. Birdman representations are common in Mexico.

There has been speculation that the religious fervor of the southern tribes was a result of a feeling of impending disaster created by stories of the Spanish slaughter of native peoples in the Caribbean and Mexico. It may be so, but human sacrifice by the Calusa predated Columbus by at least two hundred years.

European diseases, invading northern tribes, and internecine warfare took 230 years to wipe out the Calusa. Even in their waning days, they continued to resist the white man's religion. As late as 1743, they were still sacrificing children when a cacique or other important person died. Their only concession to Christianity was to call their shaman "the bishop."

That year, 1743, a Jesuit, Joseph Javier Alaño, wrote in a report that eventually made it to the King of Spain, a plea for soldiers and goods "for the preservation of the Indians." The letter, which first went to the governor in Havana, accurately predicted what was about to happen:

> These diminutive nations fight among themselves at every opportunity and they are shrinking as is indicated by the memory of the much greater number that there were just

twenty years ago, so that, if they continue on in their barbarous style, they will have disappeared with a few years either because of the skirmishes, or because of the rum that
they drink until they burst, or because of the children whom
they kill, or because of those whom the smallpox carried off
in the absence of remedies, or because of those who perish
at the hands of the Uchises [Seminoles].[21]

They stubbornly existed from the date of the first contact by Ponce de León
in 1513 until 1763, when the last eighty families of what were once the
mighty rulers of South Florida immigrated to Cuba.

Today, you can visit the Mound Key Calusa Camp, attend the Calusa
Playhouse on Key Biscayne, visit the Calusa Nature Center and Planetarium,
buy a house in the Calusa Bay development, perhaps from the Calusa Realty
Company, and even send your children to Calusa Elementary School on
Calusa Club Drive, but you will never see a Calusa Indian. These proud and
savage people are no more. Yet their fate was not unlike that of any of the
original tribes of Florida. They all disappeared or were captured and brought
into the bands of invading Seminoles.

The most powerful tribe to the north of the Calusa, the Timucuans, experienced the same sad ending as that of their southern neighbor. The Timucuans ruled central Florida. They were the first Florida aboriginals to be
hunted by the Spanish. Legend holds that it all started because of the mysterious and elusive "Fountain of Youth."

A magic place where anyone could be young again did not originate in
the imagination of Spanish nobleman Juan Ponce De León, as American
schoolchildren are taught. It was an ancient legend of the Carib and the
Arawak Indians of the Caribbean. Many years before Columbus, a party of
about one hundred Arawaks came to Florida from Cuba, presumably to find
the mythical fountain, and landed in Calusa territory.[22]

The Indian belief in the existence of a Fountain of Youth, which supposedly was somewhere north of the Caribbean Islands in a mysterious place
called Bimini, excited the Spaniards, and they eventually convinced themselves that it was not only real, but that instead of sand and coral, the won-
drous island was made of gold.

Ponce de León had conquered Puerto Rico less than nineteen years after
the first Columbus landing by either killing or enslaving most of the Indians

of the island. So, in 1513, with little else to do, he set out on his quest for eternal youth, and, perhaps a few Indian slaves.[23] He made the fateful mistake of landing near what is now Cape Canaveral, where he encountered the Timucua tribe.

As best we know, "Timucua" is a language of the Muskogan group that was spoken by many chiefdoms or sub-tribes in central Florida, including the Acuera, Mococo and Tocobaga. The Timucuans ruled the rich lands of central Florida, with villages around streams and lakes on both coasts. Handsome people, they were tall, muscular and heavily tattooed. Their round log houses were built in clusters and enclosed with log stockades, which indicate that they were not always at peace with one another. They practiced some agriculture, but the abundance of wildlife and native edible plants meant they did very little farming.[24] What farming they did do, however, they did in a way unusual for native Americans: men and women farmed together. The men broke the soil and the women planted the corn, in contrast to many other Indian groups, where farming was the sole responsibility of the women.

Like all of the tribes of Florida, they were great warriors. In warfare, their captives were scalped and mutilated. And eaten. The Timucua decidedly were Indians to avoid. In writing about tribes in the area, Harold E. Driver observes that

> . . . chiefs had absolute authority over their subjects, including the power of life and death. In this area, men were compelled to serve in the armed forces; they had no choice in the matter. The war leader was the chief himself or a lieutenant appointed by him. Scalps or heads taken in battle were treated primarily as sacrificial offers by the tribe to the supernatural rather than as appeasers of individual grief or symbols of individual war achievement.[25]

The tribe north of the Timucuans was the Apalachee. Excavations of their ceremonial mounds at the Lake Jackson site in Leon County have turned up remains of sacrificial victims and trophy skulls. The Apalachee ancestors who built these mounds probably had trade ties to some of the major mound builders in Georgia, and possibly those at Etowah, because excavators have found beautiful repoussé copper work of similar designs in both places. One relic is pertinent to the claim that these peoples were headhunters. As described by Mallory McCane O'Connor, " . . . [on] part of a magnificent costume worn by the high-ranking woman interred in the mound, the dancer is depicted wearing special moccasins, a beaded belt with a long sash, a bellow-shaped apron, a necklace of shell beads, and a feathered cape. In one hand the dancer carries a mace, symbol of authority, and in the other a severed head."[26]

When Ponce de León led the first Spanish expedition along the eastern coast of Florida into Timucua territory, the Timucuans probably knew about the Spanish and their custom of enslaving Indians. The trade routes of the Arawaks, Caribs, Calusa and Timucuans were extensive, and carried more than trade goods; information was swapped as well. As soon as the first Spanish landed in Timucua territory, the Timucuans knew what they must do.

Everywhere the Spanish went, the Indians met them with ambush and running attacks. Facing a superior force—there were about thirteen thousand Timucuans[27] in Central Florida and Southern Georgia—Ponce de León turned south, and eventually ended up on the west coast of Florida where he unhappily encountered the Calusa before returning to Puerto Rico.

It was eight years before the next conquistador sought to conquer Florida. Pánfilo de Narváez, known as "the butcher" of Jamaica and Cuba, a one-eyed veteran soldier with a red goatee who had fought against Cortéz in Mexico, had been appointed governor of Florida by the Spanish Crown. And a butcher he was. Father Bartolome de Las Casas was with a Spanish expeditionary force in Cuba headed by Narváez when they entered a large Arawak village of over three thousand Indians. Hoping for peace with the white invaders, the inhabitants offered the Spanish casava bread and fish. After accepting the food, and without provocation, the soldiers drew swords and began slaughtering the surprised Indians. Father Las Casas wrote that not a man, woman or child survived the massacre, and that all during the brutal, bloody episode, Narváez sat his horse, unmoved as though he "were made of marble."

Narváez, seeing the priest in shock, asked him what he thought of what the Spaniards had done. Las Casas shouted at Narváez, "I offer them and you too to the devil!"

Narváez left for Florida with four caravels and one brigantine, six hundred men and women and eighty horses. He landed near the entrance to Tampa Bay in 1528 with only three ships and three hundred men after a hurricane off the coast of Cuba and desertions during a stop at Santa Domingo. This was just the beginning of his bad luck. He landed near what is now called John's Pass at the entrance to Tampa Bay in Calusa territory. Wisely, the Calusa vacated their villages nearby to hide and watch. If they were gathering their forces to attack Narváez, as some historians claim, they never got a chance because the Spaniard immediately pushed his force north, away from the Calusa into the land of the Timucua.

Narváez financed the expedition himself, but he was known as truly penurious and greedy, a ducat-pincher. He was totally unaware of what was required to feed and clothe his men for a midsummer trek in an unexplored wilderness dominated by swampy terrain, snakes, alligators, mosquitoes, gnats, unbearable heat, humidity and hostile natives. Each man was allowed two pounds of biscuit and a half-pound of bacon; other edibles were to be taken from the Indians he hoped to conquer.

The Timucua seemed to sense his ignorance. They allowed the Spanish to get as far as the Withlacoochee River before their first attack. Four Indians had been taken prisoner earlier, and to save their lives, agreed to be guides for Narváez. Before they slipped away into the marshlands, the guides told Narváez about a "City of Gold" in the north called Apalachen in the land of the Apalachee Indians. It was one of the first Big Lies of the Indian-European relationship, and Narváez fell for it.

He quickly left Timucua territory. Those members of the expedition who were not killed by the Apalachee or by dysentery and fever, tried to escape Florida in four makeshift boats that were never seen again after their departure from St. Marks Bay on September 22, 1528. There were four survivors out of the six hundred who had left Cuba, but that is another story.

Our story is about the Timucua. Two Spanish expeditions had invaded their homeland and they had repelled them. The next invasion would cost them the lives of many warriors, women and children by gun, sword, battle-ax, and, eventually, by the diseases brought by the Spanish.[28] That incursion would be made by Hernando De Soto.[29]

Most of what we know about De Soto in North America comes from three sources: a writer whose name is unknown, but who called himself "The Gentleman from Elvas," and who wrote the elaborately titled book *A true relation of the vicissitudes attending the Governor Don Hernando de Soto and some Nobles of Portugal in the discovery of the province of Florida,* the diaries of Luis Hernandez de Biedma and Rodrigo Ranjel, and the stories, some in partial manuscript form, from expedition members Juan Coles and Alonso de Carmona.[30]

Garcilaso de la Vega,[31] half Inca, half Spaniard, added to these sources with information related to him by Gonzalo Silvestre, an expedition hero, and wrote *The Florida of the Inca,* recently translated by John and Jeannette Varner. The book must be read with an understanding of the times in which it was written; it often has a flowery Italian flair, and though the language posited as direct quotations may be completely accurate as to content, it is far too renaissance-romantic to be a verbatim transcript.

On May 18, 1539, Hernando de Soto set out from Havana in nine ships carrying over 600 soldiers, 213 horses, 100 or more servants and packs of killer-trained greyhounds. They landed in what the early maps indicate to be Charlotte Harbor, but based on the information in the various narratives, the landing site is now generally agreed to have been in the Tampa Bay area.

On or about the second of June, of the soldiers who were sent ashore "to perform the solemn act of taking possession of Florida in the name of Emperor Charles V, King of Spain," some took a stroll and decided to spend the night on the shore.

The following dawn, according to one account, "the Indians burst upon them with such audacity and force as to compel them to retreat to the edge of the water." [32] A long, ferocious and devastating encounter had begun.

Eight days later, when De Soto's force was rested and organized, they marched inland about five or six miles to the town of the Chief Hirrihigua.[33] "Elvas" describes the town as having eight houses with a mound at one end upon which sat a temple with a carving of "a wooden fowl with gilded eyes." It was deserted. De Soto and his officers bunked in the chief's house, and the other soldiers took whatever space they could find in the other dwellings. The temple was "thrown down" by the Spaniards in the name of their devout Christianity.

De Soto had taken prisoners that belonged to the Hirrihigua tribe and now sent them to their chief with "gifts, endearments and promises," [34] asking Chief Hirrihigua to return to his village and make peace with the Spanish. What DeSoto did not know was that years earlier Narváez had cut off Hirrihigua's nose and made him watch while dogs killed and ate his mother. Hirrihigua told the envoys that he "would willingly receive the heads of these Castilians, but he wanted to hear nothing more of their names and words." [35]

De Soto pushed on and made at least one Indian friend, the chief Mucozo, who had sheltered a Spanish captive of the Narváez expedition and who apparently was no friend of Hirrihigua. De Soto wanted to go past Mucozo's domain to the territory ruled by Mucozo's brother-in-law, Urribarracuxi. The friendly chief provided combination guide/envoys. An expedition traveled four days, only to find the village empty. The Indian envoys urged Urribarracuxi, who was hiding with his people in the wilderness, to return to meet the Spaniards, but he refused. "He did not attack the Castilians, and he did not give them malicious answers, but he excused himself with courteous words and with reasons which, though frivolous and vain, he felt were sufficient." [36] The geography of all of this is confusing. An attempt to clear it up was written early in the nineteenth century in one of the first books promoting land in Florida. Note the variable spelling of place names:

> Mucaco . . . who . . . governed a province which was situate fifty-one miles east of Hiriga, and was near the present Indian town of Hichapucksassy . . . induced his kinsman, Uribarricuxi, who governed the next district, to become an ally. Acuera, was the next province, it was divided from Uribarricuxi by a deep swamp, beyond which it extended sixty miles.
>
> De Soto also acquired the friendship of Acuera, and during twenty days that the Spanish troops traversed his dominions, he supplied them with abundance of food. The province of Acuera, probably embraced the Indian towns of Oakahumky, or Piclaklakaha. [37]

In 1837 when this was first published, there was no accurate translation of *The Florida of the Inca* available. If there had been, the author would have had a very different view of the De Soto-Acuera relationship.

With more than a little difficulty, the entire army crossed the swamp into the land of the Acuera from Urribarracuxi. Acuera is both the tribe's name and the chief's name. De Soto issued the usual *requirimento,* which was taken by captured Indians to the forest where Acuera and his people had fled. The *requirimento* was an incredibly arrogant pronouncement to native peoples finding themselves "fortunate" enough to be living in a new Spanish territory.

> I will receive you with love and charity . . . you will be converted to our Holy Catholic Faith . . .

The document then went on to tell the listeners that they were now subjects of the King of Spain and the Pope, and that if they did not accept all of this:

> We . . . shall make war against you . . . We shall take you, and your wives,

and your children, and shall make slaves of them . . . and we shall take away your goods and shall do you all the harm and damage we can.[38]

The plea to Acuera ended with "I desire to see and talk with you."[39]

Acuera's reply is one of the most memorably challenging speeches of America's past. Unfortunately, what you shall read here is a message brought back from an Indian chief by another Indian, relayed to a Spaniard who spoke Timucuan, who, in turn, translated it to De Soto, who may have told it to one of his men who years later told Garcilaso.

> I have long since learned who you Castilians are through others of you who came years ago to my land, and I already know very well what your customs and behavior are like. To me you are professional vagabonds who wander from place to place, gaining your livelihood by robbing, sacking and murdering people who have given you no offense. I want no manner of friendship or peace with people such as you, but instead prefer mortal and perpetual enmity.
>
> Granted that you are as valiant as you boast of being, I have no fear of you, since neither I nor my vassals consider themselves inferior to you in valor; and to prove our gallantry, I promise to maintain war upon you so long as you wish to remain in my province, not by fighting in the open, although I could do so, but by ambushing and waylaying you whenever you are off guard. I therefore notify and advise you to protect yourselves and act cautiously with me and my people, for I have commanded my vassals to bring me two Christian heads weekly, this number and no more.
>
> I shall be content to behead only two of you each week since I thus can slay all of you within a few years; for even though you may colonize and settle, you cannot perpetuate yourselves because you have not brought women to produce children and pass your generation forward. Therefore, all of you should go away as quickly as you can if you do not want to perish at my hands.[40]

The Spanish soldiers stayed twenty days in Acuera; they were beheaded seriatim just as promised. When a Spaniard wandered just a few feet from the main camp, soldiers heard a cry, and, rushing to the forest to come to the aid of their comrade, they found a headless body. On the night after the headless body was given a good Catholic Christian burial, the Indians dug it up, cut the body into pieces and hung the pieces on the limbs of trees for all the Spaniards to see. Acuera's warriors exceeded their headhunting quota by eight heads. A total of fourteen heads were taken to the chief; fourteen bodies were quartered and hung on trees.

As De Soto left the area, he expressed disappointment that his men had managed to kill only *fifty* Timucuan warriors. Fourteen to fifty: not a good augury for the aboriginal Americans in the inexorable tides of time, especially for those who had lived in southern and central Florida for hundreds of generations. By 1750, twenty-five years before the American Revolutionary War, most of the traditional Florida tribes had been wiped out by the white man, his swords, guns and diseases. The few native Indians who survived were either killed by invading Seminoles, or absorbed into new Seminole tribal groups.

Tribal cultures that had evolved for thousands of years disappeared in less than two hundred. It happened all around the Gulf of Mexico, from Texas to Florida. Human sacrifice, important to the religions of tribes around the Gulf, disappeared with its practitioners.

One tribe escaped destruction by leaving Texas in the 1400s and slowly migrating to present-day Nebraska. They were the Skidi Pawnees, and the next chapter explores how they brought human sacrifice with them on their long trip north.

3

Sons of the Morning Star — The Skidi Pawnee

In 1821, the prim young ladies of Miss White's Select Female Seminary in Washington DC, found themselves a hero in a Skidi Pawnee war chief— Pitalesharo, an imposing twenty-six-year- old who had traveled from the wild Nebraska plains to the nation's capital as a member of a delegation of Pawnee chiefs. Like most Americans, the young ladies had heard of Pitalesharo and his brave defiance of Skidi Pawnee traditions in rescuing a young Indian girl who was about to be sacrificed in an ancient Caddoan ceremony.

Miss White's select females pooled their money and commissioned a local silversmith to design and engrave a medal for the young warrior, which they hung around his neck in a large public ceremony. Pitalesharo sat for Charles Bird King, a fashionable portraitist of the day, and the painting appeared in a popular book on American Indian tribes.[1]

The story goes back to a trip by Pitalesharo's father, Chief Lachelesharo,[2] or Knife Chief, as he was known to whites, to St. Louis, to meet with the principal Indian agent of the Louisiana Territory, William Clark, the same William Clark of the celebrated Lewis & Clark Expedition. Clark told Knife Chief that the Pawnees' ancient custom of human sacrifice was wrong and should not continue. He explained that as more and more whites were coming "like waves of the ocean,"[3] the Pawnees would have to change and adapt to new ways. Evidently Knife Chief took this to heart and shared it with his son.

When the tribe captured a young Ietan[4] girl in 1816, the tribal priests

35

Black and white version of a portrait of Pitalesharo wearing his medal. Painted in 1821 by Charles Bird King.

began the traditional preparations to sacrifice her at planting time in the spring of the following year. Lachelesharo objected, but the spiritual leaders insisted that without the sacrifice, crops would fail and the tribe would be defeated in war and be unsuccessful in the hunt for buffalo. After the scaffold was built and the girl was tied to the upright poles, Pitalesharo stepped forth and boldly stated that he would either rescue the girl or leave his own dead body on the ground. The young chief's son was only twenty-two, but he was highly respected as a courageous and daring warrior. He cut the girl down, put her on a pony, and rode with her from the Skidi village. After two days of hard riding, he gave her a supply of food and told her the direction in which she should travel to meet her people. She arrived home safely, after meeting a war party from her own tribe.[5]

Little is known of Pitalesharo after his hero's reception in Washington. There were two other chiefs of the Grand Pawnees of the same name, but we only know that this particular war chief of the Skidi Pawnees died sometime between 1825 and 1833. The silver medal given to him by Miss White's ladies was found in a Skidi Pawnee grave excavated in 1883 near Fullerton, Nebraska, at the site of a Skidi village built in 1830.[6] He was around thirty-five when he died, probably a victim of one of the many smallpox epidemics that plagued the tribe.

Writing about Pitalesharo's adventure in *National Geographic* in 1944, Matthew W. Stirling, chief of the Bureau of American Ethnology of the Smithsonian, said that after Pitalesharo's rescue of the girl in 1818, the Skidi never again conducted human sacrifices in the morning star ceremony. Unfortunately, Stirling was wrong.[7]

The Pawnee tribe called the "Skidi," or "Skiri" originated in the western Mississippi valley along the Red River in Texas and Louisiana, where they lived near other Caddoan-speaking tribes, namely the Cadohadachos, Hasinais, and Wichitas. The Skidi maintained some the words and customs of the Caddo tribes of the south long after they migrated north. Exactly when they ended a long, circuitous migration and settled on the banks of the Loup River in Nebraska remains unclear. It may have been as early as 1400.[8] Most historians and archaeologists agree that the Skidi were well established in the north before three other Pawnee tribes—the Chauis (Grand Pawnee), the Kitkehahkis (Republican Pawnee), and the Pitahauerats (Tapage Pawnee) arrived hundreds of years later.

The Skidi Pawnee became farmers and buffalo hunters on the prairies. But tribal memories are long, and they never forgot the Caddoan ceremonial sacrifice of young girls to the morning star, a ritual in which a girl was sacrificed in exchange for the female the star had granted them at creation.

As we have seen, human sacrifice and cannibalism was an ordinary ritual by the tribes along the Gulf Coast, but few tribes matched the Caddoans' cruel forms of torture, sacrifice and cannibalism—or their fierceness in battle.

There is more than archaeological evidence of these practices. Records of the earliest contacts with these peoples are filled with eyewitness reports of unbelievable brutality.

A priest, Isidro Felis de Espinosa, was specific about their headhunting.

Upon occasion when these Indians gain a victory over their adversaries they bring back the skulls of their enemies as trophies and keep them hanging in a tree until in the course of time they decide to bury them.[9]

Writing generally of all the Caddo tribes of southern Texas, Friar Gaspar José de Solís, a Spanish priest and missionary, observed that:

They are cruel, inhuman and ferocious. When one nation makes war with another, the one that conquers puts all of the old men and old women to the knife and carries off the little children for food to eat on the way; the other children are sold; the vagabonds and grown women and young girls are carried off to serve them with the exception of *some whom they reserve to sacrifice* in the dance before their god and saints.

This is done in the following manner: they set a nailed stake in the ground in the place where they are to dance the *mitote*; they light a big fire, tying the victim who is to be danced about or sacrificed to that stake. All assemble together and when the harsh [musical] instrument, the *caymán*, begins to play they begin to dance and to leap, making many gestures and very fierce grimaces with funereal and discordant cries, dancing with well sharpened knives in their hands. As they jump around they approach the victim and cut a piece of flesh off of his body, going to the fire and half roasting it in sight of the victim, they eat it with great relish, and so they go on cutting off pieces and quartering him until they take off all of the flesh and he dies.

They take off his hair with the scalp and put in all on a pole in order to bring it to the dance as a trophy. They do not throw the bones away but distribute them and each one whose turn it is to get one walks along sucking it until he is thus finished. They do the same thing with the priests and Spaniards if they catch any. Others they hang up by the feet and put the fire underneath them . . . roasting them and eat them up. For others they do not use a knife to cut them to pieces but they tear them to pieces with their teeth and eat them raw.[10]

The Caddoans nestled around the Red River in Louisiana and Texas, and in parts of Arkansas and Kansas. Their first contact with white men occurred in 1541 when the ever determined Hernando De Soto, fresh from difficult excursions after leaving Florida, crossed the Mississippi River and pressed on to the west. The Caddoan warriors—and their women, who thrust long sharpened spears and lances at the Spanish horses and soldiers—turned De Soto back. "The Indians had no gold; and the discouraged general led his army back toward the Mississippi, where he presently died"[11] A record of one of the encounters with the Caddos was written by De Soto's factor, Luis Hernandez de Biedma:

> In attempting to seize some Indians, they began to yell and show us battle. They wounded of ours that day seven or eight men, and nine or ten horses; and such was their courage that they came upon in packs, by eights and tens, like worried dogs. We killed some thirty or forty of them.[12]

The Caddoans lived west of the Taensa and the Natchez, the mound building, ferocious fighters of the Mississippi valley, but because DeSoto's chroniclers called the tribe "Tulla," it is difficult to know which Caddo tribe was on the Arkansas side of the Mississippi River when the encounter took place. There is sufficient evidence in reports to convince historians that the Indians in this episode were indeed Caddoan.

At about the same time De Soto's men engaged the Caddos, another Spaniard, Francisco Vasquez de Coronado, approached other Caddoan Tribes from the south. Supposedly, a Caddoan had told Coronado about the prosperous villages of legendary Quivira. The conquistador was so intrigued that he left his main army, and with only thirty men pushed northward to find Quivira.

Quivira was a *group* of Caddoan Indian settlements in Kansas believed by some to have been inhabited by the ancestors of the Wichita tribe. George E. Hyde, who spent over thirty years studying the Pawnee, questions this. Hyde has suggested the Quivirans may have been the tribe known in later times as the Tawakonis. Either way, the Skidi may have been neighbors.[13]

In 1713, the first year of his appointment as French governor of Louisiana, Antoine de Lamothe, Sieur de Cadillac,[14] sent a missionary party out to the Caddo villages west of the Mississippi River. Andre Penicaut, whose accounts of Indian customs we engaged in Chapter 2, was in the group. Cadillac was responding to a request for missions to the Indians, but his real intent was to strengthen trade ties west of the Mississippi. Penicaut was an inveterate recorder of his experiences with Indians. He left us with a graphic and dramatic description of torture and cannibalism as practiced by the Hasinais.

The Indians tied captives between two poles with their feet about fifteen inches from the ground and left them for days without food or water. Penicaut's account:

> All of the men and women in the village assemble round the frames where these poor fainting persons are tied. Each family lights its fire before which they place a pot full of hot water, and, when the sun has arisen, four of the oldest savages, each one with a knife in his hand, make incisions in the arms, thighs, and lower legs of the ones hung up whose blood runs from their bodies to the extremities of their feet where four old men receive it in vessels.
>
> They carry this blood to two other old men whose duty it is to have it cooked in kettles, and when this blood is cooked, they give it to their women and children to eat. After they have consumed this blood, the two dead men are detached from the frame and placed on a table where they are cut up. The pieces are distributed to the entire assembly of the village, and each family cooks some of it in its pot. While this meat is being cooked they begin to dance. Then they return to their places, take this meat from their pots and eat it.[15]

Penicaut wrote that he was so ill after seeing this that he was unable to eat for three days.

The deep Caddoan influence on the Skidi Pawnee culture is clear, but in contrast to the religious torture-sacrifice ceremonies of other Caddoan tribes, the Pawnees' periodic human sacrifices to the morning star in the Nebraska plains were structured to be as quick and painless as possible.

The morning star ritual appears in one form or another in almost every history and ethnographic study of the Pawnee. Much has been written about the cosmology of the Pawnee, their worship of the heavens, and the origination myth in which the morning star brought the first female to earth to be

the mother of the Pawnee. Most of the monographs on the sacrifice ceremony have a single first source: James R. Murie's *Ceremonies of the Pawnee,*
some fifteen thousand words written from 1910 to 1921 and published sixty
years later (1981) by the Smithsonian Institution in two volumes. Murie's
mother was a Skidi Pawnee princess, his father a white officer with the famed
Pawnee Scouts (who fought with the U.S. Army in the Indian wars of the
nineteenth century) who left her shortly before James was born. Murie was
raised with the tribe, spoke its language, and considered himself a Pawnee.
He dealt with the tribe for extended periods, had the respect of their spiritual
leaders, and was able to elicit the most infinitesimal details of their rituals. His
account of the morning star sacrifice includes all twenty-one songs or chants
that were part of that ceremony.

According to Murie, the ceremony was not annual, nor scheduled, as
were most Pawnee events. When it did occur, however, it was timed to take
place before the planting season to insure good fortune and a good crop of
corn. The Skidi Pawnee morning star was the planet Mars. For the ceremony
to be performed, a man had to dream of the star and awaken just as it was
coming up over the eastern horizon. When this happened, everyone in the
village knew about it, for the dreamer began to weep, cry loudly, and walk
despondently about the village, distraught that he had been chosen as the instrument for killing a young girl.

In Murie's account, the dreamer finally went to the house of the Morning
Star Priest, the keeper of the secret rules of the ritual. The man and the priest
clasped each other and both cried because they knew what they had to do.
"They feel it is wrong, they know it is wrong, but they are commanded by
the Morning star and must do it," Murie wrote.[16]

The chosen one described the dream to the priest, who told him to think
continually about his task, and when ready, to come back for the tools and
instructions. From that time forward, everything done by or for the dreamer
was under the guidance of the priest: food, dress, facial paint—even down to
a prescribed formula for preparing a forest camping place from which to
scout an enemy village for the kidnapping of a young girl. Normally, the
dreamer and those who volunteered to help him traveled for three or four
days, conducting ceremonies each day as instructed by the priest.

When a suitable enemy village was located, a strategy for the attack was
planned, again with considerable ceremony. This was not to be an ordinary

strike-and-kill attack. Murie wrote that the leader—the dreamer—instructed the attackers *not* to kill.

> I will give the wolf cry; then all prepare to make the attack. When I give the second wolf cry, give a war whoop and attack the village. Do not kill. As soon as you find a girl thirteen years old, lay your hand on her and pronounce her holy for the big star. The others must assist him to bring her directly to me. Then leave the village. Do not harm any of the other people.[17]

When the girl was chosen and captured, the band attempted to escape as quickly as possible to avoid killing or being killed. As they approached their own village, they stopped to burn prairie grass for soot to blacken their faces. Choosing a location visible from their village, they rode in circles, whooping, singing and chanting, so the villagers knew they were returning.

If during the attack it had been necessary to kill some of the enemy, the women of the village held scalp and victory dances. The young girl was presented to the Morning Star Priest who—with appropriate ceremonies—gave her in turn to the care of the Wolf Priest. The latter painted her entire body red, dressed her in a long buffalo calfskin dress, gave her a new robe, and put a small soft down feather in her hair. She was given a wooden bowl and a spoon made from buffalo horn, which she was required to use and always keep with her. From this time to the sacrifice, the young girl was treated as an honored guest. She was given no information about her eventual fate.

Since the capture generally occurred in the autumn, there was a ceremony devoted to obtaining sacred buffalo meat during the winter hunt, meat to be used in the sacrifice ceremony in the spring.

The Morning Star Priest watched the skies in the spring and when the big red star appeared at dawn he declared that the time for the ceremony was at hand. The priest then ordered the dreamer to clear out his lodge and sweep it clean for the programs that would follow. For two days, the important men of the village—the dreamer, the Morning Star Priest, the Wolf Priest, and the young captive girl—participated in song, smoke and dance rituals. The girl was again painted red, but treated very kindly.

On the third day, the priest sent men to the forest to cut four poles for the scaffold. They were to cut one pole each of willow, cottonwood, box elder and elm. The men were told to select a site about a mile away from the village, erect the poles according to very specific instructions, and dig a shallow depression below the poles and fill it with white-feather down.[18] During the preparation of the scaffold, the ceremonies continued in the lodge, with the young girl joining in meals, always sitting next to the Wolf Priest who had taken care of her for the months of her captivity.

On the fourth day, she was painted again, this time half red and half black, and was given a beautifully dyed robe. On that day also, one of the priests left the lodge to tell all men, boys, and even the parents of male babies that bows and arrows must be prepared for the ceremony. After the singing of several required songs, it was time to go to the scaffold. The girl and the Wolf Priest led the procession with the other priests, chiefs, warriors, and common people in their wake. This procession took place in the dead of night, shortly before dawn. In Murie's words:

> It is now sunrise. The whole village is present. When they reach the scaffold, they pause. The maiden sees the scaffold and is afraid, but the wolf man pleads with her and coaxes her to ascend. (The idea seems to be that the captive must proceed in all things of her own free will. Hence the wolf man is credited with great skill in inducing her to do all the necessary things, in particular, to climb the frame.) She reaches to top; he ties her wrists to the last pole. She is facing east. As she stands on the crosspiece, they sing.
>
> Quickly and silently, a man rushed to the captive's side to shoot an arrow into her heart, killing her almost instantly. As the morning star rose, a man with a flint knife made a cut over the heart and put his fingers in the opening. He smeared the blood over his face and ran to a nearby ravine. As he departed, another man carried the sanctified buffalo meat to the scaffold and held it beneath the dead girl to catch drops of blood on the meat. The Skidi believed that if drops of blood did not fall on the meat, they would have a season of bad luck; but equally important, the blood must not drop on the white feathers placed beneath the girl.
>
> When the blood stopped flowing, a man with a war club approached the girl. He first pretended to strike her,

then touched her heart. With a war whoop, he turned and
ran away.

Murie observed that the idea behind this action was that by this symbolic
blow, the spirit of the sacrificed left her to go to the heavens, where it would
become a the star to watch over the people for whom she died. The sacred
buffalo meat was not eaten, but was thrown on a fire to produce smoke for
the continuing ceremony.[19]

To this point, the ceremony had been performed with sadness and a
sense of reverence. The priests and chiefs cried during some of the songs that
were sung in the lodge before the sacrifice. After the burning of the buffalo
meat, however, the mood changed and reverence vanished as each and every
male shot arrows into the girl's back and shouted and sang war songs. Even
the children were required to shoot, down to the infant males, who had small
bows and arrows especially made for them. Mothers brought their young
sons to give them an opportunity to connect with the gift to the morning
star. Finally, when there are so many arrows in the back of the girl that there
was no room for more, a priest circled the scaffold and told the people to "let
the sacrifice alone," and go home.

After the people left, four assistants to the priests untied the girl and carried the body out into the prairie where they lay it face down with the head
pointing to the east. They sang a song that included the words "the earth you
shall become a part of " . . . and promised that the ants, coyote, wildcat, the
magpie, the crow, the buzzards would find her, "and last of all . . . the bald-
headed eagle who will come and eat her."[20]

In the village, the event turned to a time of feasting and rejoicing. Men
and women danced; warriors put on their feather bonnets and grabbed their
weapons to mimic war parties. Because this was a ceremony to insure fertility,
some of the men and women took the opportunity to enjoy sexual intercourse with friends and neighbors. After a feast, the leading priest spoke to
the people and concluded the ceremony.

This highly structured ritual was probably held with slight variations for
hundreds of years before Pitalesharo disrupted it in 1816. He succeeded with
his rescue because the Pawnee believed that anyone who touched the sacrifice
would be taken away by the morning star as a substitute for the young girl.

Contrary to Matthew Stirling's assertion in *National Geographic*, the Skidi
sacrifices did not stop, though there is evidence that there were deep divi-

sions within the tribe concerning the ritual. Some chiefs, like Knife Chief, who were more politically attuned to the realities of the early 1800s, wanted it to end. The traditional priests and many of the warriors believed the chiefs were selling out to the white man.

Only two years after Pitalesharo did his heroic deed, the tribe was ready to attempt another human sacrifice. Though tradition seems to have designated that the sacrifice be of a young girl, they planned to give a Mexican boy to the morning star. In 1818, the tribe had a run-in with a group of Mexican buffalo hunters, killed seven of the men and captured a small ten-year-old boy. The warrior who captured the boy would not give him up, insisting that he be sacrificed. All of the chiefs, a French trader by the name of A. L. Pappan, and many of the tribesmen contributed goods to be used to purchase the boy from the warrior. "He refused, and Knife Chief in a blazing fury sprang at him with a war club, his son Pitalesharo shouting for him to strike hard."[21] Knife Chief restrained himself. Instead of killing the warrior, he added more of his own possessions to the purchase price. The warrior accepted and turned the boy over to the chief. Knife Chief, his warriors, and the trader Pappan took the boy to Manuel Lisa's trading post on the Missouri River. Lisa encouraged the entourage to go with him to St. Louis where they could turn the boy over to the authorities. They did so in the middle of June 1818.

There is another story reported by the *Missouri Gazette* of that same year about a young Indian girl who had been captured for sacrifice and found to be pregnant. The priests would not sacrifice her until she delivered the child. After the child was born the girl escaped, leaving her baby behind. The priests sacrificed the baby instead. This incident, reported to have taken place before 1818, does not appear in any other records.

Three of the outstanding authorities on Pawnee history and mythology—James R. Murie, Gene Weltfish, and George E. Hyde—agree on the important particulars of the morning star sacrifice ceremony: 1) The event had to begin as a result of a dream; 2) The dreamer had to find the victim; 3) The victim must be a young Indian girl of around thirteen years; and 4) The sacrifice was required to be performed as mercifully as possible. In general, the ceremonies described by these authorities are the same in details of content and timing.

Murie began his work in 1910, Hyde a bit earlier as an assistant to the renowned ethnologist George Bird Grinnell. Weltfish, a linguist and ethnologist, began her career in the late 1920s as a protégé of Franz Boas of Columbia University, the scholar often called the father of North American anthropology. It was Boas who pointed her to the study of the Pawnee language.

Grinnell had a very different version of the morning star sacrifice. He lived with the Pawnee tribes in 1872 (after a brief visit in 1870) before they made a disastrous emigration to Oklahoma, and had a longstanding relationship with many tribal members. He asserted that his information came from two chiefs, one who had seen the ceremony six times and another who said he had seen it once. Grinnell makes no mention of the morning star in his account, ascribing the sacrifice instead to an offering to Tirawa, the god of the Pawnee.

There are no dreams or weeping in Grinnell's version of the event. After a successful war party returned home with captives, one would be chosen for the sacrifice, "one who would fatten easily."[22] Like the doomed maiden in the other versions of the story, the captive was treated well and not informed of his or her future fate. Before the sacrifice, there were four days of singing, dancing and feasting, and, as in other accounts, the old men told every male in the village to prepare arrows. The males were cautioned to use only the feathers of birds of prey on their arrows and to neither cut nor burn to shape them. Instead of a ceremonial procession with the captive lead by the Wolf Priest, Grinnell has the village waiting at the scaffold for the victim. As in the other stories, the captive is shot by a single arrow through the side to the heart, and the shooter is the warrior who captured him. Other than the sex and method of acquiring the victim, Grinnell's report vaguely follows the descriptions of the actual sacrifice by the other historians, with a significant exception. His version replaces suspension over white feathers with the victim hanging over a depression filled with burning sticks and logs—in other words, a roasting fire. After all of the males in the village shoot their arrows, the arrows are removed and the now well-dead sacrifice is cooked over the fire.

> And while the smoke of the blood and the buffalo meat, and of the burning body, ascended to the sky, all the people prayed to Tirawa, and walked by the fire and grasped handfuls of the smoke, and passed it over their bodies and over those of their children, and prayed Tirawa to take pity on them and to give the health, and success in war, and plenteous crops. The man who had killed the captive fasted and

mourned for four days, and asked Tirawa to take pity on him, for he knew that he had taken the life of a human being.[23]

Grinnell knew that his version of the human-sacrifice ceremony of the Skidi differed from that of other investigators, but he believed the story because he had no doubt that the old men who told it had been witnesses to more than one of these ceremonies.

The reports of sacrifice of a baby, a captured warrior, a young girl, and the attempted sacrifice of a ten-year-old boy, plus the differing gods of the various versions, leads to the generalized conclusion that the Skidi irregularly performed human sacrifices to a god, using somewhat similar rituals. It appears that the Murie report is about the liturgy the priests would have *wished* to perform, whereas the others are accounts of actual events.

The events that have been examined here were not the last attempts at human sacrifice. In May 1833, John Dougherty, who was the Indian agent for the Pawnee, Oto and Iowa, was told of a Cheyenne woman the Skidi had captured in the winter and who was about to be sacrificed to the morning star. He rushed to the village with several of his helpers and persuaded two of the chiefs, Big Axe and Black Chief, to help him separate the woman from her captors. They spent the night in the chief's earth lodge, and by morning could tell that the situation was becoming very dangerous. It became imperative that the woman be removed from the village immediately, if she were ever to be removed at all.[24]

Facing a hostile, bunched group of warriors that had been incited by fanatical priests, Dougherty, his helpers, the chiefs, and a few loyal followers mounted the woman on a horse and started through the pushing and shoving crowd. Men stood in front of the horses of the rescuers, giving way only at the last minute as the horses slowly walked between the narrow passages between the earth lodges. Dougherty spotted one of the most rabid of the priests in an especially crowded turn, and even as the protectors gathered around to encircle the woman, he and his followers heard the twang of a bow. An arrow pierced the breast of the woman so deeply only the feathers could be seen. The dying woman and her horse were quickly separated from the protectors and disappeared onto the prairie, led by the compulsive warriors.

There was little Dougherty could do. Behind him, Black Chief had grabbed a leader of the zealots, Soldier Chief, and was choking him, seemingly with every intention of killing him for what had happened.

By the time the Indian agent and his group broke up this fighting, the dying woman and her horse were long gone. Exactly how they did what they did next to the dying woman is not known. As Dougherty left the village, he saw swarms of warriors holding up bloody parts of the sacrificed woman. Somehow her body had been torn to pieces and the pieces had been distributed among the warriors.[25]

The last known human sacrifice by the Skidi Pawnee occurred five years later on April 22, 1838, at the old Skidi village on the north bank of the Loup River fork, about five miles east of present-day Cushing, Nebraska. An Oglala Sioux girl was given to the morning star. The Skidis were then suffering the scourge of smallpox, and the priests insisted that the human-sacrifice ceremony was required for the well being of the tribe.[26]

When the Louisiana Purchase was completed in 1803, President Jefferson appointed John Sibley as Indian agent for the Orleans Territory and the lands south of Arkansas. At that point, almost constant war and two hundred years of plagues of the white man's diseases had decimated the Indians who had once boldly fought off DeSoto. Nestled away in the records of the Bureau of Indian Affairs, there is this report by Sibley:

> The whole number of what they call warriors of the ancient Caddo nation, is now reduced to about one hundred, who are looked upon somewhat like Knights of Malta, or some distinguished military order. They are brave, despise danger or death and boast that they have never shed white men's blood. Besides these, there are of old men, and strangers who live amongst them, nearly the same number; but there are forty or fifty more women than men. This nation has great influence over the Yattassees, Nandakoes, Nabadaches, Inies or Tachies, Nacogdoches, Keychies, Adaize, and Natchitoches, who all speak the Caddo language, look up to them as their fathers, visit and intermarry among them, and join them in all their wars.

Sibley wrote this about only one of the Caddo tribes, but the situation was the same with all of them, and it only got worse.

Their cousins, the northward emigrating Pawnee, too, barely survived.

Their population at the time of first contact with Europeans probably exceeded ten thousand. In the 1830s and 1840s, cholera and smallpox epidemics and incursions by warring Sioux and Cheyenne decimated the tribe. The Pawnee were one of the few tribes that never fought against the United States. They fought, in fact, for the U.S. Army as the famous Pawnee Scouts in the Indian wars against the Sioux and Cheyenne, but they were poorly treated. The government officials evidently believed that it was more important to accede to the wishes of former warring tribes than to those that were friendly. In any event, the Pawnee ceded all of their lands in Nebraska and moved to an Oklahoma reservation in 1876.

4

"Curses on You, White Men!" — Pilgrims and Indians

An examination of the invasion of North America by Europeans during the first 150 years after Columbus invites certain generalizations about the motivations and actions of the Spanish and French when compared to the English. The Spanish searched for gold, and cared little for the natives they met and showed them no mercy. The French were more interested in trade, and by the Indians' own accounts, were reasonably kind and tolerant. In a broad sense, during those early years, both the Spanish and the French came to the New World to find something of value to take home to the motherland. Not so, the English. They came to take the land.

Some three million North Americans claim an ancestor who was aboard the *Mayflower* when that ship's first few explorers came ashore at Cape Cod in November 1620, hundreds of miles from their intended destination. Their first act in the new world was robbing Nauset Indian graves of the corn that had been set on them as offerings to the dead.[1]

The stories of Massasoit, chief of the Wampanoags, and Squanto and how they helped the Pilgrims survive are familiar to virtually every schoolchild in America. How and why the Puritans killed Massasoit's two sons and mounted the head of one on a pike in Plymouth, where it was displayed for over twenty-five years, is a story no schoolchild hears. On December 6, still searching for a safe harbor for the leaking *Mayflower*, the colonists "by chance espied two houses which had beene lately dwelt in, but the people were gone." In the houses were pots, bowls, baskets and some foodstuffs. "Some of the best things we took away with us, and left their houses standing still as they were." The following day, Indians attacked, and in a short skirmish, the Pilgrims wounded the Nauset warrior who appeared to be the leader of the group. The Indian warriors fled and so did the Pilgrims. The latter named the site "The First Encounter."

Undaunted, the Pilgrims sailed across the bay. A few passengers and crew members explored on shore, then the ship was anchored, and 102[2] English men, women and children were disgorged into a deserted Indian village with cleared fields, a beautiful brook, a few dwellings and more graves to rob. The village was Patuxet, deserted because of a tragic epidemic resulting from earlier Indian contact with English fishermen along the coast. Of the 102 weary, starving passengers, only thirty-five were Puritans; the remaining sixty-seven felt that they had been hijacked because they had signed on to travel to established English settlements in Virginia, and they had not contemplated the hardships of a cold winter on the northern coast. Many did not weather those hardships that first year; half of the original settlers died of starvation and disease, ill prepared as they were for the rigors of pioneer life.

Today's Americans find it difficult to accept that these early Pilgrims—icons of piety and strength—were less than perfect. An example of historical blindness occurred in 1970 when the Massachusetts Department of Commerce refused to allow an invited guest-speaker, Frank James, a Wampanoag Indian, to give the speech he prepared for the 350th anniversary of the Pilgrims' landing. James had planned to say:

> Today is a time of celebrating for you . . . but it is not a time of celebrating for me. It is with heavy heart that I look back upon what happened to my People. . . . The Pilgrims had hardly explored the shore of Cape Cod four days before they had robbed the graves of my ancestors, and stolen their corn, wheat and beans . . . Massasoit, the great leader of the Wampanoag, knew these facts; yet he and his People welcomed and befriended the settlers . . . little knowing that . . . before 50 years were to pass, the Wampanoags . . . and other Indians living near the settlers would be killed by their guns or dead from diseases that we caught from them.[3]

The labors of Massasoit and other members of his tribe saved the Pilgrims, but the Wampanoags had an agenda of their own. Their ability to defend themselves had been diminished by an epidemic that killed nearly ninety percent of the tribe, and Massasoit feared the Narragansets who lived in Rhode Island, west of the bay that carries their name today. He saw the Pilgrims with their guns as possible future allies and as trading partners for the furs of the territory, as they proved to be. A formal treaty was made: the Wampanoags and the Pilgrims pledged to do nothing that would injure the other party, and to aid each other in the event of attacks from others. With a high sense of ceremony, the Pilgrims provided green carpets for the Wampanoags to sit on at the treaty signing, since they would not use chairs.

There was peace between the Pilgrims and the Wampanoags throughout Massasoit's lifetime, but peace did not prevail with the other tribes in the area. In 1623, just three years after the Pilgrims' landing, Governor William Bradford heard a rumor that the Massachuset tribe was planning an attack on a small, rowdy, non-Puritan English community up the coast from Plymouth. The relatively new settlement, Wessagusett, had never had good relations with its Indian neighbors. The Indians claimed that the English stole their corn.

The Pilgrims' military leader was Miles Standish. Today he is best known as the timid, frustrated suitor in Longfellow's poem, "The Courtship of Miles Standish." He should also be remembered as the first Pilgrim to cut off an Indian head. Bradford sent Standish to meet with the Massachusets. With the pretense of setting up a meeting with the Indian leader Witawamet, Standish lured the Indians out of the woods into a clearing. Then, without provocation, and with no evidence of wrongdoing—acting only because of rumor the governor had heard—the English opened fire and killed all of the Indians except Witawamet's eighteen-year-old brother, whom they hanged. Standish then ordered that Witawamet's head be cut off. The severed head was taken to Plymouth, where Standish had it mounted on an outside wall as a gruesome warning to all Indians who might be considering attacks against the Pilgrims.

Seven years later, in 1630, the English Puritans, encouraged by the success of Plymouth, began to settle Massachusetts in earnest. In just five years—by 1635—the newly formed Massachusetts Bay Colony had eight thousand residents while Plymouth Town struggled with no more than six hundred. Plymouth *Colony*, however, had grown to around five thousand in an area that includes most of what is now southeastern Massachusetts. This huge influx of settlers created ever more problems for the disease-decimated tribes of the northeastern shores, especially the Pequots. Settlers migrated to Pequot territory in the lower Connecticut River valley. Aware that they were intruding on tribal land, they built a small fort which they named Saybrook.

All contacts by the Pequots with the white colonists seemed to turn sour. A chief of the Pequots had been kidnaped by Europeans and offered for ransom to the tribe. When the ransom was paid, the Indians, expecting a joyous reunion with a beloved leader, found the chief's dead body instead. The Pequots planned a devastating reprisal, but unfortunately, they could not distinguish one European from another. There remains some question as to whether the kidnappers were English or Dutch, but whoever they were, the Pequots took their revenge on an English ship at the mouth of the Connecticut River. All on board were massacred. The English denied responsibility for the death of the kidnapped chief, and after negotiations, a fragile treaty was agreed to between the parties, with the Pequots paying a heavy indemnity and agreeing to punish the warriors who attacked the ship.

When a trader was murdered just off Block Island in Narraganset territory, this tribe pleaded innocent. The English attacked anyway, killing every male on Block Island, and even slaughtering the dogs. But for some unknown reason, the Puritans included the Pequots in their plans for retaliation. They sent a force to the mouth of the Thames River to pillage and burn Pequot villages. The war had begun.

John Robinson was a spiritual leader of the Puritans who had remained in Holland (where the Puritans had sojourned before the voyage of the Mayflower), but he was in regular communication with the Plymouth settlement. When he became aware of the conflicts with the Indians, he wrote to the Pilgrim leaders and warned them that "where blood is once begun to be shed, it is seldom staunched for a long time after." Robinson was right.

In April 1637, two hundred Pequot warriors struck back, and killed nine settlers near Weathersfield, including a woman and her child. They paddled their canoes down the river past the Saybrook fort, waving the clothing of their victims so the Puritans, watching from the bank, would know the fate planned for them by the Pequot.

Enraged by the murder of the settlers, ninety Puritan colonists under Captain John Mason—accompanied by sixty Mohegan allies and their chief, Uncas—headed toward Saybrook for revenge. When the Mohegans came upon a small party of Pequots, they broke off from the English force and attacked. They returned to Captain Mason with four Pequot heads and one captive, and chided the English for not being more aggressive.

Not accepting the taunt, the Puritans tied one leg of the captive Indian to a tree, and a loose rope to the other leg. A group of English grabbed the free rope and ripped the man into two pieces. A charitable captain ended the torture with a shot to the head of the mutilated victim.

Less than a month later, on May 25, Mason, with English reinforcements and six hundred Narraganset and Niantic warriors, attacked the Pequot fort on the Mystic River and set it afire. Inside were eighty dwellings that housed over eight hundred Indians. As the terrified Indians fled the flames, they were cut down with swords and muskets and scalped.

The hundreds of women and children who stayed inside, rather than risk the ferocity of the English and their Indian allies, burned to death. Not one Pequot escaped.

After the carnage, Captain John Underhill claimed that God had helped the Puritans. "We had sufficient light from the word of God for our proceedings," he wrote. Word of the slaughter quickly reached other Pequots in nearby villages, and they fled the muskets of the Puritans. To the colonists' credit, when they came upon the fleeing Indians, they let the elderly and the women and children go unharmed, but sixty warriors who ran to a swamp were less fortunate. The Puritans had loaded ten to twelve balls in each musket and fired point-blank at the ill-fated warriors huddled together in the water. They were torn apart by the barrage.[4]

This total, unrelenting kind of warfare by the English was new to the Indians.

During intertribal wars, total annihilation was never the objective. In their new fear, and out of eagerness to placate the English, neighboring tribes began cutting off the heads of those few Pequots they happened upon and sending them to the English leaders. Eventually, the Mohawks delivered the head of Sassacus, chief of the Pequots, who had come to the Mohawks requesting a place to hide.

The Pequots were a tribe no more.[5]

The few who survived sought alliances with the English and fought alongside the English in later conflicts. Throughout this war, the Wampanoags remained loyal to the Pilgrims, and for the next twenty-four years, there was relative peace between the Indians and the Puritans.

When Massasoit died in 1661 at the age of eighty-one, change was in the air.

The next stage is well described by historian Douglas Edward Leach:

> . . . with more experience of the white men and their ways, and particularly as the Indians came to have dealings with the Europeans in trade and settlement of land, the early sense of awe gave way to resignation, and often resentment. Resentment, in turn, easily developed into hatred. When the Indians became aware of the true consequences of the European intrusion, their natural inclination was to employ whatever forms of resistance seemed feasible at the time.[6]

At Massasoit's death, his eldest son, Wamsutta, became the grand sachem of all the Wampanoags, inheriting his father's title and responsibilities.

The colonists neither liked nor trusted Wamsutta, nor his younger brother Metacomet. Returning from a meeting with the white authorities shortly after becoming chief, Wamsutta became seriously ill and died. Metacomet became chief of the Wampanoags and was ready to employ whatever forms of resistance were available, but none seemed feasible.

Metacomet—known as Philip or King Philip to the English settlers—was only twenty-four when he assumed the hereditary title, yet even at that early age, he was feared by the growing population of New England. He believed that the Puritans were responsible for his brother's death, and with some justification—historians have discovered a "poison" item in the budget records of the day. If the English were responsible in this case, it would not have been the first time they used poison to kill Indians. In 1623, at a treaty negotiation in Virginia, a chief and over two hundred Indians had been fatally poisoned while drinking a toast of friendship.

Metacomet was bitter and enraged over the humiliations suffered by the Wampanoags. By the time he became chief of his people, the situation he faced was no longer Puritans in Indian territory, but Indians in Puritan territory.

Crimes of Indian against Indian were no longer judged by the tribe, but by the magistrates and councils of the colonists, by whose regulations the Indians were prohibited from work on the Sabbath and subject to the death penalty for blasphemy and interracial marriage, as were the settlers themselves.

For thirteen years, Metacomet seethed and schemed, always hopeful and ceaselessly seeking allies in neighboring tribes to join the Wampanoags in a force large enough to push the colonists back into the sea.

He was never able to do it, but war began nevertheless, and in an unplanned and unexpected way.

An aide to Metacomet, John Sassamon, was raised by whites and even attended Harvard for a time before returning to his people. His English was perfect and he knew the colonists' way of thinking. The chief was surprised when Sassamon suddenly returned to the white community, and equally surprised when he learned that his former friend had told the English that Metacomet was preparing for war.

Sassamon had been a spy.

Indians wandering through the countryside in January 1675 discovered his body beneath the ice in Assowampset Pond. They buried the body and went about their business, but when the colonists heard of the incident, they exhumed the body and declared that John Sassamon had been murdered. Three of Metacomet's closest friends and advisors were charged with the crime and sentenced to death. The three advisors were killed, two by hanging and the third by gunshot. This was the spark that lit the flame that history would record as "King Philip's War." The young warriors were ready, but the chief knew that without the support of all of the Wampanoag—the Sakonnets, Pocassets, and Nipmuc—and even the Narragansets, traditional enemies of the Wampanoag, the war could never be won.

Six months later, on June 20, angry, rampaging warriors shot up the colonists' cattle in the town of Swansea, and harassed the villagers to a point where they fled to the garrison house. A young colonist shot at one of the Indians and wounded him, spilling the first blood of the new war.[7]

Warriors soon swarmed around the town, hiding behind buildings and trees, waiting for the settlers to show themselves. By June 23, they had killed nine colonists and mortally wounded two others. The war was on in earnest, and Metacomet now had no choice but to fight.

When a hastily raised colonial militia rushed towards Metacomet's village, Mount Hope, near present Bristol, Rhode Island, they came upon eight poles with the mounted heads and hands of eight colonists. Metacomet had fled, and his village was deserted.

Recounting a battle with the Indians in September 1675, a writer of the time proved that the Puritan colonists were not to be outdone by heathen Indians:

Some Part of our Forces afterwards set on about Five hundred Indians, not far from Pocasset, pursuing them into a large Swamp, not far from thence; how many they killed not known. . . But in this Fight were killed King Philip's brother, his Privy Councellor . . . and one of his chief Captains; the Heads of which three were afterwards brought to Boston.[8]

With the outbreak of war, the Wampanoag began to attract allies. Other tribes like the Nipmucs grabbed at the opportunity to salve old wounds with the bitterest style of revenge. The Nipmucs burned the town of Brookfield, putting fire to every building except the garrison house, which would not catch fire from flaming arrows, or from an attempt to ignite assorted debris piled against the logs. When a wagon loaded with burning hay was pushed to the garrison house wall, rain put out the fire. Eighty village inhabitants had sought refuge in the building, and all but two survived. One was killed in the gunfire, and the other was captured. The Nipmucs cut off the captive's head, which then was "kicked about like a football until the Indians tired of this sport and stuck it on a pole in front of the unfortunate man's own house."[9]

The inhumane acts committed by both sides in this war equal the most heinous crimes of history. The hate was uncontrollable. The Indians sought revenge and a return to their way of life before colonization, and the New Englanders felt they had God on their side. The renowned Puritan preacher and scholar Cotton Mather asserted that ". . . the Evident Hand of Heaven appearing on the Side of a people whose Hope and Help was alone in the Almighty Lord of Hosts, Extinguished whole Nations of Savages."[10]

To the Puritans, every occurrence was a fulfillment of biblical prophecy.

In every way this was a war of annihilation, and there were no prisoner-of-war camps. More often than not, "captured" meant "killed" by either side and age or sex was of no consequence. Still, some Indian prisoners taken by the Puritans had a cash value and they were shipped to Bermuda, the West Indies, and even to Spain as slaves. When there was a special tax assessed to arm the militia, one merchant observed that the colonists would get their money back from the value of the lands they could confiscate as they killed the chiefs. Near the end, Metacomet's own wife and son were sold as slaves.[11]

The literature of the day—histories, sermons and civil tracts—overflows with stories of the murders of Indian and English children as mothers watched helplessly. For their part, the Indians did not kill all of their captives; some were kept as slaves and ransomed back to the English. Others were tortured. A letter written in 1676 describes the Indians' practice of tying captured English militiamen to stakes and building fires under them. As the fires burned, the torturers cut gashes in the victims and put hot coals in their wounds. The torture continued until the unfortunate soldier died.

At the beginning, The Narragansets did not enter the war on the side of their old enemies. They had a long history of profitable trade with the colonists, so they held back, content to watch developments for a while. Governor John Winthrop sent a delegation to the tribe and obtained the services of a hundred warriors, who went to Connecticut with the promise of rewards for heads and scalps. "For every Indians Head-Skin . . . they should have a coat and for every one they bring alive two Coats; for King Philips Head, Twenty Coats, and if taken alive, Forty Coats."[12]

The Indians returned in about two weeks with eighteen heads.

Eventually the Narragansets did change sides and fought the English. The Wampanoag, Sakonnet, Narganset, Pocasset,[13] Nipmuc, Niantic, Mohegan and Pequot were all Algonquians, more or less consanguineous, and spoke the same language. Tribal leadership in Algonquian tribes was hereditary, and consequently, there could be male or female chiefs, just as there were European kings or queens. Among the Wampanoags, there were numerous women known as "squaw sachems," who effectively were female chiefs. The stories of two squaw sachems who led their people in the fight against the colonists during the war, Awashonks of the Sakonnets, and Weetamoo of the Pocassets, encapsulate the tragedies of the era. Awashonks was a cousin of Metacomet, and Weetamoo was his sister-in-law, the widow of his lamented brother.

Before the fighting began, back in the days when Metacomet urged tribal leaders to join him in driving the English into the sea, peace-minded, matronly Awashonks was reluctant to bring her people into the conflict, confiding at one point to a white friend, Benjamin Church, as to what was happening. Later, however, when all the tribes massed for the major offensive against the English, Awashonks and her Sakonnets, and Weetamoo and the Pocassets were alongside Metacomet. Targets were assigned, and the Nipmucs

Illustration from a book published in 1874 of the death of Metacomet (King Philip).

and the Narragansets set out on separate missions while the Wampanoags, Sakonnets, and Pocassets joined forces to launch the main attack.

Fifty-two settlements were attacked and twelve were totally destroyed. Even sacred Plymouth was not spared; sixteen houses were burned to the ground. Those settlers who were not massacred fled to Boston and the larger towns. Absolute panic spread throughout the Massachusetts Colony. Had the Indians persisted with the same vigor they displayed in February and March 1676, they might have been the victors, at least temporarily. But they could not, for a number of reasons, sustain their war campaign.

Planting time was at hand, and most of the Indian combatants had already used up their food reserves. Because of the war, they could not go back to their homelands—that was much too dangerous—so they began to wander in search of new fields, new places to take their families for hunting, fishing, and farming.

One writer of the day claimed that the Indians were killing their own children.

> . . . they commonly kill theyr Chilldren, partly for crying whereby ye English are dereceted to them, & partly for

> want of food for them, allsoe they giue [give] a reward to a
> cruell woman among them to kill theyr Chilldren, She killd
> in one day an hundered children.[14]

The English colonists found and destroyed the Indians' storehouses and crops while the Indians died of disease and starvation. As more and more Indians left the attacking forces, the pressure lessened on the settlers. Other tribes allied with the colonists were integrated into new and bigger militia forces. With the aid of these friendly Indians, the colonists were better able to track and engage their enemies, which dampened the enthusiasm that had been fueled by earlier successes.

The beginning of the end came when Canonchet, a chief of the Narragansets, was captured and executed.

> A Pequot was allowed to shoot him, and as the colonists
> watched, his corpse was quartered and burned by exultant
> representatives of the Mohegans, Niantics, and the Pequots
> who had accompanied the Connecticut patrol. In a final ges-
> ture, the whites themselves sent Canonchet's head to the
> Connecticut authorities at Hartford.[15]

Receipt for the head was acknowledged by the Connecticut Council on April 8, 1676.

The squaw sachem Weetamoo, a queen in her own right, and her Pocassets fought alongside Metacomet from the first day of the war. After the Narragansets joined the conflict, she became one of the three wives of Quinnapin, one of the Narraganset sachems. During this period a captive by the name of Mary Rowlandson, wife of the minister of the Puritan Church in Lancaster, served as a maid to the Quinnapin household and frequently found herself in the service of Weetamoo, whom she disliked. Mary Rowlandson was eventually ransomed and wrote a short account of her experiences as a captive, providing a rare characterization of Weetamoo:

> A severe and proud Dame she was, bestowing every day in
> dressing her self neat as much time as any of the Gentry of
> the land: powdering her hair, and painting her face, going
> with Neck-laces, with Jewels in her ears, and Bracelets upon
> her hands: When she had dressed her self, her work was to
> make Girdles of Wampom and Beads . . .[16]

The squaw sachem, Awashonks of the Sakonnets, who came reluctantly into the war, was one of the earliest to surrender. Her old friend Benjamin Church persuaded her to give herself up in July 1676, and she and most of her warriors changed sides.

His allies steadily deserted Metacomet. Some Nipmuc, for instance, migrated to New York, where they were granted sanctuary. Other Indians, sensing defeat, wandered as far west as present-day Indiana and Illinois, and some even joined with LaSalle during his Mississippi River exploration, but only after they had determined that he was not English.[17]

Benjamin Church's "Rangers" chased Weetamoo and her warriors. The Pocassets fought the Rangers near Taunton, and Weetamoo, attempting to escape, shed her clothing and tried to swim the Taunton River. She drowned. When her body was found floating nude in the river, it was retrieved and beheaded.

Her head was sent to Taunton, where it remained on display for years.

Metacomet went into hiding near his ancestral home at Mount Hope, resigned to defeat. He was surrounded on August 12 and shot by an Indian, John Alderman, then beheaded and quartered.[18]

His hands were given to Alderman as a reward for shooting him; his head was mounted on a pole and displayed in Plymouth for twenty-five years. It is said that Alderman showed the famous hands to anyone who would buy him a drink at his favorite tavern. He kept them in a jar, floating in some murky preservative.

Despite the Indians' reverses and the loss of Metacomet, "King Philip's War" continued sporadically for two more years. When viewed from the perspective of the percentage of the population killed on both sides, it was one of the deadliest wars in American history. Over six hundred colonists died. By 1680, the Indian population of the area had decreased by more than ten thousand due to emigration, disease and war, and there were only four hundred Wampanoags left at war's end.

Commenting on the relationships between the Puritans and the Indians, historians Alan and Mary Simpson remind us that

> . . . we must not forget the self-righteousness of the Puritan, which was nursed on a doctrine of predestination and on a study of the Old Testament . . . sufficiently goaded, the clergy could discover a duty to exterminate the ungodly

heathens if they interfered with the enjoyment of the
Promised Land by God's Chosen People.[19]

The embarrassing facts about the Pilgrim colony and the conduct of the Puritans are disillusioning to generations of Americans taught to believe that the
humanitarian principles of these settlers formed the very foundations of freedom and justice upon which the United States was built. The Puritans came
to the New World for religious freedom, yet they offered none. To settle in
the lands of the Plymouth Colony, one had to appear before the magistrates
and prove conformity to the teachings of the Puritans. In the territory of the
Massachusetts Bay Colony during the years 1648 to 1692, twenty-five
"witches" were condemned to death: twenty-two were hanged, one was
"pressed to death," and two died in dungeons while awaiting trial.

The pious Puritans, who are credited with launching the great American
social and political experiment, beheaded the corpses of seven Indian leaders
and publicly displayed at least one head, Metacomet's, for a quarter of a century.

The gory score of severed heads for public display: Boston, three heads;
Plymouth, two heads; Hartford and Taunton, one each.

Over 150 years after Metacomet's beheading, one of the most popular
dramatic productions in the eastern United States was *Metamora; or, The Last of
the Wampanoags*. In 1829, even as the U.S. Army shot Indians in the plains, the
southwest and the west, eastern audiences relished the melodramatic heroism
of Metacomet, called Metamora in the play, wherein Metamora's son is killed,
and the chief kills his wife to prevent her enslavement by the Pilgrims. [20] Before the final curtain, the Indian hero (played by Edwin Forrest, an immensely
popular stage star of the day) proclaims:

> My curses on you, white men! May the Great Spirit curse
> you when he speaks in his war voice from the clouds! Mur-
> derers! The last of the Wampanoags' curse be on you! May
> your graves and the graves of your children be in the path
> the red man shall trace! And may the wolf and panther howl
> o'er your fleshless bones, fit banquet for the destroyers!
> Spirits of the grave, I come! But the curse of Metamora stays
> with the white man! I die! My wife! My queen! My Nah-
> meokee![21]

The curtain fell slowly. The audience—as one body—stood and cheered.

5

Promises to the Sun God—The Iroquois

The stern Puritans of Massachusetts matched cruelty for cruelty in their encounters with native cultures. To the west, in the Great Lakes region, irony becomes immediately apparent: French explorers and settlers, a far more tolerant and cosmopolitan breed than their English counterparts of the time, faced far harsher practices among the Indian tribes they encountered. The Iroquois and Huron tribes were quite different from the coastal tribes that fought the Puritans.

The bard of New England, Henry Wadsworth Longfellow, writing *The Song of Hiawatha* in 1855, chose the name "Hiawatha" as a perfect mellifluous appellation for eulogizing over the inexorable passing of noble and wise Indian cultures from the North American continent. But, the real Hiawatha—if there was one—was a much different man than is imagined in Longfellow's dramatic verse. Originally he was called "Heyanwatha," which means "wise man."[1]

The oral history of the Iroquois credits a wandering peacemaker named Hiawatha, who with the aid of a philosopher named Deganawidah, established the principles and organization of the Iroquois Confederacy, a working alliance among five often warring tribes: the Onondagas, Cayugas, Oneidas, Mohawks and Senecas. Representatives from each of these tribes met to discuss unified action in emergencies, but by their own rules, were required to meet at least once every five years, emergencies or not.

The Iroquois' traditional account of Hiawatha has him speaking to the chiefs and elders of the five tribes, saying:

> My brothers: You are from many tribes. You have come here
> for one cause. It is to live in safety. We must join ourselves
> together. The tribes that are on the warpath are strong. Not
> one tribe here is equal to that great people. Make ourselves
> a band of brothers. Then you will be stronger than they.[2]

The legend provides a shadowy glimpse into the dietary preferences of the Iroquois in pre-history. The story goes like this: After cutting up a human carcass and throwing it into the cooking pot, Hiawathia looks into the pot to determine whether the carcass had properly stewed. He sees the reflection of Deganawidah's face in the brew, for Deganawidah is watching through the smoke hole at the top of the wigwam. Surprised at so pleasant a countenance looking back at him from the pot, Hiawatha pledges to give up cannibalism then and there. And he is thus credited with ending the practice among the Iroquois.[3] From that day forward the members of the five tribes no longer ate each other, but their enemies were another thing altogether.

The Iroquois called their tribal confederacy the "League of Great Peace." It was uniquely a representative democracy that lasted for centuries before the white invaders came. It so impressed the intellectuals of colonial America that it was considered as an outline for the first confederation of the colonies. Amid all of the bickering about colonial organization in 1754, Benjamin Franklin declared, "It would be a strange thing if Six Nations[4] of ignorant savages should be capable of forming a scheme for such an union and be able to execute it in such a manner as that it has subsisted ages and appears indissoluble; and yet that a like union should be impracticable for ten or a dozen English colonies, to whom it is more necessary and must be more advantageous and who cannot be supposed to want an equal understanding of their interests."[5]

"The Great Peace" of the six tribes existed only internally; they did not fight among themselves, yet they were at constant war with their neighbors on all sides. Archaeologists have found randomly discarded bones indicating torture and cannibalism dating back to around the year 1300 in sites in Ontario.[6] The fierce warriors of these tribes appeared to have killed for the fun of it, and to have created an aura of such fear and horror that when they attacked villages, the inhabitants screamed, "It is the Iroquois. We are dead." The immediate dead were the fortunate ones, for both the Iroquois and their mortal enemies, the Hurons, gave their prisoners a long, painful death.

Before going to war, the Iroquois promised their Sun God that they would eat their captives, and upon returning to their villages, they brought the heads of their slain enemies. Sometimes they returned with scalps, but heads were preferred because they were more prestigious, and could be placed on the poles of the palisade to inspire more fear.[7]

The best and perhaps most accurate accounts of the treatment of prisoners by both Iroquois and Huron can be found in *Jesuit Relations*, a series of letters and reports made by Jesuit missionaries which were forwarded to Quebec and eventually to the headquarters of the Society of Jesus in Paris. The *Relations* of the period 1632 to 1673 were printed in Paris by the Jesuits, and eventually translated into seventy-three volumes by the historian Reuben Gold Thwaites and published in Cleveland by Burrow Brothers during the years 1886 to 1901.

On June 18, 1632, Father Paul LeJeune stopped at Tadoussac on his way to Quebec to become the second Superior of the Jesuit mission. He described his experience of seeing Indians for the first time in a letter to his superior:

> There were some whose noses were painted blue, the eyes, eyebrows, and cheeks painted black, and the rest of the face red; and these colors are bright and shining like those of our masks; others had black, red and blue stripes drawn from the ears to the mouth. Still others were entirely black; except the upper part of the brow and around the ears, and the end of the chin; so that it might have been truly said of them that they were masquerading.[8]

LeJeune further observed, mistakenly, "Their natural color is like that of those French beggars who are half-roasted in the Sun, and I have no doubt that the Savages would be very white if they were well covered."

At the time LeJeune did not realize the significance of the painted faces—blue meant health and well-being, black signified war or mourning, and red could mean either life or violent death.[9] The Iroquois were trying to tell him something.

LeJeune had hardly settled in at Tadoussac when he first faced the realities of Indian warfare. He wrote:

> Savages were coming back from a war with the Hiroquois [Iroquois], and had taken nine of them . . . I went to see

them, and found three wooden stakes erected; but news came from Quebec that a treaty of peace was being negotiated with the Hiroquois, and it would perhaps be necessary to surrender the prisoners, and thus their death was delayed. There is no cruelty comparable to that which they practice on their enemies. . . . In short, they make them suffer all that cruelty as the Devil can suggest. At last, as a final horror, they eat and devour them almost raw. If we were captured by the Hiroquois, perhaps we would be obliged to suffer this ordeal, inasmuch as we live with the Montagnards [Montagnais], their enemies.[10]

In speculating about captured Jesuits, Father LeJeune's words were, in fact, prophecy.

Leafing through these aged, crackly pages of the *Jesuit Relations*, almost every letter from the fathers to their superiors in Quebec expressed the pain, desolation, and misery that the missionaries and their flocks experienced during those times. The most familiar story in the *Relations* to schoolchildren, especially to students in Catholic schools, is the martyrdom of Saint Jean de Brébeuf, the patron saint of Canada. Brébeuf was a Jesuit missionary who lived among the Huron for fifteen years.

The Iroquois' great campaign against the Huron, which began in 1648, led them to the village where Brébeuf and his assistant Gabriel L'Alemant were living on March 16, 1649, St. Louis-de-Courville near Quebec City. The missionaries had an opportunity to flee, but decided to stay with their Huron charges. Brébeuf and L'Alemant were captured and dragged northward to St. Igance, a settlement already in the hands of the Iroquois.[11] What happened to the Fathers in St. Ignace is graphically described in a letter in the *Relations* titled, "A Veritable Account of the Martyrdom and Blessed Death of Father Jean De Breboeuf and of Father Gabriel L'Alemant, in New France, in the Country of the Hurons, by the Iroquois, Enemies of the Faith."

This is what the savages told us of the taking of the Village of St. Ignace, and about Fathers Jean de Breboeuf and Gabriel L'Alemant: The Iroquois came, to the number of twelve hundred men; took our village, and seized Father Breboeuf and his companion; and set fire to all the huts. They proceeded to vent their rage on those two Fathers, for they took them both and stripped them entirely naked, and fastened each to a post. They tied both of their hands together. They tore the nails from the fingers. They beat them with a shower of blows from cudgels, on the shoulders, the loins, the belly, the legs and the face—there being no part of their body which did not endure this torment.

The savages told us further, that, although Father de Breboeuf was overwhelmed under the weight of these blows, he did not cease continually to speak of God, and to encourage all the new Christians who were captives like himself to suffer well, that they might die well, in order to go in company with him to Paradise.

While the good Father was thus encouraging these good people, a wretched Huron renegade—who had remained a captive with the Iroquois, and whom Father de Breboeuf had formerly instructed and baptized—hearing him speak of Paradise and Holy Baptism, was irritated, and said to him, "Echon," that is Father de Breboeuf's name in Huron, "thou sayest that Baptism and the sufferings of this life lead straight to Paradise; thou wilt go soon, for I am going to baptize thee, and to make thee suffer well, in order to go the sooner to thy Paradise." The barbarian, having said that, took a kettle full of boiling water, which he poured over his body three different times, in derision of Holy baptism. And each time that he baptized him in this manner, the barbarian said to him, with bitter sarcasm, "Go to Heaven, for thou art well baptized."

The next ordeal endured by Father Brébeuf, the torture of the red-hot ax heads, is an example of the inventive cruelty of the Iroquois. The Iroquoian tribes obtained iron ax heads as early as 1580, first from the French as trade goods for furs, and later from both the Dutch and the English. They were multi-purpose tools to these creative Indians—used for cutting trees and splitting heads. There does not appear to be any record of when the Iroquois began heating them on the coals of the camp fires to apply to the bare skin of staked captives. It was already a common practice in the 1640s, and had been demonically perfected by the time Father Brébeuf was at the stake.

First they took axes, or more properly, hatchets with wood handles, and heated the iron heads in the coals, then rushed to apply the blistering-hot tools to Brébeuf's loins and armpits, extremely sensitive parts of the human body. Observers said that the Father did not scream, but continued to preach to them. Next, they took six ax heads, so hot they glowed red, and threaded them on a long green stick from a sapling to make a necklace of agony for the missionary. This collar of hot iron was designed so that he was severely burned whether he leaned forward or backward, to the left or the right. Christophe Regnaut, the Jesuit who wrote the report of Father Brébeuf's torture, said that "I have seen no torment which more moved me to compassion than that." Yet, the Iroquois were not finished:

> After that they put on him a belt of bark, full of pitch and resin, and set fire to it, which roasted his whole body. During all these torments, Father de Breboeuf endured like a rock, insensible to fire and flames, which astonished all the blood-thirsty wretches who tormented him.
>
> His zeal was so great that he preached continually to these infidels, to try to convert them. His executioners were enraged against him for constantly speaking to them of God and of their conversions. To prevent him from speaking more, they cut off his tongue, and both his upper and lower lips. After that, they set themselves to rip the flesh from his legs, thighs and arms, to the very bone; and then put it to roast before his eyes, in order to eat it.
>
> While they tormented him in this manner, those wretches derided him, saying, "Thou seest plainly that we treat thee as a friend, since we shall be the cause of thy Eternal happiness; thank us, then, for these good offices which we render thee—for, the more thou shalt suffer, the more will thy God reward thee."
>
> Those butchers, seeing that the good Father began to grow weak, made him sit down on the ground; and one of them, taking a knife, cut off the skin covering his skull. Another one of those barbarians, seeing that the good Father would soon die, made an opening in the upper part of his chest, and tore out his heart, which he roasted and ate. Others came to drink his blood, still warm, which they drank with both hands, saying that Father de Breboeuf had been very courageous to endure so much pain as they had given

him, and that, by drinking his blood, they would become courageous like him.

I do not doubt that all I have just related is true, and I would seal it with my blood; for I have seen the same treatment given to Iroquois prisoners whom the Huron savages had taken in war, with the exception of the boiling water, which I have not seen poured on any one.

In fine, I saw and touched all the wounds of his body, as the savages had told and declared to us: we buried these precious Relics on Sunday, the 21st day of March, 1649, with much Consolation.[12]

Signed by Christophe Regnaut. Regnaut was a Jesuit sent to determine what had happened to the Fathers. Regnaut had examined the bodies and verified the evidence of the tortures—the flesh-stripped arms and legs, the mutilated mouths and the scorched bodies, each with a huge cavity where the heart had been removed. Later, when it was safe to return, he exhumed the bodies and boiled them in lye to eat away the flesh from the bones. After the bones were heat treated, they were packed in silk and taken to Quebec where they remain to this day.

Regnaut said in his report that he had seen the same treatment given to the Iroquois prisoners whom the Huron savages had taken in war. Father Paul LeJeune saw even worse, and recorded it in the *Relations* of 1637. He told of an Iroquois warrior who suffered two days of torture before his eventual death. During the first day, if he grew weak, the torture would stop and he would be given water. Of his day of death, the second day, LeJeune wrote:

As soon as the day began to dawn, they lighted fires outside the village, to display there the excess of their cruelty, to the sight of the Sun. The victim was lead thither. . . Meanwhile, two of them took hold of him and made him mount a scaffold 6 or 7 feet high; 3 or 4 of these barbarians followed him. They tied him to a tree which passed across it, but in such a way he was free to turn around. There they began to burn him more cruelly than ever, leaving no part of his body to which fire was not applied at intervals. When one of these butchers began to burn him and to crowd him closely, in trying to escape him, he fell into the hands of another who gave

him no better reception. From time to time they were sup-
plied with new brands, which they thrust, all aflame, down
his throat, even forcing them into his fundament. They
burned his eyes; they applied red-hot hatchets to his shoulders; they hung some around his neck, which they turned
now upon his back, now upon his breast, according to the
position he took in order to avoid the weight of this burden.
If he attempted to sit or crouch down, someone thrust a
brand from under the scaffolding which soon caused him to
arise. They so harassed him upon all sides that they finally put
him out of breath. But he remained still, his mouth still open,
and almost motionless. Therefore, fearing that he would die
otherwise than by the knife, one cut off a foot, another a
hand, and almost at the same time a third severed the head
from the shoulders, throwing it into the crowd . . . in order to
make a feast therewith. As for the trunk, it remained at
Arontaen, where a feast was made of it the same day.[13]

The Jesuits were not alone in writing about the Iroquois and Hurons and their
atrocities. Chapter 1 introduced the French explorer Rene-Robert Cavelier,
Sieur de la Salle. Before he came to the French settlements in the New World,
he had mastered Greek, Latin, Hebrew, Arabic, Spanish and Italian. He came to
New France (Canada) in 1667, the same year the French finally negotiated and
signed a peace treaty with the Iroquois. He was twenty-four years old.

The Seneca Iroquois first told La Salle about the Ohio River, and it was
through his close association and understanding of Indians that he learned of
the Mississippi and the rivers that feed it. It did not take him long to learn
the Iroquoian language, nor to begin his famous journeys of discovery on the
Ohio, Illinois and Mississippi Rivers. In 1680, La Salle described the Iroquois
in a letter to a friend in France: "They are politically minded, wily, treacherous, vindictive, and cruel to their enemies, whom they burn on a slow fire
with incredible torment."[14]

A master of understatement, La Salle did not relate in his letter what he
had seen that same year on the shores of the Illinois River as he began his
search for the Mississippi. As his party neared a large village of the Illinois Indians, La Salle and his explorers were shocked to find that "nothing was left
to show the former extent of the village but a few ends of burnt poles. On
most of them, the heads of dead men had been stuck and eaten by crows."[15]

As they paddled further down the Illinois, they came upon another campground and were startled by the sight of several human figures standing erect and motionless. As they landed, they were revolted by the scene that met their eyes.

> The erect figures were the partially eaten bodies of women, still hanging from stakes on which they had been tortured to death. About the campground were the bodies of scores of women and children, mutilated masses of rotted flesh. Eyes had been gouged out. Limbs and breasts and vital organs had been torn from them. Here was the site on which the Iroquois had held their final orgy, a mass torture of women and children. Here they had turned back, their ferocity and demonic passions sated at last in a bloody bath and a feast of human flesh.[16]

Were the Hurons' and the Iroquois' methods of disposing of prisoners more fiendish than that of other tribes of the woodlands, or in fact, of all of the other tribes in North America? By contrast, there certainly were groups of Indians, who upon first contact with whites, appeared peaceful, and some who never knew war except for occasional wife stealing. But perhaps the reputation for ferocity assigned to the Hurons and Iroquois is overstated—in relation to other tribes—because they had the disadvantage of being written about by white observers with the ability to write lucidly about what they saw. Still, as with Le Page Du Pratz's charitable and understanding account of the fierce Natchez, some of the urbane French chroniclers may have been prepared, out of religious optimism, to soften their reports for their countrymen. For instance, Father LeJeune wrote, before he actually saw torture and cannibalism with his own eyes: "Let no one be astonished at these acts of barbarism. Before the faith was received in Germany, Spain, or England, those nations were not more civilized. Mind is not lacking among the Savages of Canada, but education and instruction. They are already tired of their miseries and stretch out their hands to us for help."[17] The wide-ranging Iroquois attempted to dominate the area marked by the Great Lakes to the north, the Ohio River to the south and the Mississippi River to the west. The success of their merciless attacks on their enemies depended on surprise. When the Iroquois ventured into the land of the Chippewa, on at least one occasion, the tables turned.

6

A Chief for Dinner — The Chippewa

When most Americans (those who are not Indian) think of Native Americans of early colonial and post-revolutionary times, they very likely visualize eagle feathers, war bonnets, animal skin tepees, and the tall, proud, noble red men who live in harmony with the animals and plants of the deep forests. Unknowingly, they are conjuring up the Chippewa. Only the buffalo skin teepee does not fit here—at least for most of the tribe.

Like the Pawnee, the Chippewa were never at war with the United States, and it is one of the very few tribes that remain today on the land it occupied in the seventeenth century.[1] Moreover, the Chippewas were the only tribe north of Mexico with a system of writing. Their birch bark scrolls were made by the medicine men and considered sacred.

History lauds the Chippewa for their hospitality, generosity and overall good sense. This was one of the largest tribes in North America, with a population estimated at 35,000 around 1650, a number probably understated because of confusion over the many names by which the tribe was addressed.[2]

Two of the most common names for the tribe—Chippewa and Ojibwa—are actually the same words, differently pronounced and spelled. Removing the "C" from Chippewa and substituting an "O" can produce a similar sounding name, and proves the difficulty of translating Indian words into standard English sounds. The popular explanation of the meaning of their name is that it describes the way they pucker the leather on the top of their moccasins.

The legendary prophet of the Chippewa, Manabozho, was born of a virgin mother.[3] He had supernatural powers and was the spokesman and representative on earth of the Great Spirit. His story is in *The Song of Hiawatha*.

Actually, the poet committed an historic gaffe: the classic poem does not follow the legend of Hiawatha, but the Chippewa prophet Manabozho. More likely than not, Longfellow's error was in accepting Henry Rowe Schoolcraft's *Algic Researches* (1839), which included the "The Myth of Hiawatha," without checking out who Hiawatha really was. Schoolcraft should have known better, too. After all, he married a Chippewa, and was superintendent of Indian affairs for the state of Michigan, where many of the Chippewa lived, when he wrote *Algic Researches.* The irony, of course, is that Hiawatha was a hero of the Iroquois, traditional enemies of the Chippewa.

Chippewa oral history says the tribe came from lands near "the great salt ocean," and it is probable that they migrated from near the mouth of the St. Lawrence River in the 1500s. There are, however, historians who believe that they came from near Hudson Bay a hundred years earlier because of climactic changes, and settled first on the north shores of Lake Huron. Wherever they came from, the early migrations eventually split into three distinct tribal groups: the Chippewa, Ottawa and Potawatomi, all speaking the same language but pursuing their own ways while maintaining a loose alliance with each other as they settled around the western Great Lakes. The Chippewa lived on both sides of Lake Superior, and around Lake Huron. The Ottawa moved to Manitoulin Island and the north shore of Georgian Bay, while the Potawatomi chose the lower peninsula of Michigan and moved to an area around present-day Green Bay, Michigan. These boundaries were elastic, as each of the tribes moved around in the seventeenth and eighteenth centuries.

The early Jesuits who traveled by foot and canoe to live with the Chippewa in New France placed themselves at the mercy of their often belligerent hosts. These missionaries were trained in the monasteries of Europe, educated in the tenets of their faith, imbued with an apostolic fervor to bring the savages of the New World to Christianity. For the most part, they were spiritually prepared for their task, but they had virtually no knowledge of the skills necessary for subsistence in the North American wilderness. The Indians with whom they lived teetered between war and famine, only tolerating the "black robes."

By the mid-1600s, the Jesuits employed "engagés," young men who would work to provision the priests and see to their comfort and safety as they lived and traveled with the Indians. Nicolas Perrot, born in 1644, entered the service of the Jesuits as an engagé around 1660 and served in that capacity for about five years in the upper Mississippi Valley and around the

Great Lakes before he left the Fathers to become a fur trader and a roving French diplomat to the Indians. He became a friend, peacemaker, and quasi-chief of the Chippewas, Ottawas, Fox, and other tribes of the territory. Fortunately for historians, he also wrote about his experiences and observations, as when in 1662, an Iroquois band of around a hundred warriors traveled westward along the Great Lakes as far as Sault Sainte Marie

> . . . to look for a village to eat; they were confident that, having carried terror among all the other savages, whom they had driven from their native lands, they would make themselves feared as soon as they came in sight. The hundred Iroquois[4] men who composed this party went above Sault Sainte Marie, and proceeded to encamp at the mouth of Lake Superior, five leagues or thereabout from the rapids; and there they descried fires along the high hills at the north, not far distant from them; they sent scouts in that direction, to ascertain who might be there.
>
> Some Saulteurs, Outaouas, Nepissings, and Amikouets[5] had left their settlement and come hither to hunt elk in the neighborhood of the Sault, and to carry on their fishing for the great whitefish, or salmon, which they catch here in abundance, in the midst of the boiling waters of those rapids. Hardly any place is known where this fish is so large or so fat as those which are found here. These people were scattered about, hunting, when one of them perceived the smoke from the camp of the Iroquois. They gave warning to one another, and rallied together to the number of a hundred men. They elected for chief of their party a Saulteur, who well deserved to be thus honored; for he had a thorough knowledge of the region where they were, having lived in it before the war with the Iroquois.
>
> This chief first sent out a canoe to reconnoiter, which was seen by the Iroquois who had been detailed for the same purpose; but the latter, believing that they had not been perceived, remained motionless, for fear of failing in their (intended) attack, and apprehensive that the Algonkins,[6] if these happened to escape from their clutches, would go to warn the entire village, whose people would immediately take to flight. The Saulteurs advanced, and proceeded

as far as the camp of the Iroquois without being discovered;
a very dense forest favored them, so that they had opportunity to count the enemy and the women whom they had
with them. The intention and plan of the people (the Iroquois) who were encamped there was, to carry away the (inhabitants of the Chippewa) villages, one place after another,
remaining in each (long enough) to consume the provisions
which they would find there, and doing the same with regard to the others.

The scouting party of the Saulteurs, having succeeded
therein, returned to their camp to report the discovery that
they had just made. Their people immediately embarked,
and proceeded all night without being able to reach the
place where the Iroquois were; they passed it, however, in a
very thick fog, without being perceived by any one. They
had gained knowledge of a little cove, quite deep, the head
of which was in the rear of the (Iroquois) camp; they gained
that location, and concluded that they must defer the attack
on the enemy until the next day. During the night they
made their approaches, and posted themselves on a small
but steep bank of earth, some five or six feet high, at the
base of which were the tents of the Iroquois, who were
sleeping very tranquilly.

Their dogs, scenting the ambushed Saulteurs, were beguiled by a little meat that was thrown to them, in order to
prevent them from barking; and when the light of day
began to appear sufficiently for discharging their arrows
with effect, the assailants uttered their usual war-cries. The
Iroquois awoke, and, trying to hasten to seize their arms,
they were pierced by the shots that were fired at them from
every side, and were forced to face about by the enormous
number of arrows that were showered upon them. When the
Saulteurs had finished shooting them, they leaped down
from the bank, entered the tents of their enemies, with clubs
in their hands . . .Those who tried to flee toward the shore
were fiercely attacked . . . none of the enemy escaping. You
see how complete their victory was.

The Iroquois who had been sent out as scouts returned
to their camp a few days after this defeat, expecting to join

their people there; but when they found only headless corpses on the ground, and the bones of those whose flesh had been eaten, they made diligent haste to carry back to their own country this dismal news. It is said that the Iroquois have not dared since that time to enter the Lake Superior (country); but in truth they have never set any limits in waging war, and, as pitiless man-eaters, they have always taken pleasure in drinking the blood and eating the flesh of all the different tribes, going to seek their prey even to the confines of America.[7]

The Iroquois who came "for a village to eat" clearly met their match in this encounter, and were themselves eaten by the Chippewa. For almost 450 years, the spur of land where the battle occurred on the shore of Lake Superior has been called Iroquois Point, and the old lighthouse there is a tourist attraction. It's about an hour's drive from Sault Ste. Marie. The Chippewa call the Point *Nadoueuigoning,* which means "the place of Iroquois bones."

From their first meeting with the French in 1623, the Chippewas were their staunchest ally. The importance of the fur trade brought new wealth to the Chippewas and resulted in major cultural and material changes in their way of life. As one of the earliest of the upper Mississippi and Great Lake tribes to have firearms—from around 1690—they pushed other tribes west and south and experienced a minor population explosion because the fur trade tended to stabilize their income and provided some protection against seasonal famine. Essentially, all of the tribes of the upper Midwest and the Ohio Valley became pawns of either the British or the French in the continuing struggle to control the fur trade. Some tribes like the Fox were almost annihilated, and others migrated west and south. Collectively, these episodes have been called the Beaver Wars, the French and Indian Wars, or in Europe, The Seven Years' War. In North America the French and Indian War is generally dated from 1754 to 1763; the wider European conflict, the Seven Years' War, did not begin until 1756.

It is difficult to point to a particular point in time, a specific incident that turned skirmishes and minor conflicts into war, but the French and Indian War may have begun with a Chippewa attack on Miami Indians in 1752. The French claimed the territory of the upper Ohio Valley all the way to Virginia, while the British openly traded with tribes in the territory. Colonel George

Washington sent Captain William Trent into Ohio. Trent was a trusted colonial officer, a friend of Washington, and later would be a business partner of Benjamin Franklin.

Only days in front of Trent, a Canadian, Charles Langlade, headed toward Pickawillany,[8] a trading post, with 240 Chippewas and Ottawas to punish the Miamis for trading with the British. Trent kept a diary as he traveled from Logstown[9] to Pickawillany, nearly 300 miles:

> July 6, 1752
>
> We arrived at the lower Shawnees town, where the Indians received us very kindly, with the firing of guns, and whooping and hollowing, according to their custom, and conducted us to the long house, where, after they had given us victals, they inquired the news; we told them the next day we would let them know everything. Then Thomas Burney and Andrew McBryer, the only two men who escaped, when the town was attacked, came to us and told us that 240 French and Indians on the 21st of June, about nine o'clock in the morning surprised the Indians in the cornfield and that they came so suddenly on them that the white men who were in their houses had the utmost difficulty to reach the fort. Three [white men] not being able to go to the fort shut themselves up in one of the houses.
>
> At this time there were but twenty men and boys in the fort, including the white men. The French and Indians having taken possession of the white men's houses, some of which were within ten yards of the fort, they kept a smart fire upon the fort till the afternoon, and had taken the three white men who had shut themselves up in one of the houses.
>
> The French and Indians in the afternoon let the Twightwees [Miami Indians] know that if they would deliver up the white men that were in the fort, they would break up the siege and go home. After a consultation it was agreed by the Indians and Whites that as there were so few men, and no water in the fort, it was better to deliver up the white men with beaver and wampum to the Indians not to hurt them, than for the fort to be taken, and all to be at their mercy.

> The white men were delivered up accordingly, except Burney and Andrew whom the Indians hid. One of the white men that was wounded in the belly, as soon as they got him they stabbed and scalped, and took out his heart and eat it. Upon receiving the white men they delivered up all the Indian women they had as prisoners, and [then] set off with the plunder they got out of the white men's houses, amounting to about three thousand pounds. They killed one Englishman, and took six prisoners, one Mingoe [Seneca Iroquois] and one Shawnee killed, and three Twightwees, one of them, the old Pianguisha king called by the English Old Britain, who for his attachment to the English, they boiled and eat him all up.[10]

The Chippewas who claimed he had taken Chippewa scalps hated Pianguisha, but the act of boiling his entire body and eating it was one of the more unusual and gruesome acts of cannibalism in North American history. The Miami Indians suffered even more in 1867 when Senecas captured their women and children from a village near present-day Chicago. As the Senacas fled the pursing Miami warriors, they left the remains of partially eaten Miami children on the trail.

The question remains, were the Chippewas cannibals? The Smithsonian Institution's Bureau of American Ethnology in a bulletin dated 1910,[11] said yes and no:

> It is affirmed by Warren,[12] who is not disposed to accept any statement [that] tends to disparage the character of his people, that, according to tradition, the division of the tribe residing at La Pointe [Wisconsin] practiced cannibalism, while Father Belcourt affirms that, although the Chippewa of Canada treated the vanquished with most horrible barbarity and at these times ate human flesh, they looked upon cannibalism, except under such conditions, with horror. According to Dr. William Jones (1905) the Pillagers[13] [band of Chippewa] . . . assert that cannibalism was occasionally practiced ceremonially by the Chippewa of Leech lake, and that since 1902 the eating of human flesh occurred on Rainy Reserve [in Canada] during stress of hunger.
>
> On January 29, 1855, President Franklin Pierce signed

a treaty with the Chippewa wherein the tribe traded title to the valuable mineral and timber lands on the western shores of Lake Superior for guaranteed permanent residence on much of their homeland. Individual heads of households of the tribe were paid a share of the annuities that were given to the tribe by the government in payment for the land. The first annuity payment was scheduled to take place around La Pointe, Wisconsin, during the summer of 1855, just six months after the treaty went into effect.

German travel writer, ethnologist and geographer Johann Georg Kohl decided to visit the Chippewa of Wisconsin and northern Michigan as they gathered to receive their first payments. He went to La Pointe well prepared. He had read everything he could find in Europe and the United States on the tribe,[14] and, once there, he spent every day talking to the Indians and every night composing his notes. He published his book *Kitchi-Gami* in Germany in 1859, and an English edition appeared the following year. This book is a mostly sympathetic, uncritical examination of a culture—hardly an unbiased scientific report. Yet, as an understanding, investigative document it is useful even today for its view of the Chippewa after their first experience on the new reservations.

Johann Georg Kohl, 1854

Like many foreign travelers and Americans of the time, Kohl had no doubt that he was seeing the last gasps of a people who would soon lose their culture, and would in the next hundred years or so die out completely. This belief created an urgency for Kohl for recording the present and digging even deeper to discover the past. Before cultural disintegration and before the memories of the past faded from the bands Kohl lived among, he listened and wrote down what they said about war and revenge:

If they are lucky in their prophecies, and at the same time
victorious in their action, they hang up after the engage-
ment some deer-skins, or other matters, in the trees on the
battlefield, as a species of expiatory sacrifice; for they appear, to certain extent, to regard their murderous attacks as
something godless, and hope by such sacrifices to prevent
the manes of their murdered foemen, and the spirits in
heaven, being too angry at their barbarous cruelty. Many of
them will bring locks of hair, cut from their deceased relatives, on to the battlefield, and have a habit of thrusting
them into the wounds they have dealt on the enemy.

I have been assured that they will frequently cut fingers,
arms and other limbs from their enemies, which they carry
home to show to their families. These limbs, which finally
grow quite dried up, they carry about with them for a long
period. Like the scalps, they are produced at the war dances,
and the braves will grow so excited over them as to break
off and swallow a finger.[15]

Kohl forthrightly noted that "It frequently happens, too, in these barren and
poor countries that men are so reduced by hunger and want, that in their de-
spair they shoot down their fellow-men like game, and eat them in the same
way."[16]

Kohl did not like the stories he was told. He said his ears tingled at the
tragic stories. His Chippewa hosts told him of a man who shot and ate his
two squaws and then each of his children in succession. There was the tale of
a starving Indian who killed and ate his best friend, and an even more
macabre story of a man who had developed a taste for human flesh and
scoured the north woods for victims.

The Chippewa had a name for those who ate human flesh: Windigo.
Among their legends "of a long time ago," there were giant cannibals, Windigos, who, like the giant in "Jack and the Beanstalk" sought little people to eat.
The Chippewa, in common with many other tribes, believed that dreams
were prophecies, visions of the future, or orders from their Manitou (guardian
spirit) to perform or become what a dream depicted. The fables and legends
of the giant Windigos, the war stories of stripping the flesh from arms and
legs for a victory feast, and the more desperate accounts of starvation cannibalism were everyday stories for this woodland tribe. As Kohl wrote:

> At times a man will merely dream that he must kill so many persons during his life; another dream adds that he must also devour them; as these strange beings believe in their dreams as they do in the stars, they act in accordance with their gloomy suggestions.[17]

The question persists: were the Chippewas cannibals? The answer lies in the definition of the word. Some Chippewas at certain times under particular circumstances ate human flesh, but in their cultural traditions this was an abhorrent practice. The charge of cannibalism is no more nor no less applicable to the Chippewas than to any of the tribes in the central regions of North America. Near the end of his book, Kohl wrote of an old Indian woman, called "Old Auroa" who gave him her version of the history of the Chippewas and their relations with white men. She began by recalling the stories of the early relationship with the French:

> The Frenchman began to give them presents, but not such presents as at the present time. The French presents were good and solid presents, wholesome food, fresh pork, stout knives, lasting guns, and good clothes. The savage loved the Frenchman, and accepted the French religion and the French trade; and the French "black coats"[Jesuits] took good care of the Indian, and lived with him in his wigwam. And the savage went hunting for the Frenchman, and so he hunted the game for him for a long, long time, and both lived together in peace and friendship.
>
> At length, however, the *Yaganash* [English] came. He took away the whole lower land from the French. The Indians, because they loved the French, all dug up the tomahawk for them, and many braves set out too from Lake Superior to help the Frenchman. But the Englishman at last conquered everything.
>
> At first the Indians did not love the *Yaganash*. He also brought much ishkotewabo (fire-water) with him. The Frenchman had also fire-water with him, but not so much as the Englishman. Hence things have now grown much worse in the country. When the Indian had many furs, he drank much fire-water. And my grandfather who was very old, often told me this sorrowful story. He often told me that

more than one-half of the Indians died of this "whisky water." And would to God we had taken an example from it! Like the men the animals die out; and in the English time already there were many hunting districts where no game was to be found.

But the long-knives [Americans] brought us even more whiskey-water than the Englishman, and these killed more men and animals for us, and the times always became worse, worse. The presents and the salt pork grew ever worse, and the hunting grounds have failed: besides, more and more land was taken from us.[18]

The Chippewa population in the United States and Canada, estimated at 35,000 for 1650, as mentioned earlier, seems to have remained fairly constant through 1905. The tribal population fluctuated during times of famine, disease, and war, but began to stabilize at the beginning of the twentieth century. By 1923, there were about 45,000 Chippewas in the United States and Canada. Today there are almost four times that number, still living mostly on the lands of their ancestors. The present population, however, like all of North America, contains thousands of mixtures with other tribes and mixtures with whites dating from as far back as the seventeenth century. Many of the tribes that were neighbors to the Chippewa in the eighteenth and nineteenth centuries are now almost nonexistent, or live in relative isolation in Oklahoma.

It was the skin of the beaver that the Chippewa sold and traded to the French that bound their alliance. At the time the Chippewa "dug up the tomahawk" for the French and joined in the campaign to oust the English from the lands north of the Ohio River, another equally ominous and destructive Indian-European relationship had begun about 1,700 miles to the northwest. On the coast, it wasn't the rodent beaver that the fur traders wanted, it was the mustelid sea otter, a cousin to the mink, ferret and skunk. Russians traded with the tribes on the northwest Pacific shores for this furry creature, which floated on its back, eating crustaceans and shellfish or carrying its young.

7

Arms and Legs for Sale — The Nootka

When the indomitable British explorer Captain John Cook anchored the *Resolution* and the *Discovery* off Vancouver Island on the morning of March 30, 1778, he had already visited Australia, Tasmania, New Zealand, Tahiti and the Hawaiian Islands on this, his third voyage to the Pacific. Like many explorers before him, he headed into the cold northern seas seeking a navigable passage across North America, searching the western shorelines to find a river that connected to the inland lakes that might open to other rivers flowing to eastern shores. Cook stopped for four weeks, anchored, and tied up to trees on the shores of Vancouver—not to explore, but to repair his leaking, rotting ships; he wrote in his journal that he was fortunate to have found a place where wood was so plentiful.

Captain Cook named the place where he landed "Nutka" on his early maps, which may have been his misunderstanding of instructions the natives gave him to "go around" Bligh Island to Yukuot. They shouted "itchme nutka"—go around—and even though Cook did not go around and anchor at Yukuot (he anchored at Ship Cove, now called Resolution Cove), he thought the natives were identifying the location as "Nutka." So the Mowachaht tribe became the Nootka. A later expedition, one led by James Strange, renamed Yukuot, which was the spring fishing camp of the Nootka. He called it "Friendly Harbor."

Ship's carpenters from the *Discovery* and *Resolution* were often on shore, cutting and stripping trees alongside blacksmiths with their fiery forges beating the iron rings for the main mast and later for the mizzen mast, which was damaged during a gale strength storm while they were anchored in Resolution Cove.

British explorer, adventurer, Captain James Cook from a portrait by Nathaniel Dance, 1776.

The Indians they met may have been as Cook wrote "mild and inoffensive," but one member of Cook's crew gave a more comprehensive description:

> They were a short-statured people, dirty beyond measure from head to foot, smelling strongly of fish, oil and smoke, their broad faces painted thickly with ochre, red white or black; their legs bowed with long sitting in their canoes. . . . These women, at any rate, had no attraction for the British seamen, except for some of the more experimentally-minded young gentlemen, who went to work to see what they could do with a tub of warm water and soap, and scrubbed down the startled ladies to a very satisfactory result.[1]

It did not take long for Cook's crew to conclude that their friendly native hosts were cannibals. They offered cooked human arms, decaying skulls and leathery hands to the sailors as items for trade. Cook stayed for less than a month before he sailed off to his fate in the Hawaiian Islands. When his ships *Resolution* and *Discovery* reached England without their famous captain in 1780, the interest in Cook's discoveries led King George III to issue a royal order to print Cook's log and journal of the voyages. It was published in 1784 in three volumes and titled *A Voyage to the Pacific Ocean; Undertaken by Command of His Majesty, for Making Discoveries in the Northern Hemisphere* .

In this journal, Cook, writing of his experience in Nootka territory on the west coast of Vancouver Island, stated that "the horrible practice of feeding on their enemies is as prevalent here as we found it to be at New Zealand and other South Sea Islands."[2]

Later explorers had the same experience of being offered human parts as trade goods. Over time, it became obvious that the Indians of the Northwest did cut off and keep the heads of their enemies, but whether they engaged in gustatory cannibalism—that is, eating human flesh as food—was never settled definitively by the early explorers. Some historians suggest that the Indians offered human parts in the belief that the Europeans were cannibals and needed food. Others speculate that hands and heads were offered because the Indians were clever enough to discern what the Europeans wanted as curios and souvenirs.

These suggestions attained greater credence when a re-study of the original Cook journals and logs proved that the accusation of cannibalism was not made by Cook, but by the editor of the journals who had heard the cannibalism claim by sailors and officers.[3]

The Nootka are linguistic cousins of the neighboring Kwakiutl and shared many customs, ceremonies, and spiritual and ritualistic practices. The Nootka were in contact with Europeans early in their history because of their location on the Pacific Ocean side of Vancouver Island.

Cook may have been the first European to visit the Nootka. The Indians may have seen European ships as early as 1542 when the intrepid Spanish explorer of the Pacific coast Juan Rodriguez Cabrillo sailed north from San Diego. Some historians believe Cabrillo got as far as Victoria. The next sailor to sail near Vancouver Island was Juan de Fuca[4] for whom the strait between Vancouver Island and the mainland is named. De Fuca mistakenly believed the strait was the beginning of a west-to-east waterway across the North

American continent. Juan de Fuca was there in 1592. Juan Perez in the ship *Santiago*, loaded with trade goods, arrived four years before Cook, in 1774. A vague historical record does not indicate that any of these intrepid adventurers—other than Cook—ever left their ships. Cook did some trading, too, in his turn, mostly for sea otter furs. Focusing on a chief, possibly Maquinna,[5] Cook wrote on May 14, 1778, about the trading practices of the Indians:

> Amongst those who came on board, was a good-looking middle-aged man whom we afterward found to be the Chief. He was clothed in a dress made of the sea-otter's skin; and had on his head such a cap as is worn by the people of King George's Sound,[6] ornamented with sky-blue glass beads, about the size of a large pea. He seemed to set a much higher value upon these, than upon our white glass beads. Any sort of beads, however, appeared to be in high estimation with these people, and they readily gave whatever they had in exchange for them, even their fine sea-otter skins. But here I must observe, that they set no more value upon these than upon other skins, which was also the case at King George's Sound, till our people set a higher price upon them, and even after that, the natives of both places would sooner part with a dress made of these, than with one made of the skins of wild-cats or of martins.[7]

The blue glass beads were probably those traded by Juan Perez four years earlier.

Alexander Walker, an ensign who commanded the East Indian Company soldiers on James Strange's British trading expedition to the area, wrote about his experience with the Nootka [Mowachaht]:

> We saw many bare skulls in the possession of these people and with the flesh and hair upon it, and which was still bloody. They ate part of this raw before us, and as usual expressed the highest relish for the food. Upon another occasion they produced an arm half roasted, feeding on it in the same manner. . . . Although at first the natives shewed no inclination to expose these things, yet as soon as they perceived us willing to buy them, they brought such numbers

as became disgusting, and forced us to drive them away from the vessels.[8]

Walker eventually had a change of heart. He wrote later that a shipmate who was left for a year with the Mowachahts maintained that they were not cannibals, and that he—Walker—felt that the longer experience of his shipmate required a change of mind. But even with softer attitude toward the Nootka and their dietary preferences, Walker nevertheless purchased several dried hands, which he took home and later gave to a friend.

The accessibility of the Indians plus the aggressiveness, greed, and ambition of one of their chiefs created the circumstances that allowed the early explorers to know much more about the Mowachaht than they knew about the Kwakiutl or any of the other nearby tribes. The chief was Maquinna, and his desire to be the principal conduit for trade with the white men put him in frequent contact with sailors, adventurers and traders who would later write about the man and his people. Maquinna ruled when Alexander Walker saw the skulls, hands and arms.

The Spanish claimed all of the West Coast of North America. By 1789, they realized that fortunes were being made in the Northwest in the trading of sea otter skins. To enforce their claims and keep out the British and Russians, they sent several ships to the area. One, a frigate, was commanded by Jacinto Caamaño. Caamaño admittedly did not like the Indians, and his dislike of the Mowachaht culture may have tilted his writings toward distortion of the nature of Maquinna and his people. Caamaño wrote in his diary:

> There are only two chieftains who eat human flesh. One lives in Tahsis, at the foot of a very high mountain of this name, which one reaches by one of many arms of the sound and is about eight or nine leagues away. The other is called Maquinna: one of the most prominent and closest to our establishment. This cruel man has eaten eleven children, which he bought for this purpose and raised to seven or eight years of age, executing this detestable act when it seemed to him that they were ready, or his evilness prompted it.
>
> Placing this unfortunate victim before him and closing his eyes, as if to symbolize the horror that such an abominable deed caused his nature and humanity, he began to

beat the air with a club until one of the blows struck a head. At once he quartered and cut it into strips, separating flesh from bones, eating it raw in great mouthfuls, shouting and making fearsome gestures and grimaces.

After we had confirmed this with Englishmen of the Argonaut, Maquinna came by and we gave him to understand, as well as we could, the great evil in this and if we heard he repeated the practice, we would go to this village, burn it and kill everyone there.

This admonition had the desired effect. Previously it had been determined he should be whipped, but this was not put in practice to avoid driving the Indians away. After three or four days he brought a little girl to sell, whom I bought for a sheet of copper and gave the name Delores. Since she was of the said age, I inferred that she was being kept for such a depraved objective. This he denied and he assured was only a charge made against him by those of other villages. What is certain is that before this they brought the legs and arms of children to our ships in order to sell them to us.[9]

Numerous slave children were sold to the Spanish and English during this period; the Europeans claimed that they were buying these boys and girls to protect them against the cannibalism of their owners. Caamaño admitted that the story he told was one told to him by other Indians. As an offset to this hearsay, it is possible that the sources were other chiefs who were jealous of Maquinna's monopoly of trade with Europeans. There is one other possibility: a third of the population of some of the villages was slaves, and in Maquinna's household alone fifty, of the residents were slaves. To the Indians, slaves were a commodity. What better way to sell them than to convince the visitors that they would die and be eaten unless they were purchased? Caamaño also may have been one more European who markedthe "otherness" of the barbarian by calling him a cannibal.[10] He did not see Maquinna kill and eat children, but the accusation took on a life of its own and was repeated in the writings of various observers throughout the life of the chief. There is no way to know the truth of it, but there is no real evidence that Maquinna killed and ate children.

Relations between the Indians, the English traders, and the Spanish who

Nootka Chief Maquina. A sketch of a 1780 painting by a Spanish artist.

claimed the territory were fragile, at best. The traders wanted the outrageous profits from the skins of the sea otter; the chiefs and the Indians wanted the beads, knives, tomahawks, and guns of the trader; the Spanish wanted control of the land and the commerce. The conflicts between the Spanish and the English over control of the territory almost led to another war, and the conflicts among the tribes could often be traced to European trading rights. In the midst of all of this stood the chief of the Mowachahts at Friendly Bay—the egregious Maquinna, who seemed to rule wherever the white men turned.

And there was a steady stream of white men. The sea otter skins that were sold in Europe, the United States and China brought at least $300 each, and there are reports of some sales as high as $4,000 for a single pelt in China, a fortune of a lifetime at the end of the eighteenth century. Eventually, of course, the slaughter of these animals brought them to the edge of extinction.

On March 12, 1803, the fur bonanza was still in full swing when the American trader ship *Boston* tied up to some trees about five miles north of the village at Friendly Bay. The captain, John Salter, was leery of the Indians, and avoided dropping anchor right in the middle of their bay.

Maquinna came aboard the following day.

> The king . . . was a man of dignified aspect, about six feet in height and extremely straight and well proportioned. His features were good, and his face was rendered remarkable by a large Roman nose, a very uncommon form of feature among these people. His complexion was of a dark copper hue, though his face, legs and arms on this occasion so covered with red paint that their natural colour could scarcely be perceived. His eyebrows were painted black in two broad stripes like a new moon, and his long black hair, which shone with oil, was fastened in a bunch on top of his head

and strewn or powdered with white down, which gave him
a most curious and extraordinary appearance.[11]

Salter entertained Maquinna and traded with him for fresh food for the ship
while the crew made water casks and cut timber for yards and spars. The chief
took an interest in the work of the blacksmith on the ship, John Jewitt, a
young Englishman recruited in Hull during one of Salter's trips to England.
When visiting the *Boston*, Maquinna liked to go to Jewitt's forge and watch
him shape knives and daggers, repair firearms, and manufacture tomahawks.

John Jewitt's skill, wit and considerable luck later saved his life.
Maquinna often dined with Salter, bringing warriors and noble relatives with
him. The crew of the *Boston* was pleased with the large store of fresh fish provided by the Mowachaht. In a friendship gesture after entertaining Maquinna,
Salter offered the chief a double barreled "fowling piece" which he suggested
would be an easy way for him to add geese and ducks to his table. This occurred on March 19, 1803.

Two days later, just as the ship was ready to leave, Maquinna returned to
the ship with eighteen wild ducks as gifts for the captain, and a broken gun.
One of the locks no longer worked. The chief told Captain Salter that the
weapon was *peshak*, bad. The captain was insulted, and, according to Jewitt,
called Maquinna a liar and "other opprobrious terms," grabbed the gun from
the chief, and put it in his cabin with instructions to Jewitt to fix it.

Possibly Salter did not realize that Maquinna had been dealing with
English-speaking traders for almost twenty-five years, and knew enough of
the language to understand the insults shouted at him. In any case, Maquinna
left the ship. On the following day, he was back with more fresh salmon for
the ships crew, but this time he wore an animal mask and had with him a
large number of his men. They danced and otherwise entertained the sailors,
and seemingly in the best good humor suggested that since the ship was
about to leave that the captain should send some men to Friendly Cove to
catch a supply of fresh fish for their journey. Accepting this gesture of good
will, Captain Salter sent his chief mate and nine crewmen away in a yawl.

John Jewitt, who recorded these events, went below to his workplace,
and did not see what happened next. He heard unusual scuffing and shouting
on deck, and when he stuck his head out the hatch to see what was going on,
he was grabbed by the hair and struck on the skull with an ax. Jewitt fell
backward, tumbling below decks, unconscious.

When he recovered, the hatch was closed and all he could hear were the yells of the Indians. The hatch opened. With a huge gash in his head and one eye swollen shut, Jewitt was ordered on deck. Blood splattered Indians surrounded him with daggers in hand, but the chief interceded, offering the blacksmith a choice between slavery or death.

Jewitt was washed, given rum and a coat, and his first assignment: identify by name each of the dead crewmen whose heads were lined up on the deck. As the heads were brought to Jewitt one by one, he recited to Maquinna the names of all of the crew members except for a few whose heads were so mangled and disfigured that he could not recognize them.[12]

Had the young blacksmith known more about the war practices of the various Mowachahtn tribes, he would not have been surprised that his shipmates were beheaded.

Many tribes in North America took heads instead of scalps. The Mowachahtn [Nookan] practice of saving the heads of the enemies they killed was recorded by the earliest explorers in their stories of bloody heads for sale. The collection of heads continued long after Jewitt. The early reporters of the tribal wars in the 1860s and 1870s did not refer to warriors killed, only heads taken. A notation of a battle in 1868 reads "35 heads, 13 slaves."

Phillip Drucker began an exhaustive study of the Nootka in 1935, which years later, was published by the Smithsonian Institution as *The Northern and Central Nootkan Tribes*. In the section on "war," Drucker explained:

> Warriors beheaded their victims—not just war chiefs, but all men, women and children that they killed. The heads were taken home, to display and rejoice over; they were out on a rock at one end of the beach for 4 days, after which they were hidden in the woods. The custom of setting them up on poles is said to have been practiced only by the tribes of the Barkley Sound district.[13] The Chickliset[14] had a special method of stringing heads like beads on a long cedar withe (apparently punching holes through the cranium to insert it), and hanging them on a tree near the village. . . . Only women and children were taken as slaves. Sometimes they were sold, sometimes they were taken to the home of the raiders and clubbed to death.[15]

Maquinna's interest in iron weapons and the blacksmith's ability to make and repair firearms saved Jewitt. The Indians beached the *Boston* and stripped it of its cargo, cut loose the sails, and chopped down the mast and spars. Most of the cargo and all of the weapons in or on the ship were transferred to Maquinna's house. During the looting, Jewitt found the captain's desk, some paper and blank account books.

Using berry juice and quills from ducks and geese, the lost blacksmith began the diary that almost two hundred years later remains the best and most exciting authority on the life and ways of the Mowachaht.

Several days later, two trading vessels came near the cove, and the Mowachaht used their new rifles and blunderbusses to fire at them. The traders returned the fire with grapeshot, but no one was hurt. Maquinna must have realized a mistake had been made; these traders would tell others, and the fur trade of the Mowachaht and other nearby tribes could dry up. Representatives of most of the Mowachahtn tribes canoed to Friendly Cove for a feast to celebrate Maquinna's victory over the traders, and the chief made them beneficiaries of the slaughter by distributing over a hundred rifles, four hundred yards of cloth and forty casks of powder to these guests. If Maquinna was worried that traders would see the beached *Boston* and be frightened away, he need not have been. One Indian scrounging around the dark hold of the ship for more plunder carried a flaming torch and accidentally started the fire that engulfed and destroyed the vessel.

John Jewitt was a slave to the chief of the Mowachaht for two-and-one-half years. He learned the tribal language and eventually married—at Maquinna's insistence—a princess of a nearby friendly tribe. With his bride, paid for by Maquinna, he also acquired two slaves and a somewhat easier life.

Jewitt's diary provides some of the earliest information about slavery as practiced by the Mowachaht tribes:

> Their slaves form their most valuable property. These are either captives taken in war or purchased from the neighboring tribes. They reside in the same house and are usually kindly treated. They are compelled, however, at times to labor severely and the females are prostituted by their masters whenever they think proper, for the purpose of gain. None but the king and chiefs have slaves. Maquinna had

nearly fifty, male and female, in his house, a number about one half of its inhabitants.[16]

When Maquinna sensed that Jewitt was tempted to escape to another tribe, he told him the story of seven seamen who deserted the ship *Manchester* and came to the Mowachahts for refuge. Refuge with the Mowachahts was slavery, so after some consideration, they decided to try another tribe, but were captured by allies of the Mowachahts and returned to Maquinna. The chief sentenced them to death. As the deserters watched their desperate plight unfold, one by one, they were held down by warriors who forced open the victims' mouths and pushed stones down their throats until they choked to death.

During the later part of July 1804, sixteen months after his capture, Jewitt, now a trusted slave and companion, was told by Maquinna that he had decided to go to war with a tribe because of an .insult or some disagreement that occurred during the preceding summer. Jewitt was to go along, and was encouraged to participate in the war preparation rituals of the Mowachaht. Warriors went to the beach with boughs of bushes intermixed with briars, walked into the salty water, and washed themselves with the thorny greenery until they had bleeding scratches over their faces and bodies. With the pain of the salt water in their wounds, they sang "Great God let me live, not be sick, find the enemy, not fear him, find him asleep, and kill many of them." This occurred several times a day for up to four weeks before they went into battle.[17]

During this preparatory period, they stayed away from their women and avoided feasts and any other pleasure-giving activities. According to Jewitt, on the last three days before the attack the Indians were in the water almost constantly, beating themselves with the briar bushes. Maquinna said that by following this routine, their skin was made so tough that no enemy weapon could penetrate it.

The Mowachaht attack on the village was ferocious and unmerciful, but not unusual. During the night, the Indians silently rowed their war canoes almost thirty miles south and landed near the sleeping village. Near dawn, they slipped into the village. One or two warriors crept into each house as others waited outside to kill or capture those who might attempt escape. At the war wail of the chief, clubs crashed down on sleeping heads. The few who got out of their houses were stabbed or shot. Some prisoners were taken, but those who were old, sick or injured were killed. After the village was looted, it was set afire, and the victors packed their canoes and paddled home to a victory celebration. Five hundred warriors in forty canoes slaughtered a village population of around four hundred people.[18]

The Indians were not sharpshooters; guns were used in close-up warfare, loaded almost to the end of the muzzle with small shot. Before the tribe had a supply of rifles and blunderbusses, Alexander Walker of the Strange expedition, writing about twenty-six years before the battle just recounted, vividly described the fighting mode of the Mowachaht:

> The spears which these people use in war are pointed with bone three or four feet long, but without barbs. This bone is probably a Whale's. Their daggers are also made of bone, and are about a foot long. They asserted that they sometimes made them from human thigh bones, most probably as an object of triumph from those of their enemies. They were proud of speaking of their enemies, who according to their account were very numerous and frequently employed in making war. Although they took no care in the village to guard against surprise, nor fenced it in any manner so as to resist the attack of an enemy, yet from the character of the people, I suppose, that they chiefly carry war on by surprise and stratagem . . . They carry their resentment against their enemies so far as to devour part of them—to what remains, they seem to pay no attention. We saw the remains of one they had killed while we were here. He was discovered by accident, lying in the woods at the back of the village. Part of the body was covered with a course mat, and it appeared to have been carried to the place where we found it, in a fish basket, which was left behind. His toes were wanting, and the hands had been cut off by the wrists. The face was much mutilated and the skin was taken off from the forehead.[19]

Both the Mowachaht and the neighboring Kwakiutl held winter festivals, but contrary to most of the early reports, the Mowachaht festival did not include ritualized cannibalism. The singing and dancing lasted for fourteen or more days and ended when a young man or a boy was carried among the celebrants with knives, spears or bayonets piercing his arms, legs, and the area near his ribs. Maquinna told Jewitt that by ancient custom the ceremony ended with a human sacrifice, but that his father had changed the ritual, substituting for the sacrifice an exhibition of courage and endurance.

Endurance was a singular feature of Mowachaht women, who were sold to husbands-to-be by their fathers. Jewitt told one story about a stubborn new wife who refused to have conjugal relations with her new husband:

> I was sent for by my neighbor Yealthlower, the king's elder brother, to file his teeth, which operation having performed, he informed me that a new wife, whom he had a little time before purchased, having refused to sleep with him it was his intention, provided she persisted in her refusal, to bite off her nose. I endeavoured to dissuade him from it but he was determined and, in fact, performed his savage threat that very night, saying that since she would not be his wife, she should not be that of any other, and in the morning sent her back to her father.
>
> He afterwards told me that in similar cases the husband had a right, with them, to disfigure his wife in this way, or some other, to prevent her from marrying again.[20]

Jewitt, who spoke highly of his own selected bride, in time deserted her and had her sent back to her village when the Mowachahts finally determined that with Indian bride or not, he could not really be part of the tribe. When Captain Samuel Hill of the brig *Lydia* out of Boston finally rescued him, he left behind a five-month-old son, who was adopted by Maquinna. The rewrite of Jewitt's diary by Boston merchant Richard Alsop (under Jewitt's supervision) romanticizes his captivity and has a Robinson Crusoe flavor that made it one of the best sellers of the early 1800s. John R. Jewitt spent most of the rest of his life promoting his book, and once played himself in a dramatization of his experiences. He died at the age of thirty-eight in Hartford, Connecticut, in 1821.

Maquinna was succeeded by his eldest son, who married a princess of the Muchalaht, a tribe whose territory adjoined the Mowachaht. They had two sons; the eldest took the name of his father, Tsaxhwosip, when he succeeded him. The younger brother was Ciwuc. Tsaxhwosip ruled only for a few years before he died, and because he had no sons, the office passed to Ciwuc.

Tsaxhwosip's body was wrapped in sea otter skins and lashed high in a tree near the coast on Hectate Channel so that all of the members of his tribe and the neighboring tribes could see his body and mourn. Sometime later it was noticed that the lashings holding the body in the tree had been tampered with, and a man climbed the tree to investigate. The prime sea otter skins were missing. There was a report that a man of the Muchalaht was seen nearby, so Ciwuc assembled his men to go to the Muchalaht village. No one was there, but they came upon a man and his son fishing nearby whom they beheaded and left in their canoes.

So began what historians call the Muchalaht wars. Maquinna's grandson Ciwuc led the Mowachaht in a war of attrition that lasted for years and had a single objective: to wipe out the Muchalaht. Some years after hostilities began, Ciwuc developed a ruse to get him and his warriors in to the principal Muchalaht village: he would go ostensibly to buy a Muchalaht wife. When it seemed that the Muchalaht were convinced of his peaceful intentions, he and his warriors would surprise their hosts and kill them. It did not work. As Ciwuc was being taken across a river to get his canoe, the plot was discovered, and Ciwuc, after a companion was shot, jumped in the water. Swimming for shore, he was intercepted by the war chief of the Muchalaht who picked him up and repeatedly threw him against the large rocks on the shore. The story goes that Ciwuc said, "I thought no one would dare kill so great a chief as I," and the Muchalaht rejoined with, "You killed many of our people. This is the revenge of the Muchalaht." He battered Ciwuc to death.[21]

Though without a chief—for Ciwuc had no sons—the Mowachaht raged against any tribe that came near, but they never again mounted a serious attempt to battle the smaller tribe of the Muchalaht.

Peace came in the 1870s when three chiefs met and pledged to war no more.[22]

Today, over 130 years later, Friendly Cove—once Friendly Harbor—is a Canadian national historic site. The old "Nootka" plaque has been replaced by a Mowachaht marker. The Mowachaht are now called the Nuu-Chah-Nulth tribal group, and the old enemies have combined under the name Mowachaht-Muchalaht First Nation. And it is reasonable to assume that somewhere on Vancouver Island there are great, great, great grandsons and granddaughters of John R. Jewitt.

Well over a hundred years ago, on the other side of the island, a young German anthropologist began taking notes about a most unusual culture—the Kwakiutl, the subject of the next chapter.

8

Life for Life — The Kwakiutl

In 1886, a twenty-eight-year-old German anthropologist began what was to become a forty-year study of the Kwakiutl Indians of British Columbia, Canada. His name was Franz Boas, and he is regarded by many as the real father of anthropology in North America. The next year, 1887, he joined the faculty of Clark University in Worcester, Massachusetts, and by so doing became one of the first academic anthropologists in the United States. Eight years later, he became the first professor of anthropology at Columbia University.[1]

His first major paper on the Kwakiutl was the most exhaustive study of any culture conducted up to that time. It was titled *The Social Organization and the Secret Societies of The Kwakiutl Indians*. A significant contribution to the 1895 Report of the U.S. National Museum, it was printed in Washington by the government printing office in 1897.

During his visits to the Kwakiutl in 1886 to 87 and again in 1893, Boas, who had learned the Kwakiutl language,[2] enlisted the help of George Hunt,[3] whose mother was an Indian, the wife of the Fort Rupert Station manager of the Hudson Bay Company.

The Kwakiutl, neighbors of the Nootka, lived on the eastern shores of Vancouver Island and on the western shores of the mainland. The traders and adventurers who anchored off Vancouver Island to trade for sea otter pelts generally overlooked them. The first European contact made with the Kwakiutl[4] was in 1786—by the same trader, James Strange, who had visited the Nootka. Six years later an American, two Spaniards[5] and the man for whom their island was eventually named, George Vancouver, separately established contact with the Kwakiutl. Frequent and regular white contact and trade began in the early 1830s, a direct result of new trading posts by the Hudson Bay Company.

Boas made no claims to being a historian, and his extremely detailed study of Kwakiutl culture lacks a timeline. For instance, there is no hard evidence that the tribes of the Kwakiutl ate human flesh as food; there is an abundance of evidence that they engaged in ritual cannibalism. Did this practice continue until the time Boas was with the Kwakiutl, or did it end with settlement pressure, Canadian law, and the establishment of missions in the 1850s and 1860s? The evidence is inconclusive. Other anthropologists who have studied the tribe assert that they resisted European pressure much better than their neighbors,[6] and there are records of prosecutions by the Canadians for ritual cannibalism up to the 1890s.

The Kwakiutl, Nootka, and other tribes in the area around and on British Columbia's Vancouver Island raided indiscriminately for slaves, took the heads of their enemies in war, or tied their captives to stakes and split open their bellies to drink the blood. Their vicious war practices gave way to the famous potlatch[7] contests where the victorious clans were the wealthiest, because they could give away the largest number of valuable blankets and slabs of copper. A Kwakiutl speaker at the winter ceremonies at Fort Rupert in 1895 put it this way:

> "When I was young, I have seen streams of blood shed in war. But since the time the white man came and stopped up that stream of blood with wealth, now we are fighting with wealth."[8]

Isolated, nestled between the sea and the mountains, they knew nothing of the cannibalism of the Iroquois, nor is it likely that they had ever heard stories of human flesh-eating by the Chippewa. Yet, cannibal stories are as common in Kwakiutl legends as they are in early Greek mythology and in the scary children tales of medieval Europe. The Kwakiutl had their own "Hansel and Gretel" tale about a witch-spirit named Tsonoqoa, who lived on a diet of little children. Visitors to the northwestern coasts of North America most likely have seen Tsonoqoa carved on house posts, in masks, and in other totem carvings. She has enormous breasts, her mouth is open with her tongue extended down her chin, her eyes are hollow, and she carries a basket.

In the legend, Tsonoqoa puts children in the basket, children she has carried to her house in the woods with a secret red chewing gum over their eyes. There were over thirty-six different Kwakiutl villages, and each of them had a favorite version of the story. Boas translated the version wherein two of the children she captured were sons of a tribal chieftain. As the distraught mother of the children cried, she threw mucus on the floor, which miraculously turned into the small body of a child. In only four days, he grew fast enough to master the bow and arrow and go into the forest to free his brothers and destroy Tsonoqoa. After finding her house, he was told she was at the lake getting water. He silently stalked her, spotted her, and climbed a nearby tree.

Here the English translation of the legend becomes a little confusing. Franz Boas wrote it as: "The Tsonoqoa saw his image in the water and made love to him. She looked up and discovered him." This happened before she spoke to him and he came down from the tree. She asked him how and why he was so beautiful. He replied that it was because he put his head between two stones. She liked this idea, and went to the edge of the lake and got two large stones for herself. The boy instructed her to lie down with her head on one of the stones and to close her eyes. He then smashed her head "and her brains scattered." He then used the stones to break all of her bones, which he threw into the water.

Returning to the house in the woods to rescue the children he was told by a woman that Tsonoqoa cannot be killed. She will return. You must shoot her "life" when she enters a knothole in a nearby hemlock tree. Even as the boy receives the message, he hears the cannibal witch chanting,

> I have the magical treasure,
> I have the supernatural power,
> I can return to life.

The boy shot her "life" with an arrow. She fell dead and was thrown into the hole of the tree where she had intended cooking the children. The boy washed the eyes of the children with urine and took them home. Those who were dead came alive again. And the boy, actually a god in disguise, went back to heaven.[9]

The Kwakiutl institutionalized cannibalism and may have eaten their enemies during their earliest history, a history that archaeologists speculate may go back as far as five thousand years. During the late prehistory period and later, after the first contact by white men, a select few were cannibals, but they did not do it for nutrition, nor to render deep insult to those they hated, nor to gain the powers and courage of the victim. The Kwakiutls who dined on human flesh did it as an obligation and as a privilege granted to only a few by the Manitou—the guardian spirit—of the clan.

Throughout North America, young warrior initiates sought their personal guardian spirit, a protector who granted supernatural powers, and after fasting, ceremonies, and often physical endurance tests, the spirit entered into the warrior. In most cases and in most Indian tribes, the spirit was as individual as the person it inhabited; not so with the Kwakiutl. Instead of personal guardian spirits fashioned to the personality and way of life of the individual, the Kwakiutl spirit was inherited. It was the living spirit of the clan passed down through the generations. Because heredity was the determinant, the number of warriors receiving a particular guardian spirit was limited.

It is a common belief in primitive and many modern religious groups that when one enters into reenactment rituals, with costumes, words, objects, songs and dances, and the participant uses the items and the ritual to personify the spirit, he acquires the spirit's powers. Examples abound in Christianity, starting with the communion celebration and extending at the extreme to devotees having themselves crucified.

The Kwakiutl fervently believed that reenacting the dramatic performance of their central myth (the story of the ancestor's acquisition of the spirit powers) gave those supernatural powers to the actor-initiate. In imagery peculiar to the northwestern tribes, the costumes of the various spirits were made of cedar bark dyed blood red. The cedar was soaked in the red sap of alder bark.

The Kwakiutl believed in four main spirits, but there are others only half recognized by the early anthropologists who studied the tribe, spirits never completely understood.

There is Winalagilis, the war spirit, whose name literally means "making war all over the earth." Matem is the magical spirit of flight, illustrated as a bird; Matem gives the power to fly. Also, there is a spirit of ghosts who can give the power to return to life after violent death (Boas does not provide a name for the ghost spirit), and the cannibal spirit, Baxbakualanuxsiwae, "the first one to eat man at the mouth of the river."[10]

Baxbakualanuxsiwae continually pursued men. He had a wife and female slave to help him find human food. His house emitted red smoke, and in it lived a raven that pecked out the eyes of the people his master ate. Another

A Hamatsa, a Kwakiutl Indian of the cannibal spirit.

bird, bigger, sucked out the brains. This ghoulish menagerie also included a grizzly bear, a close friend of the cannibal spirit.[11]

Not every clan member living under the cannibal spirit, however, was a cannibal. Only the hamatsa and the less violent hamshamtses were given that privilege. Other followers of the guardian spirit took the form of bears who killed for the hamatsa or acted as his servants with responsibility for obtaining flesh for him to eat. Some recipients of the spirit had little connection to cannibalism—their forte was the ability to eat fire and touch it without being burned.

In the myth of the cannibal spirit, Baxbakualanuxsiwae was tricked into falling into a hole lined with fire-red rocks. In some versions of the myth, additional heated stones were thrown on him to assure his death. A woman who lived with the spirit and who was rooted to the floor gave instructions on how to kill the spirit to young men who had been sent to find out why tribal members were disappearing. To deceive the cannibal spirit, the appearance of the young men is explained as food the woman has gathered for Baxbakualanuxsiwae. Baxbakualanuxsiwae is described as having bloody mouths all over his body.

When the cannibal spirit died, a young warrior took his costumes, masks, whistles, the hamatsa pole, the raven mask and the bear mask home to his father. The father and son then returned to the cabin of the dead spirit and were told the secrets and ceremonies of Baxbakualanuxsiwae by the woman who turned out to be the lost sister of the slayer and daughter of the father. She could not leave the cabin, however, because she was rooted to the floor, and cutting the roots would kill her.

She told the young warrior brother about Qominoqa, the woman who gathered the corpses for the hamatsa to eat, and the parts played by the raven and the bear. She told them to hold winter ceremonies and what the young man must do to become a hamatsa.

Incongruity abounds here. The Kwakiutl's hate and fear of Baxbakualanuxsiwae, which leads to his death, and the instant and eager acquisition of his cannibal powers by his slayers is a cultural puzzle, explained by a few contemporary anthropologists as a dramatization "of life giving power and destructive human desire" brought under control.[12]

Versions of the story vary by clan. The Awikenox version explains the creation of one of the Northwest's greatest pests. After the death of Baxbakualanuxsiwae, his bones are taken from the hot rock pile, cut into small pieces and thrown to the wind with the instruction "Baxbakualanuxsiwae, you shall pursue man!" His bones turned into mosquitoes.

In the Baxbakualanuxsiwae legend of the Nimish clan, the ancestor returned to his home after slaying the spirit, and bird-like, flew to the graveyard, dug up corpses, and ate them.

There were only two ways to receive the honors, rights and privileges of a hamatsa. To be a hamatsa, a Kwakiutl must be from a clan of the cannibal sprit, and must replace a present hamatsa. The novice either married the daughter of a hamatsa who relinquished his rights and gave them to his son-in-law, or he killed a hamatsa and stole his masks and whistles. He could also kill a novice undergoing initiation in the forest and gain the right to take his place.

The family of the murdered initiate was not allowed to revenge the death. Under this system, the total number of hamatsas in the Kwakiutl and other nearby tribes was always constant.

Franz Boas explained the confusing changes among the Kwakiutl from tribal and clan units to adherents and possessors of a special spirit:

> . . . a number of spirits . . . appear to the Indians and are supposed to bestow supernatural powers upon them. From the legends which I have been told, it appears that these spirits appeared first to the ancestors of the clan, and I have stated that the same spirits continue to appear to the descendants of these mythical ancestors. The number of spirits is limited, and the same one appeared to ancestors of various clans of different tribes. But in these cases he gave each of his protégés his powers in a slightly different form. In fact each name of the nobility has a separate tradition of the acquisition of supernatural powers, and these have descended upon the bearers of the name.
>
> As indicated in some of the traditions, the spirits give new names to the men to whom they appear, but these names are in use only during the time when the spirits dwell among the Indians, that is, in winter. Therefore from the moment when the spirits are supposed to be present, all the summer names are dropped, and the members of the nobility take their winter names.
>
> It is clear that with the change of name the whole social structure, which is based on the names, must break down. Instead of being grouped in clans, the Indians are now grouped according to the spirits which have initiated them. All those who are protected by Baxbakualanuxsiwae form one group; those who stand under Winalagilis form another group, etc., and in these groups divisions are made according to the ceremonies or dances bestowed upon the person.
>
> The social system changes at the beginning of the winter ceremonial. The complete social and governing structure regroups into societies, each of which has as its members those to whom the special power or secret has been bestowed.

The Kwakiutl have a different name for the time before the winter ceremonials, which translates as "profane." The time of the winter ceremonials was called "the secrets," and "making the heart good."

George Hunt transcribed a story in 1895 from an older Kwakiutl who said it occurred at the time "when we were still naked," probably around 1845.

The storyteller and his companions and a friend and his companions were in their canoes, pursued by enemies from the north. Paddling as fast as they could, the two groups went in different directions, to escape death or slavery. Their enemies stopped at a sandbar and set up camp on the edge of the woods. The storyteller and his companion later decided to attempt to find the enemies to see if they had captured their friend and companions.

In Hunt's transcription, the storyteller related what happened next in this way:

> We paddled to the island. When we arrived there, I took my gun and went ashore. I went to where the fire was burning on the beach and saw that the warriors had unloaded their canoes. I said to my companion: "take care, my dear, I am going to shoot them." We hauled up our canoe and hid. As soon as we reached there, we sat down close to them. They were eating. There were five men in line from my seat and my friend said that there were three in line from his seat. We put thirty balls of buckshot each in our guns and fired both at the same time. I had killed three and wounded two others. My friend had killed two and wounded the third man. And I saw two more men running away. Then we ran to the wounded ones and killed them. One man and four women we took alive and made them our slaves. We took the property of the northern people. I looked into a large box, and when I opened it I saw much red cedar bark and abalone shells which were attached to it, and whistles of a hamatsa. I asked one of the women: "what is that in this box?" She only replied: "Hom, hom, hom, hom, ham ham, ham, hu, hu," and she bit her own arm. Then I knew that one of these men who we shot had been a hamatsa. I cried "hap" right away. ["Hap" translates as "eat" or "eating."][13]

Thus, the storyteller became a hamatsa by killing one.

One of the best known war stories of the tribes of the Northwest, including the Kwakiutl, tells of a conflict between the Bilxua (more commonly referred to today as the Bellacoola) and the Kwakiutl and their allies. The version of the story told to George Hunt illustrates the no-mercy warfare common in this part of the world in the early 1800s. The Bilxua sought revenge for the theft of a hamatsa whistle, and attacked a village on what is now Gilford Island, a heavily forested, mountainous, twenty-by-thirteen-mile island near Vancouver Island in British Columbia. This event probably occurred in 1857.

The Bilxua stayed in their canoes not far from the beach until it was almost daylight. It was foggy. As soon as it grew daylight, they landed and many men went to the rear of the houses. As soon as they were ready, the most courageous warriors broke into the doors of the houses and speared men, women and children. Whoever tried to escape through the rear door was speared by the men stationed there. Others of the Bilxua looked after the valuable property and put it into their canoes . . . Then the Bilxula set fire to the houses. Their canoes were deeply loaded with mens' heads.[14]

The Kwakiutl and three other tribes pledged to fight together to annihilate the Bilxula. The Kwakiutl chief, in his revenge pre-battle speech given before his allies, said, "Fathers, uncles, brothers, children, thank you that you have come. Now let us go and look for our exterminated tribe . . . who were eaten by the Bilxula. Let us make them vomit our tribe!"

It didn't turn out that way, at least on this outing. The Kwakiutl, while searching an island for the Bilxula, ran into a party of Heiltsuq (now known as Bellabella) Indians. The Heiltsuq were not enemies, but their chiefs and captains were all hamatsas, so they were slain by the Kwakiutl for their masks, bark, and whistles—for in those days, to be a cannibal, you had to kill one. After the battle, the chief said "We have done a great thing." The Heiltsuq are relatives of the Bilxua, he proclaimed. Then the victorious warriors gathered up their newly found ceremonial loot, and went home.

The purpose of the winter ceremonies, according to the Kwakiutl, was to purify and return to a normal life those initiates who had absorbed the spirits. Or, as Boas wrote: "when he has returned in a state of ecstasy, to exorcize the spirit . . . and to restore him from his holy madness."

The hamatsa initiate spent three to four months in the wilderness prior to the winter ceremonies, and during that time, he became a cannibal in fact.

When hungry, he appeared at the edge of the village, sounded his whistles and shouted "hap, hap, hap," a call for his "kinqalalala," the person, generally a female relative, who was required to procure food for him.

Two early observers of the tribe reported that upon one occasion when hamatsas returned to the village, a slave was shot and dismembered and fed to them in the order of their rank as they squatted down and shouted "hap, hap, hap." In memory of the event, the Kwakiutl carved on the site—on a sandstone rock on the beach—an image of the face of Baxbakualanuxsiwae. A photograph of the carving appears in the 1895 Annual Report of the Smithsonian.[15]

Boas recorded another killing of a slave, as told by one of the participants:

> A female slave was asked to dance for the hamatsa. Before she began dancing she said: "Do not get hungry, do not eat me." She had hardly said so when her master, who was standing behind her, split her skull with an ax. She was eaten by the hamatsa.[16]

The same old Indian who told this story, Qomenakula, reported that it was the custom to take the bones of the slaves eaten by the hamatsas and bind them and hide them on the shady side of the house where the sun would never see them. Then after four days, they were weighted with a stone and thrown into deep water. The Kwakiutl feared if the bones were buried, they would return and take the soul of their master. She also said that it was very hard to eat fresh human flesh. It was much easier to eat dried corpses.

George Hunt, whose mother was a Tingit Indian noblewoman and whose father worked for the Hudson Bay Company, proved to be a rich source of information to Boas. It is probable that Hunt was a hamatsa, because he was arrested by Canadian authorities for participating in a hamatsa ceremony when he was working as an Indian agent. He was neither convicted nor dismissed from his job, because all of the Kwakiutl said that he was not guilty of the charge against him—cutting up a corpse for the ceremony.

There is a story from Hunt, which he told to the famous photographer and writer Edward S. Curtis, about a winter dance he observed in 1875. The dance was being held by the Owikeno clan and the Nakwoktak had been invited, but when the guests paddled to shore, they did not bring the customary corpse.

Beach rock carving of the face of the Hamatsa's spirit god.

Hunt told Curtis:

> After they had entered the dance house, their hosts brought
> forth a mummy and it was eaten in the usual way. During
> the feast Yahyekulagyilis was evidently revolving something
> in his mind while he regarded a female slave belonging to
> one of his companions. Soon he directed one of his atten-
> dants, in a whisper, to go and ask the owner if he would
> take a hundred blankets for his slave. This was a generous
> offer and was quickly accepted. . . . After the mummy was
> eaten, [he] rose and led the other hamatsas in a rapid dance
> round the fire. Four times round they went, and then sud-
> denly he leaped upon the slave woman, who fell on her
> back.
>
> Quick as a flash he fastened his teeth on her throat. She
> struggled and scratched his face, but he kept his hold, and
> other hamatsas seized the woman's legs.
>
> When she ceased struggling, Yahyekulagyilis cut a hole
> around the navel, severed the intestine, placed an end be-
> tween his teeth, and ran around the fire dragging out the in-
> testine like a rope. While he was doing this another hamatsa
> was cutting the woman's throat and catching the blood in a
> wooden dish, which was passed among the hamatsas to
> drink. Then the flesh was cut into pieces and distributed,
> and as there were many hamatsas among the Owikeno,
> there was no difficulty in consuming all the flesh and leav-
> ing only the bare bones.[17]

The hamatsas ate corpses. Following is the written report of Franz Boas to
the Smithsonian about this cannibalistic practice of the hamatsa after his initiation and before his dance. Changes made to the original text are only in its
paragraphing and the emendations in brackets.

> Besides devouring slaves, the hamatsas also devour corpses.
> When a new hamatsa, after being initiated, returns from the
> woods he will sometimes carry a corpse, which is eaten after
> his dance. The bodies are prepared for this ceremony. The
> skin is cut around the wrists and ankles, and they must not
> eat the hands and feet. It is believed that else they would die

immediately. The hamatsa must use for this ceremony the corpse of one of his deceased relatives, which the heliga must prepare. [The heliga are a group of from six to twelve "healers" who protect the tribal members from the flesh eating urges of the hamatsa, but who also assist him in this gruesome task with corpses.]

The Kwakiutl used to bury their dead on trees. The body was placed in a box, and these boxes were placed on branches a considerable distance up a tree. There the boxes were piled one on top of the other. The bodies, who so exposed to the action of the freely circulating air, mostly mummify. A corpse is taken down from the tree and is soaked in salt water. The heliga takes hemlock twigs, the leaves of which have been removed, and pushes them under the skin, gradually removing all the decayed flesh until nothing but the skin remains. [In this report, there is no mention of the bones, or what happens to them.] After this is done the body is placed on top of the small hut in which the novice [called a "giyakila"] is living while he is staying in the woods. The hands of the body hang down. Its belly is cut open and spread with sticks. The hamatsa keeps a fire under it and smokes it. Four days before he returns to the village he sends for all the old hamatsas. When they come, he tells them: "These are my traveling provisions, which I received from Baxbakualanuxsiwae." He asks them to point out what share they desire to have when he will return. They take the body down and place it on a clean mat. Each points out what he desires to have.

[When returning to the village] his kinqalalala returns with him. She carries the corpse which has been prepared. She goes backward, facing the hamatsa. When she reaches the right side of the fire [in the ceremonial house], the hamatsa enters the house. He stoops so that his face is close to the ground. On entering, he turns four times, descends to the middle of the house, and when he is four steps away from the door, he turns again four times. When the kinqalalala reaches the rear of the house, she turns again.

A drum is placed in the middle of the rear of the house, bottom up. The kinqalalala pretends to put the corpse on the drum, but walks past it, the hamatsa following her. At the door she turns again, proceeds around the fire, and when she reaches the drum a second time, she turns again and pretends to put the body down. At this time all the old hamatsas, who have been outside the house, jump down from the roof and rush in through the doors. They are all naked and follow the kinqalalala in a state of high excitement. When they have run around the fire four times, the body is put down on the drum. The master of ceremonies begins to cut it and distributes the flesh among the hamatsa. But first the kinqalalala takes four bites. The people count how many bites each of them swallows. They are not allowed to chew the flesh, but they bolt it. The kinqalalala brings them water to drink in between.

After this part of the ceremony is finished, the heliga rise, each takes one hamatsa at the head, and they drag them to the salt water. They go into the water until it reaches up to their waists, and, facing the rising sun, they dip the hamatsa four times under water. Every time he rises again he cries hap. Then they go back to the house. Their excitement has left them. They dance during the following nights. They look downcast and do not utter their peculiar cries, hap, hap. They do not dance squatting, but in an erect position.[18]

Winter ceremonies included songs. One of the songs for Baxbakualanuxsiwae went like this:

You are looking for food, you great magician.
You are looking for men you want to eat, great magician
You tear men's skins, great magician
Everybody trembles before you, you great magician, you
who have been to the end of the world

An equally ghastly song originated when a hamatsa named Wanuk cut off the head of an enemy, another hamatsa, and was holding the dripping head in his teeth. Wanuk mocked his dead enemy by singing:

That is the way of the real Baxbakualanuxsiwae.
Are you the real Baxbakualanuxsiwae?

Songs were proprietary. They were the personal property of the hamatsa singer, and could not be sung by any one other than the owner, who often was the composer. Older songs could be bequeathed to a new hamatsa or acquired when the owning hamatsa was killed. One such song was composed by a hamatsa warrior who killed the chief of the Qoexsotenox:

> I have the winter dance song,
> I have magic powers.
> I have the hamatsa song,
> I have magic powers.
> I have Baxbakualanuxsiwae's song,
> I have magic powers.
> Your magic power killed the people,
> and therefore they hide before you,
> fearing your great power.

The warrior lost the song when he was killed by a member of the Qoexsotenox tribe, who then owned the song.

The mysteries and songs of Baxbakualanuxsiwae go beyond that of the creation of the hamatsa and his eagerness for human flesh. And just as the songs were different for the members of this unearthly cast, so were the masks and costumes. Second only to the hamatsa, the woman, qominoqa, had tasks similar to that of kinqalalala, and where the hamatsa wore a costume of red bark, qominoqa, who gathered the bodies for the hamatsa to eat, wore red and white.

Like the hamatsa novice, a qominoqa novice was required to disappear in the woodlands. In the woods, she is initiated by Baxbakualanuxsiwae. When she returns to her tribe she is a terrible sight—her hair is mostly gone and her head is covered with blood from the actions of Baxbakualanuxsiwae. She has a partially decomposed human head in each hand. When she enters the ceremonial house, the hamatsas who gathered to greet her begin a trembling, squatting dance with outstretched arms to accept the gift for them she carries. The qominoqa dances, too, and is joined by other qominoqas, and even other women who had given up their qominoqa status.

The women who join in hold out their hands as though they too have decomposing skulls to offer. As the pace and frenzy of the dance builds, the hamatsas finally take the skulls from the qominoqa's hands to "lick them and eat the maggots and the dry skin attached to them."[19]

The Kwakiutl Indians and most of the tribes of the Northwest developed ceremonies and rituals unlike any in all of North America, with guidelines and rules of conduct so strict a fallen dancer could be clawed, even killed, by ceremonial attendants dressed in bear costumes. During the winter ceremonies, when they gathered in the assembly house, even coughing or throat-clearing were forbidden when the hamatsas were present. During feasting, no one was allowed to eat until the hamatsas had eaten.

The disciples of the cannibal spirit Baxbakualanuxsiwae ranked higher than any of the members of the other secret societies. Though the winter ceremonies included dances, songs, and rituals directed toward other spirits, the main event was the initiation of new hamatsas. All of the ceremonies were heavily dosed with magic and illusions. In one, a participant was be-headed and his blood spurted on the onlookers as the severed head fell into the fire. What really happened in the dimly lit room is this: a bladder filled with animal blood was pressured to burst, and an amazingly lifelike wooden carving of a head tumbled into the fire. All of this happened rap-idly. Even the unharmed participant who fell quickly into a hole dug in the dirt floor—with his head intact—produced the illusion of a decapitated torso disappearing.

Many of the rituals featured voices and sounds apparently coming from nowhere or from the flames of the fire. Sometimes the sounds originated with participants hidden in the rafters of the large assembly hall, or from long tubes inserted in tunnels dug under the building that were shouted into by members of the societies hidden in another room. They made the fire "talk."

In another ceremony, a man standing at the edge of a forest was made to disappear and reappear hundreds of feet away. Man One stepped behind a tree, and man Two, identically dressed and decorated, stepped from behind another tree far away.

Obviously, the nobles of the tribe conspired to make the magic and per-form the illusions for the common people they ruled, even as they initiated a near relative to a higher rank. Even the biting of individuals was staged; cer-tain people were seated near the action of the ceremony so the newly initi-ated cannibal could nip a breast or chomp into an arm or shoulder without venturing too far from the dancing ring.

The words of one song repeated endlessly by the shaman (paxalas) adds some meaning and understanding to the worship of the cannibal spirit:

Baxbakualanuxsiwae made me a winter dancer.
Baxbakualanuxsiwae made me pure.
I do not destroy life, I am the life maker.

The song appears to go to the duality of life and death, summer and winter, the good and the bad, proclaiming that by consuming death, life is given.

When the novice or initiate hamatsa was about to reappear from the woods, the people were cautioned, "Take care! We want to save our great friend." And the kinqalalala (young women who served the hamatsa) sang: I am the real tamer of Baxbakualanuxsiwae. I pull the red cedar bark from Baxbakualanuxsiwae's back. And a second kinqalalala chants: It is in my power to pacify you, when you are in a state of ecstasy.

When the novice arrived, he began his disappearing act. The first "sighting" was not the novice, but a young man chosen to look like him. This stand-in quickly took off his costume and adorned red cedar bark, so as to blend with the people who pursued him.

After several sightings of this kind, a man took off all of his clothes to tempt the new hamatsa to come out and bite him. As the hamatsa took the bait and actually bit the nude man, he was captured by the people and taken to a house. Then the kinqalalala entered naked as they sang their songs. The hamatsa was released and ran around the assembly, biting people, until the audience shed the hemlock branches they wore and threw them into the fire. The smoke from the green branches was supposed to smoke out the wildness of the hamatsa.

The ceremony that lasted for nine or more days ended with the "waleqa," the first meal of the hamatsa after his return from the bush. The kinqalalala accompanied the hamatsa into four houses successively, where the cannibal was required to eat all that was put before him. So ended the winter ceremonies. The people took off their red cedar bark head rings and threw them in the fire. They burned the sticks with which they had pounded the planks in the assembly house. The winter mysteries, the songs, the dancing, the invariant routines were remembered, but put away for a year until another hamatsa father-in-law sponsored a new member.

When the hamatsa ate slaves or the bodies of deceased relatives, the Kwakiutl knew from experience that this practice could bring serious disease and death to the cannibal. Immediately after ingesting a corpse, the hamatsa was forced to drink seawater to induce violent vomiting. Aides counted the pieces of human remains they regurgitated, and, if they did not add up to the amount eaten, excrement was examined to make sure that all of the human flesh had left their bodies. These methods were feasible because the hamatsa was not allowed to chew what he ate.

The fathers-in-law paid off those tribal members who were bitten, but the newly initiated hamatsas began a yearlong period of ceremonial repentance, a hard-and-fast regimen where every normal act was dictated by ritual. They were not allowed to go out of the front or main door of the house in which they were billeted, but exited and entered through a secret door at the rear of the house. When one of the new hamatsas had to go outside to defecate, even that most fundamental function was ordered; all of the new hamatsas had to exit with him, each carrying a small stick. They sat in a line on a large log, then rose three times, and settled down on the fourth time, turned around four times. When they were finished, they turned around four more times before they arose from the log. When they got to the secret door, they turned around four times again before entering the house. They were not allowed to look back.

For four months, each hamatsa had his own kettle, spoon, and dish, which were thrown away at the end of the period. No one could enter the hamatsa's bedroom, and a grizzly bear dancer stood guard at all times to see that the rule was followed. For sixteen days, the hamatsa was not to eat hot food, and was not allowed to blow on hot food to cool it for four months. When he drank from his cup, he had to first dip it into the water three times, and drink on the fourth, but no more than four mouthfuls, and since his lips could not touch the cup, he used the wing bone of an eagle as a straw.[20]

He could neither work nor play for one year, nor could he touch his wife. He pretended that he had forgotten all ordinary ways of living, and that he must learn them all again.

With the "turning four times" and so much four-this and four-that, it is no surprise that the winter ceremonies—the dancing season—lasted about four months, the rough, cold and dangerous months when these men who lived by the sea and from the sea dared not to go too far out in their canoes. The dates do not appear to be fixed, but Boas indicated the ceremonies started sometime in November and ended by March.

The Kwakiutl are survivors. From first-contact in the late 1700s to 1929, population decreased from the diseases brought by the European, Canadian and American traders and settlers. From 1929 to the present time, population increased, but the Kwakiutl have lost much of their identity. As an anthropologist who lived among the Gilford Island group wrote:

"The Kwakiutl are no longer exceptional because of their economic activities, their religious practices and beliefs, their social or ceremonial life; their house style or the food they eat. In most ways, in fact, they live in a style very similar to the White fishermen and loggers who also reside in the area. Therefore the Indians can be viewed as a rural, working-class, sub-cultural variant of the North American class structure, rather than being a distinctive cultural group."[21]

They survived by adapting to the sometime intolerant rules of the Canadians, who outlawed many Kwakiutl traditional ceremonies and customs. To prevent the reoccurrence of these ceremonies in future generations, the authorities sought to acculturate Kwakiutl children by forced education in residential schools. To make matters even worse, the British stole their land. In 1849, they gave title to Vancouver Island to the Hudson Bay Company in an effort to promote white settlement. Conflicts began with the white authorities in the 1850s and continued into the 1860s. In 1881, there were forty settlers, and by 1921 that number had increased to five thousand. No one was granted permission to settle by the Indians, nor was any land ceded to the white man through treaties or as a result of war. Today the Kwakiutl occupy a portion of their original homeland, which remains some of the most beautiful, awe-inspiring real estate in North America.

The Indians of British Columbia had a hard time of it, but they did not have to endure being hunted down like animals by militia and vigilante gangs as did the California Indians—as explained in the next chapter.

9

Anomalous Californians — The Yuki and Their Neighbors

Yukian speech and physiognomy so differed from most of the tribes of California that the foremost authority on that state's native peoples, Alfred L. Kroeber, called the Yuki "autochthonous Californians" and "anomalous."[1] They were shorter, had longer faces, and spoke a language that could not be identified with any other major linguistic group.

The Yuki lived in one of the most idyllic valleys of all of North America, Round Valley in northeastern Mendocino County in California. Snuggled between the snow capped Yolla Bolly peaks and the coast range spurs, the Eel River flows among giant oaks and a verdant plain which in prehistoric times provided all the Yuki required in game and plant food. This tribe of hunters and gatherers was strongly territorial, and many of their conflicts with nearby tribes were to protect the land they claimed, or to wreak vengeance for some wrong done to them. The Yuki were headhunters. And so were many of their neighbors and enemies.

Most of the tribes in North America that beheaded their enemies were cohesive, highly organized hierarchal groups with strong and powerful leaders. Heads were taken and exhibited as a grisly object lesson by some tribal rulers, just as they were under the authority of European monarchs, by the U.S. Army,[2] and by the Pilgrims of New England. Heads were not to dance over, but to frighten. With most tribes across the continent, scalps were the real trophies of successful battles and raids, of victory and vengeance, though to be sure, the ceremonies and customs associated with them varied more

116

geographically than by tribe. The tribes of central California took scalps, but they preferred heads. In this and in many other ways, they were different from the continental norms.

Some of the California tribes, notably the Pomo, Valley Maidu, Wintun and the Yokuts were known not to take either scalps or heads, nor did they have victory dances. These tribes sometimes held what have been called "incitement" dances, which were conducted with their enemies before a battle. These dances began when hostile parties gathered to settle a feud, danced with their weapons in hand, and in their anger, ended up using them.

Most of the other tribes in California gathered scalps, tied them to poles, and held loosely organized ceremonies around them with yelps and stomping. Except for the Mohave and Yuma, the scalp dance did not follow any traditional or prescribed form, though generally it was a loud and wild celebration. When it ended, the scalp was disposed of, either thrown away or burned. The Janeño around San Juan Capistrano were an exception; they saved scalps for future ceremonies.

The very definition of "scalp" varied among the California tribes. The tribes that took scalps in most of North America cut the flesh around the hairline of their dead enemy, grasped the hair, and pulled for their trophy. Californians took more time to attain a larger scalp. They decapitated the dead warrior and took the head to their village where it was skinned to include the top of the head and the ears, eyes, and nose. The Mohaves differed even among the California tribes. They took the entire skin of the head except that triangle that includes the eyes, nose, and mouth.

Intensive and extremely ruthless warfare prevented most California Indians from dying of old age, and equally ominous practices caused some to die before they were the critical three days old.

Most all of the California tribes practiced infanticide in some measure, especially with newborns who were deformed in any way or in the birth of twins. Killing newborn twins seems to have been restricted to brother-sister twins; in those cases, the female infant was killed. Male twins were often allowed to live. There is one known case where triplets were not killed, even though custom demanded it. Among the Yuki, ever different, twins were cherished and thought to be a special blessing.

As a young warrior-to-be grew into young adulthood, assuming he was fortunate enough to escape the dangers of constant warfare, accidentally broken bones, and natural disasters, he could look forward only to later years of misery and mistreatment. Outside of California, semi-nomadic southwestern and plains Indians were known to leave the very old with food and water, alone, waiting to die when the tribe or group moved on. This probably also happened among some tribes in California, but the information available indicates that in most tribes of that region, the elderly were cared for, especially those who remained in a family group. Yet the old got the last food, the worst clothes, and little respect.[3]

There exists an eye-witness report that the Gallinomero (Southern Pomo) Indians, who lived around what is now Sonoma County in California, sometimes killed aging parents who were unable to carry their share of the labors of existence, as in this case:

> He puts his decrepit mother or father to death . . . when the former can no longer feebly creep to the forest to gather his back-load of fuel or a basket of acorns, and is only a burden to his sons, the poor old wretch is not unfrequently [sic] thrown down on his back and securely held while a stick is placed across his throat and two of them seat themselves on the end of it until he ceases to breathe.[4]

How often this occurred and how widely it extended to other nearby tribes in the Somoma area is unknown. In any case, it is clear that those who killed, whether the victims were children, enemies, or the old, believed that the killings were justified. These killings were institutionalized; the society in which they occurred approved of the acts.

California Indians killed their enemies and sometimes killed their relatives, but they did not eat them. With the rare exceptions found in any population, California Indians did not engage in cannibalism. That does not mean that they did not accuse their enemies of being cannibals. Cannibalism was something someone else did, someone or some people who were feared and generally far away. Cannibals were always the next tribe up the mountain. In reality, the Indians of California so abhorred the idea of cannibalism that they even refused to eat bear meat, fearing the bear they killed might have been a bear shaman who had changed himself into a bear. By eating the bear, they might be committing cannibalism, or the bear, particularly a grizzly, might have eaten a person, so eating the bear would be like eating a person.[5]

There is one reference in Stephen Powers' *Tribes of California* about early

California Indians engaging in cannibalism. It is certainly not as authenticated as the Jesuit reports of cannibalism of the Iroquois, thousands of miles to the east. The account has to do with the cremation ceremonies of the Gallinomero, a wild, frenetic dance around a pyre, accompanied by screams and howls of mourning by friends and relatives with black pitch in their hair and on their faces. In a hypnotic, wild-eyed, feverish state, dancers were seen grabbing the flaming flesh of the deceased and eating it.[6]

The second reference to cannibalism is vague. The California Costanoan Indians who lived around San Francisco cut off the heads of prisoners and dismembered the bodies. The scalp or the entire head was given to the parents of the warrior who killed him, and "it is said" that the parents ate some parts of the body of the victim.[7]

The Yuki, too, have been accused of cannibalism. In an account compiled by Stephen Powers in 1871 to 74, the first attempt at a comprehensive study of California tribes, the Wintun Indians described the Yuki as ". . . savage giants, living in the coast range mountains, dwelling in caves and dens, horribly tattooed . . . and cannibals."[8] The Yuki were certainly not giants; in fact, they were shorter than most California Indians. They may have had a few caves, but like most of their neighbors, they lived in wood, dirt and sapling houses. The men were indeed "horribly tattooed," but the indictment of cannibalism is probably a metaphor for fear and disgust. The only other time it appears is in an interview with a Nomlaki in the mid-1930s, who related a story told to him by his grandparents wherein the Yuki had killed a family group and "cut up our people and made 'jerky' of them."[9]

Prisoners taken by the California tribes were almost always killed, and attacking warriors did not care about the sex or age of their victims. The northern California Maidu tied captives to poles inside the tribal dance house where they were mutilated and burned to death. "Several of the devices . . . show some ingenuity of cruelty, but the torture gives the impression of a spontaneous expression of hatred rather than of a refined system of prolonging anguish."[10] The Apache and other war-like tribes captured young boys and raised them as tribal members, but some California Indians took young girls instead and raised them as slaves. Most reports say that they were not molested, and treated rather well. There are, however, also stories of them being killed.[11]

These few observations are not in any way an ethnographic outline of the war and killing practices of California aboriginals. The statements are far too broad for that, and anyone who studies California Indians soon realizes that the only safe generalization is that they are different from each other, and from the rest of the tribes of North America. In California, during the periods of early European contact, there were around five hundred different Indian territories with villages—some anthropologists call them *tribelets*—and over one hundred languages and dialects were spoken.

It is the Yuki and their enemy neighbors who were the most unique of all. These tribes were headhunters. For them, to win a battle, you must collect one enemy head.

Alfred L. Kroeber, a star pupil of Franz Boas at Columbia who became the first dean of anthropology at the University of California, interviewed hundreds of Native Americans and recorded their oral histories. He began his work in California in 1901 and for seventeen years assembled the stories, history and data that were eventually published as the *Handbook of Indians of California* in 1923. Here is a portion of what he wrote about the wars of the Yuki and the Kato, using information gleaned from the grandchildren of the participants:

> Word came to the Yuki on Eel River that if they would come to the Kato village of "redrock-creek," they would receive gifts; that is, that the Kato wanted to trade, making a donation first and then accepting presents in return. When the Yuki arrived an old man and two of his sons were killed and two other young men captured by the Kato. A brother and a son of the old man, named, respectively, Titopi and Pitaki, escaped. The former had indeed been seized, but broke away. As he fled up the canyon he was shot through the hand with an arrow. But he made his escape, and when he arrived on top of the mountain sat down and mourned his brother.

The Yuki apparently knew the Kato man who was responsible for the attack, because the story teller called him Palmi. At no time in this long interview was Kroeber told of the fate of the two men captured by the Kato. This was not unusual, though, since "capture" meant "death by torture." Like the Yuki, the Kato were headhunters, so they chopped off the head of one of the dead Yukis to take back to their village.

Of course this meant war. War Yuki-and-Kato style, more often than not, consisted of fast, small raids or ambushes where the attackers attempted first to get hold of a victim and then dispatch him at close quarters. Then if other opponents had fled, the victim would be beheaded. Both tribes engaged in some stand-up fighting, but Kroeber's interviews revealed that these battles were long-range affairs "with arrows and infinite dodging" with few casualties and inconclusive results.

Kroeber related how.

> The Kato, anticipating reprisals, came to a Yuki settlement on Eel River, and succeeded in killing an old Yuki and carrying off his head. This was "too soon," according to the narrator, for the Yuki had not yet made an attack in return for their first loss. But after this they went out.
>
> The Yuki scouts were run on to by a young Kato known to them as Hutichpalsi. He was seized, bound, his arms stretched out, and his head cut off. There may have been more fighting; but apparently the Yuki having got a head for the one that they had lost, were satisfied and went home. At Tamahan [Yuki village] they built a dance house for the occasion and celebrated over the trophy.

The Yuki and the Kato sporadically engaged in conflicts such as this. When the heads had been collected, the associated ceremonies completed, life returned to normal for both tribes. That would have happened after this short conflict, but peace was upset when the sister of the old man killed in the last Kato attack sought revenge.

She had a plot:

> . . . and pretended a revival of friendship. Supported by a party of Yuki in hiding, she followed her husband to a Kato house. When he had entered, he made as if he were having difficulty passing through the door a large basket of buckeye porridge which his wife had brought up; until one of the two Kato men inside said: "Set down this Yuki blood." At once the husband leaped upon them, his wife rushed in, and between them they overpowered and killed the two inmates. A Kato woman seized up her baby and fled, but the Yuki amazon ran her down at a near-by spring and brained both her and the Infant. The main Yuki party probably came

up after the affair was over, since the narrative does not
mention them again; and if there were Kato in near-by
houses, they probably fled at the first alarm, knowing that
an attack would not be made without an equipped and out-
numbering force in reserve.

These bellicose societies could not stop fighting. Now it was the Katos' turn
to go on the offensive. The Yuki narrator admitted that eleven of their people
were killed. After organizing another war party and traveling toward the Kato
villages, the Yuki "hesitated whether to attack or to treat for settlement." They
did neither.

The majority of the Yuki went home or turned aside. Two Yuki bear doctors, shamans of unusual ferocity, who had the grizzly as their protector and
could more or less completely turn themselves into this dangerous and vindictive animal, in native belief, trusted in their power or the fear of their re-
pute, and boldly went or remained among the Kato. The latter took one of
the two brothers fishing, and after cooking one of the catch offered it to him.
The Yuki, however, knew in his heart that the fish had been poisoned by one
of the Kato who could exercise magical control, and refused; whereupon a
Kato came up to hold him, no doubt preliminary to the others dispatching
him. The unarmed bear doctor, however, seized his bone hairpin, and using it
as a bear would use his teeth, killed the man who had grasped him and several others after him, until the Kato, recognizing his supernatural abilities and
invulnerability, desisted.

Bear doctors existed in the lore of all of the California tribes, except for
the Colorado River tribes in the south and a few groups in the most northern
corners of the state. The bear shaman had the power to turn himself into a
grizzly bear; he was invulnerable as a grizzly: stronger, more destructive than
any normal man. When assuming this power, he wore a bearskin. In European folklore, the most comparable animal-person-creature is the werewolf.
Kroeber continues:

> A true bear shaman cannot, in fact, be killed with weapons;
> but they may have been unconvinced that his powers were
> complete and genuine. About the same time his brother was
> attacked at the Kato village where he had remained behind,
> but saved himself by recourse to similar faculties. The Yuki
> of today believe that between them the two medicine men

disposed of six of their foes before they returned home, and that so strong and bear-like was the frenzy of the one brother that he chewed and actually devoured part of the arm of the rash man who ventured to be the first to hold him.

The story told to Kroeber had some holes in it. The Yuki admit that during this incident they lost two men. Both the Yuki and the Kato ran away, but on the next day the Kato returned to find the two Yuki corpses. True to form, they cut off their heads. Kroeber summed up the story:

> The count stood 17 or 19 killings for the Kato, only 11 for the Yuki, in half a dozen or more encounters, though without a pitched fight, during a period that very likely covered two or three years. Excitement must now have been at a point where larger undertakings might be attempted; and in fact all the Yuki talked of combining for one great expedition into Kato territory. Talk and deliberation are, however, the necessary and almost endless preliminary to any joint action of California Indians, however swift and resolute they may be in crises as individuals; and talk it remained. For the whites appeared in the country, upset the native life, and gave Yuki and Kato alike more pressing problems to meet than even their feud.[12]

The Yuki, Steven Powers wrote, "were indisputably the worst tribe among the California Indians."[13] "Yuki" in the Wintun language literally means "stranger," and that translates to "enemy." Recall that it was the Nomlaki group of the Wintun tribe that claimed the Yuki made "jerky" of Nomlakis they had killed. The Wintuns lived somewhat north and east of the Yuki on the other side of the coast mountain range. There were no cushioning tribes between them, and they were often at war in the summer, when they both climbed the 7,500-foot slopes to hunt and gather plant foods.

In a story told by the Nomlaki Wintuns, the Yuki killed a large number of their people and stole their food. This story purports to tell of the last big fight between the two tribes and is to have happened about three years after the Americans came to the area. Three years after the Americans dates the battle to around 1850. The Nomlaki found the Yuki in Round Valley having a scalp (or war) dance, a ritual celebration for killing many of their enemies. The Nomlaki split their party, sending one group to gather the stolen food-stuffs and another to attack and kill the Yuki and burn their houses. In the ensuing battle, so the Nomlaki story goes, all of the adult Yuki were killed, and eighteen girls and three boys were captured and brought back to the Nomlaki camp.

A Nomlaki, Joe Freeman—his Indian name is not known—told the rest of the story this way:

> On Thomes' Creek they [Nomlaki] kept the [Yuki] girls a couple of years and made them work. They built a big sweat house there. They set a war dance for the spring of the year, for they were going to kill those girls. The Nomlaki set a pole in the ground and attached crosspieces, like a ladder, so that they could make the girls climb up there. Then they dressed the girls in feathers, painted their lips and cheeks, and tied their hands in back of them. As they put each girl on the pole they tied her leg on each side of it and stood her up. They had gathered up a pile of small rocks and a lot of wood, and a big fire was built as soon as night fell. They started to yell and run around the girl they had upon the pole. They danced, and made the other girls dance too . . . They circled around her, stopping to give a whoop and to shoot arrows into her. They all took a shot at her, and she was quite a while dying. They didn't quit dancing until she died. Singers changed off and never stopped singing until she died. When she was dead they put another one up the same way. The girls that were to be killed were forced to dance, too.
>
> My grandfather had one of the boys who had learned to talk Nomlaki. He was a good boy, so my grandfather told him that he was to be killed in the same way. He sent the boy after water and told him to run away, and to stay in the canyons so they wouldn't find him. When the Nomlaki noticed that this boy was gone they told my grandfather, and made him go out to look for the boy with them. So he went out on a ridge and watched the trail on the summit by Log Springs, and when the boy came up the ridge he told him to get down in the canyon. Then my grandfather returned and

told the people he hadn't seen the boy, and they gave up the hunt.

After all had been killed they took the girls and the two boys and laid them down with the heads to the west and the feet to the east, on top of the ground. Then they took the white rocks and laid them on all around. That was the last fight they had with the Yuki. My grandmother was a young lady at the time. She danced in the war dance and showed me the place. The sweat house and the rocks were still there.[14]

Is the story true, or an "old Indian tale" told to a wide-eyed young Indian on the reservation by his aging grandparents, and repeated as fact to inquiring university ethnologists almost seventy-five years later? The ethnologist in this case, Walter Goldschmidt, did not accept it as real history but acknowledged that the story did have its origin in actual conflict. Goldschmidt and his team recorded four different stories of war between the Yuki and Nomlaki that claimed to be the "last Nomlaki-Yuki fight."[15] Another of the "last Nomlaki-Yuki fight" war stories from 1850 was told to ethnologist George Foster by the nephew of the Yuki warrior. The story is not the same as the Nomlaki narrative, but it does have some of the same features, including a bear shaman:

A Yuki man and his woman became angry at their parents, so they left home and climbed up the mountains to the east, camping near the crest in Yuki territory (probably just below Black Butte). Here they made a rough shelter in which to sleep. In the afternoon the woman looked up toward the summit and saw something move. She said to her husband, "Old man, let us go back; there are people above us." But the man said nothing; he was mad at everything and everybody, and didn't care even if he died. At dusk they built a fire, ate, and went to bed. But the woman was restless. "Don't sleep. I feel uneasy," she said. But toward morning, both finally dozed off. Then something came into the shelter, stirred up the fire and sat down. The woman awakened and saw it, and awakened her man. He grabbed for his bow, but the stranger, who was an "Indian bear," jumped on him. This "Indian bear" was a Nomlaki doctor [shaman, medicine man] covered by a thick bear hide which protected him from danger. He was naturally a very strong man. Both fought for a very long time, and by and by the Yuki man became exhausted, and he turned to his woman who had been helping as best she could. "Go home, I'm done. Go home to your people."

She was stubborn and would not go home, but finally she slipped out of the shelter and hid herself to watch what was going on. The "bear" killed the Yuki and came out to look for the woman. He hunted everywhere, but she was hidden behind a tree and he couldn't find her. So he dragged the body of the Yuki man out of the shelter, and with his knife cut it all up. He took off the scalp and kept it, and spread the rest of the flesh, skin and entrails over the ground and bushes. When this was all done, he went to the stream and took off his bear hide. Then he washed himself thoroughly, packed his hide on his back, and struck off over the mountain. Then it was that the woman knew it was an "Indian bear" and not a real grizzly bear. After this the woman went home to her people, and said, "My man was killed. A Nomlaki 'Indian bear' killed him, and hung him all over the ground and trees, and cut his guts out."

So the warriors gathered, and she led them back to the spot, where they examined the remains which proved that the killer had been an "Indian bear." They gathered up the remains of the man and burned them, and took his ashes home for burial; after this they had a big "cry" [period of public mourning] for everyone felt very bad. Then after a few days they talked things over and sent word to the [war] chief. He told them to get ready, and have plenty of arrows.

Then everyone started up the mountainside—everyone who could go, women and children too. They were afraid to stay at home for fear the Nomlaki would attack them while their men were away. At the top of the ridge at a place called Government Flat they stopped and sent word to the Nomlaki chief to come up there for a council. The Nomlaki chief asked what was wanted, and the messenger said that his chief wanted to talk about payments. So the Nomlaki chief came with all his warriors, and both sides drew up, with their chiefs in front.

Then the Yuki chief addressed the Nomlaki, and told them what had happened, and asked that they pay for the murder. The Nomlaki chief asked his people, "Did any of you do this?" One doctor (shaman) answered, "yes." But the Nomlaki refused to pay; three times they refused, so finally a Yuki warrior stabbed a Nomlaki, and the battle was on. It began in the evening, and lasted for most of the night. The Nomlaki chief and all of his people were killed, all except one young boy (Jim Haley) who escaped. Many women helped in the battle, too. Women who had lost their men were even more terrible as fighters than the men. Many Yuki were killed, but not so many as Nomlaki.

When the battle ended, the Yuki gathered their dead and wounded, burying the former and carrying home on stretchers the latter. [Stretchers were made by lashing wild-grape vines between two poles] They took the scalps and the heads of the dead Nomlaki, and just let their bodies lie on the field. Scalping was done by cutting across the fore-head and peeling to the rear. [Other accounts state that the cut was made on the neck, and the scalp peeled forward so as to include the entire face.] When they got home they had a big war dance, and danced with the scalps and heads on poles, carrying bows and spears and imitating shooting and stabbing the enemy. After this there was a big feast. The reservation was founded soon after this fight, so the Nom-laki, who were severely reduced in number, didn't have an opportunity to retaliate. But the two peoples have never got-ten on very well in Round Valley [which became the reser-vation], to which the Nomlaki were brought.[16]

George Foster, the recorder of this war story, later wrote *A Summary of Yuki Culture*, published in anthropological records by the University of California Press in 1944. This excerpt from the "warfare" section details how the Yuki took scalps and heads:

These [scalps] included the face from chin to the back of the neck, or even the entire head. The account of the war with the Nomlaki indicates that in more recent times at least, the true scalp, though of larger size than a Plains scalp, was also taken. Scalps were rubbed with deer marrow to make skin and hair soft, and then stretched on frames; heads were also rubbed with marrow and mounted on tall poles. The populace taunted these symbols, as well as the enemy. Widows or orphans of warriors might pick up the trophies in their mouths and dance until exhausted, or until the scalps began to go to pieces. Scalps were not kept permanently, and the person who took the scalp seems to have received no special honor . . . not all of the slain were necessarily scalped and . . . even one specimen was sufficient to express the dominant feeling of revenge. This is in line with the general tenor of attitudes toward war and victory. After the victory dance came the feast that terminated all Yuki group undertakings.

Actual peace negotiations were carried out in the rancheria [camp or village] of the victors, and implied, curiously, payment on the part of the winning side. Satisfied with winning, a side would not want to jeopardize its position through further warfare. The losers, however, would be burning with a desire for revenge, and anxious to fight again after renewing their forces. Thus, the payment was actually a bribe to the losers to accept settlement.[17]

That Yuki war widows danced with heads and scalps held in their teeth could have caused the cannibalism stories that all of their enemies believed.

And this postscript: When they were not fighting, the Yuki warriors were hunting. When they snared or chased down a deer, it was slaughtered on the spot and divided up among the hunters. The man who actually killed the animal took the heart, head and shoulders and gave the rest to his companions. He had one further duty. He sucked out the eyes of the deer with his mouth and swallowed them—taking care not to break them, for if any of the fluid from the eyes were to fall on the ground hunting would be bad in the future.

Most of the war stories material herein about the Yuki was gathered between 1909 and 1937, one to two generations later than the events recounted actually occurred. The early population of the Yuki has been estimated at two thousand. By 1937, there were only ten full-blooded Yuki alive, and about twenty-five mixed-blood Yuki. Most all lived on the Round

Valley Reservation where the government had shoehorned neighboring tribes into the Yuki homeland.

In 1969, the California State Department of Public Health reported that "the California Indians are the poorest, least educated, worst housed, and most neglected minority in the state." This should elicit little surprise. In just one twenty-two year period, 1848 to 1870, 50,000 California Indians died of starvation, disease or just cold-blooded murder by the white man.[18] During this period, there were armed settlers and miners ranging the backcountry with the sole intent of killing any Indian they stumbled upon, and some of the expenses of these groups were subsidized by the state of California.

From 1542 to 1849, California Indians were invaded by Russians, Spanish, Mexicans and Americans; the invaders greatly altered the Indian way of life. The white men brought a new kind of slavery, new rules, forced white schooling, missionaries, diseases, guns and knives. What were they like before first-contact? We will probably never know. Robert F. Heizer explains the disappearance of the native values and cultures of California Indians as another catastrophic consequence of white incursions into Indian lands. "These values come to mean less and less as the whites fought and killed them off, took their lands, and forced [them] to accept the white man's values at the same time excluding them from entering as participants in a new culture."[19] While Heizer was writing specifically about the Mohave, his words ring true for all of North America.

10

"But, If Not Starvation, What?" — The Anasazi

Around three hundred years after the birth of Christ, while the Visgoths were sacking Athens, Sparta, and Corinth, on the other side of the world near a cave in Kinboko Canyon, Arizona, an Indian had taken the skin from a severed head, sewn the cut skin back together, and painted the skin with broad stripes of green, yellow and white. He had made a trophy mask from the head-skin of his decapitated enemy. In 1915, about 1,600 years after it was painted, archaeologists discovered the mask under the mummified remains of a young girl and a child in the cave. Today, the mummies and the trophy skin-mask rest in a temperature and humidity controlled archival chamber of the Peabody Museum of Archaeology and Ethnology at Harvard University.[1]

There is a cliff on the San Juan River outside the little Utah town of Bluff that is covered with petroglyphs scratched or pecked into the soft rock sometime before 500 A.D. by a little-known group of prehistoric Indians called the Basketmakers.[2] The Bluff site contains drawings of birthing poses, animal-costumed shamans, the mysterious "triangle people,"[3] and several images of faces in what were once believed to be drawings of masks. Similar stylized art, depicting hunting scenes, spirals, wavy lines, and faces is found throughout the San Juan basin. Petroglyphs in the Butler Wash area show full-body images seemingly wearing masks. In Canyon del Muerto[4] there is a rock painting of a man who appears to be carrying a head or a mask. At Sand Island there are two petroglyphs of masks with loops at the top of the head.

In 1984, archaeologist and rock art specialist Sally J. Cole pointed out significant similarities of the mask rock art at the Green Mask Site in Grand Gulch, Utah,[5] to the specimen discovered in 1914 in Kinboko Canyon in Navajo County, Arizona, "of an entire head of skin." As Cole indicates, the face drawings may represent masks, but if so, they are masks made of the decorated human heads the Basketmakers carried with them.[6] The evidence that the heads were carried is strong; the petroglyphs show a thong at the top of the head, and several of the actual heads were discovered in the 1880s in caves in New Mexico. They were in a mummified state and held by a thong in the hand of a mummified male, painted in the same striped pattern depicted on the cliff faces at Bluff. In the mid-1990s, rumors circulated in the Four Corners area (where Colorado, Utah, New Mexico, and Arizona meet) that another decorated head had been discovered by an employee of the Bureau of Land Management, the U.S. government agency that overseas most of the land where the Basketmakers once lived. So far, inquiries to the BLM and other authorities in the area have not turned up any evidence of the rumored discovery.

The best documented indication that the Basketmakers were headhunters is the evidence referred to above from Kinboko Canyon, evidence discovered by archaeologist Samuel J. Guernsey of the Peabody Museum of Harvard in 1915, and reported in a 1919 publication of the Smithsonian Institution's Bureau of American Ethnology:

> It is the entire head skin of an adult, with the hair carefully dressed. In its preparation the scalp proper, including the ears, was removed from the skull in one piece; the face to the mouth in another; and the chin with the lower cheeks in a third. After drying or curing, the three sections were sewed together again, one seam running across the forehead and one down each side in front of the ears; the horizontal seam which joins the upper and lower face pieces crosses at the region of the mouth, but the skin along this sewing has been so trimmed, probably in order to insure a straight seam, that no sign of the lips remains. The eyes and nose, though shriveled, are plainly recognizable; the eyebrow and eyelash hairs are still in position. Although thorough examination under the brittle "side-bobs" of hair is impossible, one can make out the shrunken ears; through the lobe of

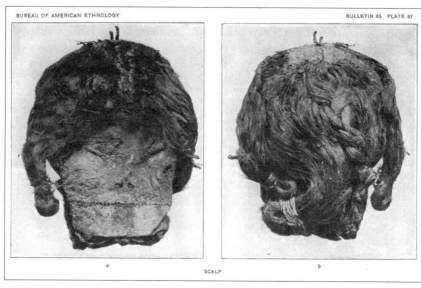

Basketmaker trophy from the head-skin of a decapitated enemy with fragments of a carrying loop.

each there runs a bit of yucca string, the attachment cords presumably for pendants which have now disappeared . . . .

The face has been colored rather elaborately: the "part" and tonsure are painted with a pasty, greenish-white pigment; up the center of the "part" and across the tonsure runs a narrow streak of yellow. Just under the forehead seam there is a thin, horizontal band of red. From this to a line drawn across the face half an inch below the eyes is a zone of white. A band left in the natural color of the skin extends from here to just below the nostrils, whence to the bottom of the white paint is continuous, except for a broad median band of red running downward from the mouth seam.

Rove through two small holes in the tonsure is a narrow thong for suspension. In this part of the scalp there is a short rent carefully sewed up, probably a wound or a cut made in skinning.[7]

The fact that the Basketmakers were a cruel and violent people became evident with the early excavations in the Four Corners area. A rancher, Richard Wetherill, wandered into the canyons a few miles west of Mancos,

Colorado, seeking stray cattle, and became the first Euro-American to see the cliff dwellings of the prehistoric people the Navajos called the Anasazi, which in the Navajo language means "enemy ancestors."[8] Wetherill's ordinary day in 1887 set off a fifteen-year frenzy of grave pillaging and commercial artifact collecting that muddled the evidence of three thousand years of habitation of peoples generally acknowledged as the ancestors of many of the modern Pueblo tribes of the Southwest. And though Wetherill's discovery eventually led to the establishment of America's first national park dedicated to a human historical site, Mesa Verde, and a new discipline in American archaeology—the study of the life patterns and migrations of ancient southwestern native peoples—comparatively little exploration and study has been done by trained archaeologists on the Anasazi ancestral group, the Basketmakers.

We do know the Basketmakers were early horticulturists, planting corn and squash possibly as early as 1,500 B.C. to supplement hunting and gathering. We know somewhat more about them than we do about other early Americans of the same period because they spent at least part of each year in the dry caves of the Colorado Plateau, where their remains were often mummified. The dry caves also preserved wood, fiber and feathers—materials lost in other ancient cultures by time and exposure to the weather. Like many early semi-nomadic farmers, they lived in small groups, probably as extended families of several generations, and dwelled in the caves at harvest time and during the cold winters. They got their "Basketmaker" name from the early collectors, who found beautifully crafted baskets at their living sites, but no pottery.

Their weapons were simple. They did not have the bow, but they were proficient in making deadly projectile points and knives from obsidian and flint, which were fastened to long sticks and used as jabbing or throwing spears. They were one of the early peoples to use the atlatl,[9] a carved stick which extended the leverage of the arm to propel spears or darts greater distances with considerable accuracy. Throwing-sticks were also in their arsenal. Basketmaker throwing sticks are quite similar to those still used by some Pueblo peoples of the Southwest to hunt rabbits.

Many of the relics assembled by Richard Wetherill and others from the canyons and caves in the Four Corners area, made their way to the World Columbian Exposition in Chicago in 1893 and were displayed in the Utah and Colorado exhibits. Public interest in this new "lost race of Indians" spurred even more relic hunters and grave robbers to dig in the Southwest. By 1897, Wetherill was writing that there wasn't anything to find anymore. But he was wrong.

A Basketmaker cave explored and reported by Earl Morris, an archaeologist working in the 1920s and 1930s, contained

> ... clear evidence of a dreadful prehistoric massacre. There were a large number of broken and cracked skulls. The nature of the fractures showed them to have been made with heavy stone axes—even children and babies had not been spared this brutality. There was one old lady who had been done to death in this summary fashion in the final hand-to-hand stage of the fighting .[10]

The discovery was made in Battle Cave in Canyon del Muerto, now part of the Canyon de Chelly National Monument inside the Navajo Indian Reservation.

Sixty years before Morris found Battle Cave, Wetherill noted in his records that thirty-three caves were explored in the 1893 to 1894 expeditions, and wrote brief descriptions of the discoveries in each cave. "Cave 13: Headless mummy. Cave 19: Mummified remains of arms and hands from elbows and legs and feet from knees showing evidence of having been cut off before burial. Mummy in bottom of circular grave. Man nearly 6 ft. tall. Was cut in two at loins and sewed together again with hair string"[11] By far the most dramatic find by Wetherill's party was the now famous Cave 7 in the north fork of Whiskers Draw near Bluff, Utah. Ninety-seven skeletons were taken from the site (some reports say ninety-two), and at the lowest level of excavation, there was evidence of a massacre.

Wetherill wrote:

> The number of skeletons found at one level and in one place would suggest a sudden and violent destruction of a community by battle or massacre. Many of the skulls are broken, as well as the ribs, and the bones of the arms and legs. In the backbones of two different skeletons we found the ends of spear points firmly imbedded; in one case the break in the bone was partially healed, showing that the person must have lived for some time after the wound was inflicted.[12]

He noted that ". . . one interesting group, a mother with an infant on each arm, and another lying on her breast with its head under her chin" was found.[13]

In the decade after Richard Wetherill discovered Mesa Verde, expeditions commissioned by some of the most prestigious museums in the country scattered Basketmaker relics from Chicago to New York in the archives of these same museums. Like many relics collected during this period, they were put on shelves or in boxes, sometimes poorly cataloged, and stored in remote wings of museums to remain there, unstudied, for over a hundred years.

Wetherill's ninety-seven skeletons from cave 7 did make it to a museum. The Wetherills sold the collection to two wealthy brothers, C. Fred and P. T. B. Hyde, around 1897, and the Hydes donated the collection to the American Museum of Natural History in New York. Christy G. Turner, professor of anthropology at Arizona State University, has published an analysis of the skeletons in the collection. The report included observed details of the condition of the skeletons of thirty-seven males, fifteen females, and seven of indeterminate sex.

Several of the specimens are of particular interest: the skull numbered 104 had significant perimortem (around-time-of-death) damage. Turner observed that: "Skull and mandible are complete. Nose is totally crushed and broken away from face. There are cut marks on the right temporal line near the brow ridge. Other cut marks occur on distal aspect of the right parietal. Scalping is indicated."[14]

Specimen number 128 examined by Turner had chopping marks on and near the left mastoid. These marks probably indicate an effort to sever the head, although they could also be from scalping. Some of the skulls are so heavily damaged from severe beating and mutilation that they have large holes in the vault, and in one skull, the blows were so damaging that they separated the face from the vault.

Turner speculated on what weapon could have caused this degree of damage: "Head damage is . . . brutally severe. Fracture patterns indicate that both clubs and hammer-like weapons were used to beat the victims."[15]

One dismembered leg found by Wetherill had indications of flesh-stripping, possibly meaning quick, on-site cannibalism, since this particular specimen has no sign of bone-crushing or burning. Cannibalism has been documented as occurring among the later Anasazi by archaeologist Tim D. White, anthropologist Christy G. Turner, and others. Although White and

Turner have gained the most attention, many other archaeologists also have investigated evidence of cannibalism in the Southwest.[16]

Turner and Winston B. Hurst's paper, *Rediscovering the Great Discovery: Wetherill's First Cave 7 and its Record of Basketmaker Violence*, suggests that these discoveries "should have alerted us to the reality that prehistoric southwestern populations shared a universal human talent for cruelty and violence, but that insight was quickly submerged by an interesting need in the Euro-American psyche to perceive Puebloan peoples as being more noble, humanistic and peacefully inclined than other human populations."[17]

The brutality of the Basketmakers persisted through the generations of their progeny to the people who are called the Anasazi.

Around 950 A.D., eleven persons, including women and children, were killed and butchered, cooked, and eaten on Burnt Mesa in New Mexico north of the San Juan River. At a site near the Hopi villages in Arizona, a group of thirty individuals, forty percent under the age of eighteen, were slaughtered and eaten. In a Colorado rock shelter, a large jar was found filled with splintered human bones. Thirty-three victims were found in a Pueblo-period burial in Mancos canyon with bones split apart to get the marrow. Fifteen fragmented skeletons with split bones and evidence of burning were found in Sambrito Village, a site near the San Juan River in New Mexico. By late 1997, there had been at least twenty-six separate sites discovered with evidence of cannibalism. By the year 2000 the number had increased to forty.

Tim White's book *Prehistoric Cannibalism at Mancos* in 1992, and Christy Turner's *Man Corn, Cannibalism and Violence in the Prehistoric American Southwest* in 1999, further ignited the growing dispute over cannibalism in the Southwest. Leaders of the present Pueblo peoples, the Hopi, Zuni, and others, have long denied any claims of cannibalism by their ancestors and have been joined by sympathetic archaeologists and anthropologists. Fragmented skeletons and split bones, unusual cut marks, and cooking pots with bones have been explained away as artifacts of witchcraft; or, it has been suggested, bones were damaged by scavenger animals after burial. There is a myriad of somewhat illogical though empathetic explanations.

The controversy was put to rest in the well-publicized work of molecular biologist Richard A. Marlar and his associates at the department of pathology at the University of Colorado School of Medicine. Marlar tested preserved human feces, called coprolites by archaeologists, that were found

Photo of one of the hundreds of petroglyphs of trophy heads with a carrying loop in the San Juan River Basin. Photo by George F. Feldman.

near disarticulated bones at the Cowboy Wash site in the Four Corners area of Colorado near Delores. By testing the feces for human myoglobin, a protein used by the body to carry oxygen, he proved that the person who deposited his waste near the remains of four slaughtered adults and three children had eaten human flesh. Human myoglobin was also inside the cooking pot found at the site. The bones of the massacred Indians held cut marks that indicated that they had been de-fleshed. The human waste had human tissue in it, and it could have come from no other source than from eating another human. Marlar and his associates demonstrated in test after test that the myoglobin could have not come from animals, nor from some bodily defect of the person who deposited the waste.[18] So far, no qualified scientist has challenged Marlar's methodology or his conclusions. The residues of butchery at Cowboy Wash are so similar to indications of cannibalism found at other sites that now there is no question that cannibalism was widespread in the Southwest.

Marlar settled the cannibalism dispute, but as yet no one has come up with a convincing theory as to what *really* went on at Cowboy Wash 850 years ago.

The entire Cowboy Wash site consists of nine room-clusters.[19] In the four that have been excavated, there are cannibalized remains of twenty-four individuals. The archaeologist who excavated the site, Brian L. Billman, estimates that the four room-clusters housed about thirty-five people, so over two-thirds of the population of the excavated site were processed and eaten. It has been estimated that the total population of the nine room-clusters would be close to one hundred individuals, so it is reasonable to expect that the total feast consisted of at least fifty people or more.

Anthropologist Steven A. LeBlanc estimates that the cannibal raiders processed more than 1,200 pounds of human flesh from the individuals in the four excavated room-clusters. It follows, then, that the total amount of human remains processed—including those in the unexcavated rooms—could have been in excess of 2,400 pounds. The evidence of bones scattered everywhere indicates the human processed meat was consumed at the site. If that was the case, then the attacking force had to have been enormous: three to four hundred warriors. This is a number so improbable for the time and the place that LeBlanc and others rule it out. Nor do they consider the event starvation-driven. But, if not starvation, what?[20]

No one knows, or probably ever will know, all of the reasons for the savagery and cannibalism practiced in the Southwest. Growing and hunting conditions in the Southwest are extremely volatile, many times for long periods the area suffered from severe drought. Cannibalism at Cowboy Wash occurred in the midst of the most severe drought periods (1130 to 1180 A.D.) in the Four Corners area.[21] Drought is acknowledged as one of the factors that led to the increased warfare that possibly caused the mass migrations of the Anasazi from their Colorado Plateau homeland from about 1300 A.D. Several abandoned Pueblo villages in the Cortez, Colorado, area appear to be massacre sites from this period. At Castle Rock, burning was evident, and forty-one damaged, unburied skeletons were found. Nearby Sand Canyon Pueblo was partially excavated by archaeologist Bruce Bradley at about the same time as Castle Rock (1983 through 1994) and produced twenty unburied bodies; because of the large size of the settlement, this number extrapolates to a massacre of over two hundred individuals.

It is not difficult to imagine starved warriors seeking meat wherever they could find it. Nor is it coincidental that the dating of cannibalized bones often matches the dates of severest drought. But however ameliorating drought may be for cannibalism, it does not necessarily correlate with times of wanton warfare and massacre. When times were good and there was evidence of adequate food supplies, entire communities were wiped out, children were killed and stuffed into storage cists, and old ladies were battered to death with stone axes.

Today, archaeologists search the Mesoamerican records for similarities between the northern Mexican Toltecs and the Anasazi and their Basketmaker ancestors. Whether by coincidence, cross-cultural influence, or simply similar but separate cultures acting in the same way, there is parallel art of decapitation at several Mexican sites that are contemporaneous to Basketmaker head-thong rock art. There is also reliable evidence of trade between prehistoric Native Americans and Mexican tribes in the Anasazi/Basketmaker area.

The early Southwestern Basketmakers collected heads. Like most historical societies where headhunting was practiced, these early Southwestern settlers may have been motivated by greed, vengeance, or the practice of shamanistic sacrifice. Some investigators do not agree with that thesis. They maintain that the Basketmakers kept the skulls or the skin of the heads of venerated relatives, just as the Manus peoples of New Guinea treasure the skulls of relatives and use them in rituals. If this is true, it means that the Basketmakers were the only group of American Indians who scalped their dead relatives in a form of early North American family values. Impossible? No, but highly improbable given the known ferocity of these early dwellers of the Southwest.

And cannibalism? Marlar's conclusive work with myoglobin is forcing Southwestern anthropologists to consider a new question: was it starvation cannibalism or gustatory, the breakdown of an established cultural and social order, or simply the introduction of a frightening new one? Could the Cowboy Wash cannibalism be punishment dealt to a small community that would not conform to the social or religious dictates of a stronger more dominant group?

If the Cowboy Wash cannibalism was punishment, the orders probably came from a Chacoan Great House at Aztec Springs about five miles away. Many Southwestern archaeologists maintain that from around A.D. 900 to about 1300, much of the area of the San Juan River basin was under the control of the people who built the magnificent structures in Chaco Canyon, New Mexico. Nestled in this barren place is an awe-inspiring building of stone construction that covers almost two acres. It was up to four stories high in some places and held 650 rooms. It is called Pueblo Bonito and recognized as a center of political and religious power.

Pueblo Bonito is reminiscent of a European medieval town, a place where the ruling elite lived in luxury nearby smaller more humble dwellings.

Over centuries, the pattern repeated itself throughout the Four Corners area and south, deep into Arizona and New Mexico: well built large stone structures nearby or easily accessible to smaller communities. Southwestern archaeologists call them "outliers."

Steven A. LeBlanc suggests that the Chacoans gradually expanded and the other great houses like the one at Aztec Springs were built as headquarters for a localized ruling elite that used terrorism to enforce orders, even if it meant the massacre of entire communities.

LeBlanc wrote: "Such terrorism included some form of processing the bodies of individuals, or sacrifice, or other forms of violence."[22]

LeBlanc's model of Chacoan expansion and terror is supported by maps that illustrate Chacoan Spheres of Influence and pinpoint the locations of cannibalized remains. Christy G. Turner states: "The sites where cannibalism has been or can be hypothesized are strongly linked with the Chaco phenomenon, both in physical proximity to great houses within and outside the canyon and in time—that is, the period from A.D. 900 to 1300.[23]

Because of the distinct similarity between the incidents in the San Juan basin and the activities of the Mexican Xipe Totec and the Tezcatlipoca-Quetzalcoatl, plus the identification of distinctive skeletal remains with traditional Mexican dental disfigurement, Turner posits a hypothesis that cites "maniacal" Mexican cultists and their descendents as responsible for the Chacoan phenomena. He suggests that the Mexican cultists brought a "harsh, totalitarian, and fatalistic Mesoamerican worldview" to the San Juan basin.[24]

The Chacoan influence began breaking down around A.D. 1200, and the scattered pueblo farmers coalesced in fortified villages. Yet even that was not enough. The warfare and massacres continued. So the ancestors of the people who now make up the Pueblo tribes—Hopi, Zuni, Laguna, Acoma, Zia, Jemez, and all of the others—did the only thing left for them to do. They left. They fled from terror, war and famine to join other settlements to the south. By around 1300, the San Juan basin was an area of ghost villages—homes left with pots on the floors, homes left vacant except for those household items too big or too heavy to carry on the long trek to safety.

The Pueblo Indians of today should not be shamed by the cannibalism of a thousand years ago. After all, they are descendents of the refugees who fled from it.

11

"Go Warpath to Texas" — The Commanche

They have been called the "Spartans of the Prairies," and "Lords of the South Plains." When around 1991, they sought words to sew on a new flag, the Comanches chose "Lords of the Southern Plains." That they were.

They had fought and decisively defeated Pawnees, Utes, Navajos, Osages, Apaches and Tonkawas. They raided all the way down in Old Mexico to Durango, and when the Anglo-Americans came to the Comanche Southwest in the 1820s and 1830s, it was not a safe place for them to be. Ever larger numbers of Americans invaded Comanche territory after the U.S. war with Mexico (1846 to 1848), and by so doing, became fair game for the adventurous, raiding tribe. Comanches fought the white intruders for almost forty years.

Two generations of conflict began with a Comanche attack on a small homestead fort, Fort Parker, near the Navasota River in what is now Limestone County, Texas. John Parker and his family, settlers from Virginia who had lived in Tennessee and Illinois, decided that the lush valley of the Navasota was a perfect site for a farm, but they knew about the Indian problems, and better to protect themselves they built a stockade wall around their homes. Several other families joined them, and at the time of the attack, Fort Parker had a population of thirty men, women and children.

On May 19, 1836, most of the men were working in the fields when a mounted band of around a hundred Comanches[1] rode up to the fort waving a dirty white rag. With the stockade doors wide open, Benjamin Parker, one of the elder Parker's sons, walked out to meet them. When he returned, he told the waiting anxious settlers that the Indians wanted beef and directions to a water hole. Parker said he didn't think the Indians were friendly, but he had refused the beef, and he was going back to talk to them to try to avoid a fight. As he strolled near them, the Indians whirled their horses around and repeatedly speared him with their lances. Before the stockade doors could be closed, the warriors were inside. John Parker was pinned to the ground with lances, scalped, and his genitals were cut off. His wife was also pinned down and raped by several attackers.[2] They chased the fleeing settlers and ransacked the fort.

The men in the fields worked with their guns nearby at all times. Hearing the screams they rushed with rifles in hand to save their families. Seeing the armed farmers, the Indians remounted and rode away with five captives, two women and three children. They had killed five men and mauled several women, who later died. When they stopped for the first night they repeatedly raped the two captive women while the children watched.

Scavenging the pile of loot from the raid, they discovered a container containing white powder, and using fingers and saliva, four warriors made a white paste and decorated their faces and bodies. They soon died a painful death. Unknowingly, they had ingested arsenic.

Both of the women were eventually ransomed. Rachel Plummer died within a year of returning to her relatives, and Elizabeth Kellogg disappeared after being turned over to Texas authorities. Two of the boys were also found and ransomed in 1842, but one, John Parker, ran away from civilization to find his sister, Cynthia Ann Parker, who, at age fifteen was the wife of an important Comanche. He never found her.

When Texas Americans held councils with the Comanches, the fair, white wife of the warrior Nokoni was often seen. She had small children of her own and considered herself Comanche. Her first born was named "Quanah," who in his later years became a Comanche chief.

As one historian wrote:

> That she [Cynthia] was a Comanche "squaw" continually fed dark racial and sexual angers across the Texas Frontier. A spark of violence and hatred had been lit at Parker's Fort that would burn for forty years. The raid had spawned a tragedy that dogged the Parker blood, and its continuing reverberations would last till the twilight of the Texan-Comanche wars.[3]

The Comanches split off from a larger group of Shoshones, perhaps before 1541 when the Spanish explorer Coronado, seeking cities of gold, met and described a people who "do not have any crockery . . . do not make gourds, nor sow corn, nor eat bread . . ." He said they lived on the flesh of buffalo and heated themselves with fire made of their dung. He described their tents, and had some understanding of the sign language they used to communicate with other-language tribes.[4] Whether Coronado met the Comanches or not (and several eminent historians do not believe he did),[5] the Comanches were in the southern plains at least by 1700. The Comanches claim they went to Rocky Mountain country near the headwaters of the Arkansas River when they left their Shoshone brothers. They migrated south over the years, seeking horses and following the buffalo into the southern plains.[6]

In a study that began in 1933 and resulted in the book *The Comanches, Lords of the South Plains*, a book that has been continuously in print since its publication in 1952, the Comanches' motives for war are listed as "plunder, love of fighting, a desire for glory as a means for achieving personal status, eagerness for revenge, and a determination to take and afterwards to hold free from all trespassers, both white and red men, the hunting grounds of the South Plains."[7]

When the first white American immigrants began to drift into Comanche territory, there was bound to be conflict. Typical of the thousands of incidents in the early to mid-1800s is the story of four soldiers, a guide and a drummer boy who foolishly left Fort Davis, Texas,[8] in 1855:

> Sergeant Love . . . three privates, and Sam Cherry as guide, started out to scour the country for timber to enable the post to prepare for the coming winter, which was expected to be very severe, as the site upon which the fort was built was some five thousand feet above sea level. On reaching the entrance to Limpia Canyon, also known as Wild Rose Pass, some six miles from the post, about thirty Comanches dashed out from the mesquite brush and cut off the retreat to the post. Sam Cherry at once wheeled his powerful horse and dashed through the savages and ran for his life out into the plain with a number of yelling savages after him. Sam would have made good his escape, but his horse stumbled and fell, breaking his neck, and falling upon him. In an instant he was surrounded by exultant savages. Raising himself up as best he could, he fired five shots from his six-shooter in rapid succession, each one with deadly effect; and turning the muzzle of his pistol at his own temple, fired his last shot into his own brain, thus escaping the terrible tortures of his enemies. Baffled and terrified, the savages fled without touching the body or the arms. The three soldiers were shot and riddled with bullets after they had fallen to the ground. The savages captured a drummer boy, aged about twelve years, who had slipped away from the post and joined the party for a day's boyish sport.
>
> The Comanches had meditated an attack upon the post, with the view of its destruction, as it would be a continued menace to them. The drummer boy spoke Spanish fluently, and on being questioned at length by the captors, through a Mexican boy captured some years before, he satisfied them that their scheme of destroying the post was sure to prove disastrous to them: They grew angry and turned him over to the squaws, by whom he was tortured to death.[9]

The Apaches took captives, as did most of the Southwestern tribes, but few were as intent upon getting Mexican and American children into their tribes as were the Comanches. There is an instance on record in 1848 of their torching a schoolhouse in Mexico to capture the children as they fled the fire.

Around the same time, a six- or seven-year-old Mexican girl was captured and lived her entire life as a Comanche with the name "Carrying Her Sunshade." When she was ninety years old, in 1933 she told her story to anthropologist/ethnologist E. A. Hoebel:

> I was captured in the summer by a war leader, Tawyawp, who was himself a captive—It's funny they had no pity on their own people. I was sitting in my grandmother's arms on a log outside our house. An Indian came and pushed our fence down. He rode up, grabbed me from my grandmother's arms and put me behind him on his horse. I was the only one in my family who was captured, for my parents were gone that day.
>
> When it was nearly night, we joined up with some Indians. They came on a boy sheepherder, whom they killed, and they ate his lunch. Then they rode on toward the high mountain. It was a four-day trip, and when they ran out of food, they killed a horse. When we finally got there, it was raining hard, and I went to bed soaked. As soon as we had entered the camp, other Indians had run up and snatched off my earrings and clothes for souvenirs. Other little captive girls told me not to be afraid, "They won't hurt you," they said.
>
> The next morning the sound of a wagon moving at the foot of the mountain was heard. Four men were sent down to see about it. Then we heard shots. After a while the scouts came back, bringing some food and Mexican blankets. I knew from this that they had killed some more Mexicans.
>
> It was a big camp there on the mountain, and we stayed there quite some time while the Comanches made some more raids about the country. They didn't seem to be the least bit afraid. We captive girls had to eat by ourselves so we would not disturb the men's medicine.
>
> On the last raid, all the Comanches went, including the women. They left us captive children in charge of one man, himself a captive. He cooked a whole horse for us, and we ate as much as we could.

When the raiding party returned with more horses, they all got ready to go back north. It was probably in September.

Each family camp left when it got ready, driving off its own bunch of horses. Tawyawp, my captor, had about thirty people in his camp. He was not satisfied with his horses; he wished to capture more; so his bunch stayed behind. Everybody had gone, but a man named Wahaawmaw came back to get something. As he rode by me Tawyawp said to him, "We are going on another raid. This girl is in the way, so we are going to kill her."

Wahaawmaw felt sorry for me. He thought of his own children; his wife was dead. So he picked me up and put me on his mule. He gave Tawyawp a few arrows, and Tawyawp gave him three blankets, put one for me to ride on. On the road we passed a girl lying on the road about to die; she had been raped. Later we passed a boy captive—dead.[10]

Nowhere, not in the swamps, the mountains, the forests or the plains were people more free than the Comanche. Like many tribes, their name for themselves meant "The People"; they proudly knew their tribal affinity, and this established a bond among them that made more formal political and social organization unnecessary. The Comanche's spiritual life was based on a search for power. Like many other plains tribes, a young aspiring warrior was sent to an isolated place with tobacco and a buffalo robe to fast and await the arrival of his personal vision, his *puha*. He sought his power for four days and nights, and if unsuccessful, returned to the teepees of his band and tried again another time. Ghosts also gave special powers. A Comanche named Post Oak Jim told this story to Hoebel:

> A ghost came to a young man and told him "Bullets will never kill you. Keep a white ball of clay with you. When there is going to be a fight, paint yourself white all over [with the clay.] Never go into battle first. Wait until your friends retreat. Then go right in." According to the tale, the young man went out the next day on a raid for a herd of Mexican horses, but when the battle turned against them and the other Indians were retreating, the young man and a friend, painted white, charged the pursuing Mexicans and turned the tide of the battle by killing several of them.[11]

It is difficult, perhaps impossible, for a Euro-American raised in a severely structured religion, living in a country with regularly elected officials who promulgate and enforce written statutes, to understand the religious and organizational systems of the people called Comanche. Their society was fluid, organized only when necessary to meet a threat or profit from opportunity. And when these times came, the leaders were always there. Like many people of the plains, they lived in extended family and clan groups, but they could leave without enmity to join another band. In fact, a determination of the number of Comanche bands and their leadership at any particular time in history continues to puzzle anthropologists.

"Medicine power" or *puha* was attained by the vision quest, the search for spiritual power, and to be a great leader, a Comanche must have *puha* and be the man who killed the most enemies in battle.[12]

Only in their later years, suffering defeats and the disappearance of the buffalo, did they have chiefs strong enough to convince their brothers of the need to unite and act as an "organized" people. Ten Bears was one such chief, a true statesman and a brilliant speaker. In 1864, he visited Washington where President Abraham Lincoln showed him a globe in which Comanche territories were so labeled. Three years later, he was one of the Comanche representatives at the truce negotiation in Kansas where the Comanches and their allies, the Kiowa, were granted a three-million-acre domain in Oklahoma. His speech at the Council of Medicine Lodge Creek in southwestern Kansas on October 20, 1867, is one of the most often quoted speeches by a Native American. Ten Bears eloquently told the assemblage what had happened to the Comanches, and what his people had done and would do. It follows in its entirety:

> My heart is filled with joy when I see you here, as the brooks fill with water when the snows melt in the spring; and I feel glad as the ponies do when the fresh grass starts in the beginning of the year. I heard of your coming when I was many sleeps away, and I made but few camps before I met you. I knew that you had come to do good to me and to my people. I looked for benefits which would last forever, and so my face shines with joy as I look upon you. My people have never first drawn a bow or fired a gun against the whites. There has been trouble on the line between us, and my young men have danced the war dance. But it was not

begun by us. It was you who sent out the first soldier and
we who sent out the second. Two years ago, I came upon
this road, following the buffalo, that my wives and children
might have their cheeks plump and their bodies warm. But
the soldiers fired on us, and since that time there has been a
noise like that of a thunderstorm, and we have not known
which way to go. So it was upon the Canadian. Nor have we
been made to cry once alone. The blue-dressed soldiers and
the Utes came from out of the night when it was dark and
still, and for campfires they lit our lodges. Instead of hunting game they killed my braves, and the warriors of the
tribe cut short their hair for the dead.

So it was in Texas. They made sorrow come in our
camps, and we went out like the buffalo bulls when the
cows are attacked. When we found them we killed them,
and their scalps hang in our lodges. The Comanches are not
weak and blind, like the pups of a dog when seven sleeps
old. They are strong and far-sighted, like grown horses. We
took their road and we went on it. The white women cried
and our women laughed.

But there are things which you have said to me which I
do not like. They were not sweet like sugar, but bitter like
gourds. You said that you wanted to put us upon a reservation, to build us houses and make us medicine lodges. I do
not want them. I was born upon the prairie, where the wind
blew free and there was nothing to break the light of the
sun. I was born where there were no enclosures and everything drew a free breath. I want to die there and not within
walls. I know every stream and every wood between the Rio
Grande and the Arkansas. I have hunted and lived over that
country. I live like my fathers before me and like them I
lived happily.

When I was at Washington the Great Father told me
that all the Comanche land was ours, and that no one
should hinder us in living upon it. So, why do you ask us to
leave the rivers, and the sun, and the wind, and live in
houses? Do not ask us to give up the buffalo for the sheep.
The young men have heard talk of this, and it has made
them sad and angry. Do not speak of it more. I love to carry

out the talk I get from the Great Father. When I get goods
and presents, I and my people feel glad, since it shows that
he holds us in his eye.

If the Texans had kept out of my country, there might
have been peace. But that which you now say we must live
in, is too small. The Texans have taken away the places
where the grass grew the thickest and the timber was the
best. Had we kept that, we might have done the things
you ask. But it is too late. The whites have the country
which we loved, and we only wish to wander on the
prairie until we die.

Any good thing you say to me shall not be forgotten. I
shall carry it as near to my heart as my children, and it shall
be as often on my tongue as the name of the Great Spirit. I
want no blood upon my land to stain the grass. I want it all
clear and pure, and I wish it so that all who go through
among my people may find peace when they come in and
leave it when they go out.[13]

Who fired the first shot between the Americans and the Comanches is hardly
relevant; the Americans settled on land the Comanches believed was their
own and they fought. Yet the Comanche had taken much of this same land
away from the Apaches and many of the original Texas tribes, the Caddos
and the Tonkawas, and they, too, fought. There was war in this land long before the white Americans or even before Coronado and his Spaniards. Of all
the tribes the Comanches fought, the one they hated most was the Tonkawa.
The ate human flesh and killed children.

Some Kiowas—the Comanches' only allies—called the Tonkawa the
Kuikogo, other Kiowas referred to them as the *K'inahi-piako,* the Comanche
called them *Kariko*—all of these words mean either "man-eaters," or "man-
eating men." The first contact the Tonkawa had with a white man was with a
Spaniard, Alvar Nunez Cabeza de Vaca, a shipwrecked survivor of the ill-
fated Narvaez expedition in Florida in 1521, who trekked across Texas to
Mexico. To stay alive in this barren country, he often spent long periods with
the Indian tribes of the region. Cabeza de Vaca later wrote of his experiences
during an eighteen-month stay with the tribe he called the Mariames, but
who were more aptly named man-eaters by the Kiowa and the Comanche.
We know them today as the Muruam Tonkawa. Cabeza de Vaca cannot be

Comanche Chief Ten Bears, statesman and brilliant speaker.

considered a "reliable reporter," and what he wrote about the Mariames' life ways may have been one more fictional dramatization he presented to his superiors to explain his long absence.

He claimed the Muruam Tonkawa were the most primitive of Indians, heartless and without compassion for their own children. Infanticide is rare among North American tribes, but according to Cabeza de Vaca, the Muruam Tonkawa without exception would not allow a newborn girl to live. He wrote that they had a taboo on marriage between tribal members, so they believed that any girl who was allowed to grow to maturity would marry in another tribe and be the mother of future enemies. When a female baby emitted its first whimper, proving it was alive, it was tossed outside for the dogs to eat.[14] Male children did not fare much better. Allowed to live at birth, they were nursed by their mothers until twelve years old, if they lived that long. The Muruam Tonkawa had no rituals or ceremonies, no identifiable religion, but they believed in the spirit power of dreams, and when either parent had a "bad dream," it usually meant death for the boy. During Cabeza de Vaca's eighteen months with them, he wrote that twelve boys were killed, some buried alive by their parents. Based on Cabeza de Vaca's numbers, this band of around two hundred individuals murdered one or more of their own children, male or female, once a month.[15]

Like other members of the Tonkawa in desolate, inland south Texas, the Muruam spent all of their waking hours in search of food. Rats and mice were hunted. Snakes were eaten and their bones were saved, pulverized and eaten. Insects and spiders were also in their diet, some in egg or larval form. In periods of starvation, even earth, wood, and deer droppings were sometimes on the menu.[16]

But it was not infanticide that created the intense hatred the Comanches had for the Tonkawa. In fact, by the 1700s, when the Comanches were in Texas the Muruam band of the tribe was extinct. The surviving Tonkawas were cannibals, and equally amazing, they were cannibals working for and with the United States Army, fighting the Comanches and the Apaches.

More often than not, accusations of cannibalism by one tribe against another is based upon fear and loathing, rarely on fact. It is what one anthropologist aptly calls the "boogieman" syndrome, and it very well could have remained that except for a series of unusual circumstances wherein a white man was captured in childhood, became a Comanche warrior, and later returned to his own people with this story:

> One day three warriors came rushing into camp almost exhausted and told us that they with three other warriors had been surrounded and overpowered by about thirty Tonkaways who were well armed and equipped, and in the fight the three had managed to escape to bring us word of the attack. We had more than three times that number, so we mounted and rode out to meet them. After riding about three hours we located them in camp, having a feast.
>
> The Comanches and Tonkaways had been at war for a long time and the Tonkaways had been nearly exterminated. The hatred the Tonkaway had for the Comanche was fierce, for they blamed the Comanche for all of their misfortunes and eventually made a treaty with the white people and

combined with them to exterminate the Comanche, acting
as scouts and trailers and warriors for the whites.

Our chief gave the war whoop and we all joined in one
continual yell as we charged that camp. They fled at the on-
slaught and several of them were killed. We took possession of the camp, and what do you suppose we found on
that fire roasting? One of the legs of a Comanche! A warrior of our tribe!

Our chief gave the cry for vengeance and we all joined
the chorus. We immediately gave chase. . . . The Tonkaways
had collected in a ravine and were prepared to receive our
charge with a deadly fire, which for a moment checked our
onrush; down would come horse, over would tumble the
rider, but on, on, we came, in our frenzy. At first I was terrified, and it seemed like I could not face death that way, but
I was in the front rank and my comrades in the rear pressed
me onward. Then I caught the spirit of vengeance. I became
enraged, spurred on my steed and fought courageously. One
of the Tonkaways rode out of the canyon to challenge a single combat. A Comanche made a dash for him, but fell mortally wounded. Another went and received a death-blow. It
seemed like human blood had made the Tonkaway bold,
and somehow our shields would not ward off his bullets,
but the third warrior to advance got him.

At this single combat by seemingly general consent, a
cessation took place and at this recess every warrior loaded
his gun and prepared for eventualities . . . in a very few sec-
onds we were in a hand-to-hand conflict with these Tonkaways and they were soon vanquished. Those cannibals
fought bravely, and eight of our men lay dying on the battlefield, while forty or fifty were more or less desperately
wounded. But our work was not finished.

A great many of the dying enemy were gasping for
water, but we heeded not their pleadings. But we scalped
them, amputated their arms, cut off their legs, cut out their
tongues, and threw their mangled bodies and limbs on their
own campfire, put on more brushwood, and piled the living,
dying and dead Tonkaways on the fire. Some of them were
able to flinch and work as a worm, some able to speak and

plead for mercy. We piled them up, put on more wood, and danced around in great glee as we saw grease and blood run from their bodies, and were delighted to see them swell up and hear the hide *pop* as it would burst in the fire.

Some of the enemy may have escaped, but we never saw any signs of them. We had twenty-eight scalps, thirty-five split-eared horses, thirty long-range guns, some saddles, a number of blankets, many bows and arrows, besides a great quantity of ammunition and other trophies as a reward for our vengeance, which in some respects partly satisfied our blood-thirsty band.[17]

The Comanches, perhaps more than any tribe of Indians in North America, typified the Indian of the plains. They had the four important ingredients: horses, buffalo, teepees, and the spirit and fervor of unfettered freedom. When invaders killed their buffaloes and attempted to harness their freedom, these invaders faced the most fierce and implacable of enemies. The Comanches had a special hate for the white buffalo hunters, whether they were the so-called sportsmen or professional skinners. Whenever and wherever the Comanches found them, they tried to kill them, and in most cases they were successful.

All of the plains Indians depended upon the buffalo for food, clothing and housing. (The teepees were covered with ten to twelve buffalo hides.) The Comanches were the first tribe in what is now the United States to have horses, which made them efficient harvesters of the buffalo. Every part of the huge animal was used by these nomadic hunters: fur for robes and bedding, horns for spoons and other utensils, hooves for glue, and leather for saddles, bridles and canteens. The number killed each year by the Comanches and the other Indians of the Plains was less than the reproductive capacity of the herds. In 1800, there were sixty million buffalo. Around 1840, the killing began as the white man's sport. Even then, the impact on the economies of the tribes in the plains was negligible.

Two years after the 1867 Council of Medicine Lodge Creek, an eastern inventor was granted a patent that would create circumstances so detrimental to the Comanche way of life that in six short years they would move to the Oklahoma reservation. The patent was for a process to tan buffalo hides into supple, soft leather, quickly and economically. An eastern tanner using the new process created an immediate market, and in the economic doldrums of the times, gave opportunities for quick money to any hunter who had the new .50-caliber Sharps rifle and a willingness to travel to the great American plains. Between 1872 and 1874, 4,274,000 buffalo were slaughtered by professional hunters. The famous Buffalo Bill Cody killed 4,300 in just eight months. Wyatt Earp, Pat Garrett and Wild Bill Hickock joined in the killing spree. The rapid destruction of this great natural resource alarmed even the Congress of the United States, who, in their collective wisdom, passed legislation to protect the buffalo. Ulysses S. Grant, who vetoed more legislation than that of the combined seventeen presidents who preceded him, vetoed this bill, too.

Grant, the former general, may have been influenced by General Philip Sheridan, who encouraged the hunters. Before a joint meeting of the Texas senate and house of representatives in 1875, Sheridan repeated what he had told anyone who would listen to him:

> These men [buffalo hunters] have done more in the last two years and will do more in the next year to settle the vexed Indian question than the entire regular army has done in the last thirty years. They are destroying the Indian's commissary; and it is a well known fact that an army losing its base of supplies is placed at a great disadvantage. Send them [buffalo hunters] powder and lead, if you will, and for the sake of lasting peace, let them kill, skin and sell until they have exterminated the buffalo. Then your prairies will be covered with speckled cattle and the festive cowboy, who follows the hunter as a second forerunner of civilization.[18]

Ironically enough, it was the vagarious U. S. Grant who signed a bill on March 1, 1872, that established Yellowstone National Park, which protected the park's meager twenty buffalo. When the bill was signed, the massive slaughter had already begun in the western plains.

U.S. army posts popped up everywhere to protect ranchers, miners, and farmers from "the red horde." Repeatedly defeated in their battles with the army, the Comanches became elusive and concentrated on small pockets of civilian population, isolated farms, and especially the white professional buffalo hunters.

Herman Lehmann, a white man raised as a Comanche, told the story of the Tonkawa massacre; he also related this account about his band and the white buffalo hunters:

Herman Lehmann, the former white Co-
manche photographed in his Comanche
garb years after he left the tribe.

We rob buffalo hunters and leave them naked, penniless and
afoot out there on the plains hundreds of miles from home
to die of thirst, starvation or sunstroke.

It was good fun to us to see those palefaces, those city
born and tenderly reared fellows running barefooted and
clothe-less through grass-burs and briars; to see them
scratched and bruised with blood and perspiration trickling
down and leaving purple stains on the grass and sand. We
would follow them and see that they did run and if they
checked we would feign our approach to see those poor fellows already wind-broken put forth their last energy and

utmost effort and endeavor, but at last to fall breathless, exhausted and lifeless on the ground.

We would then ride up and punch them and if life were
extinct, scalp them; if not, we would torture them to death
and their scalps would go to adorn the belt of our chief,
while their lacerated bodies would be left as food for vultures or wild beasts; thus perished many valiant hunters and
"Cuckoo European-Americanoes." We continued north and
many, many hunters fell victims to our sleuthhound vigi-
lance and daring bravery.[19]

Hunters simply disappeared. Bodies were not often discovered, and although
it was believed the missing hunting parties were massacred by roaming Indians, who the Indians were, or where they were, mitigated reprisals. Attacks on
farmers and ranchers seemed to occur in series. The raiding Comanches
would start at point "A" and kill and loot everything they found between "A"
and "Z". This left them vulnerable, because the first victims, if any were left
alive, could alert the army or the Texas Rangers. It was under these circumstances that the man who was to become the greatest Comanche chief became a leader of a raiding band.

Quanah, as he was known to the Comanches, or Quanah Parker, as he
become known to the whites, was the first son of the captive girl Cynthia
Ann Parker and a warrior-headman Peta Nocona, who later became a chief in
his own right. Quanah was a human product of the bitterest territorial and
racial strife ever to hit the Southwest.

He was only seventeen years old when the reservations were set up in
Oklahoma. Like most of the bands, Chief Nocona rejected reservation life to
continue traditional hunting and raiding. In fact, over a third of the Comanches refused to "put their mark" on the treaty that created the reservations. When Quanah was eighteen or nineteen years old, he was with other
warriors raiding in the area from the Pease River to Gainesville. They had hit
the small ranchers and farmers and had gathered a large herd of horses and
mules before they started back to camp. Near Jacksboro, soldiers stationed at
Fort Richardson heard about the raids and set off to find the Comanches.
When the Indians got near Red River, the soldiers attacked, galloping and firing. Bear's Ear, the band's leader, was one of the first to fall. With the raiding
party in confusion with the death of their leader and under fire from the U.S.

Comanche Chief Quanah Parker

cavalry, Quanah took charge, shouting, "Spread out . . .turn the horses north to the river." Quanah stayed behind while his companions urged the stolen livestock north. A cavalryman rushed Quanah, firing his six shooter. Nicked in the thigh, Quanah notched an arrow, shot and hit the soldier in the shoulder, forcing him to drop his revolver and flee.

That evening, safe from the soldiers, the band chose Quanah as their new leader.[20]

The raids—theft of horses, torture of Texan men and capture and rape of their women—continued all along the frontier. The most humiliating defeat for the Comanches was at Adobe Walls, where twenty-eight buffalo hunters protected by thick walls drove back seven hundred warriors. The high-powered, long-range rifles of the hunters and skinners demoralized the attackers. Quanah was wounded twice. After the battle, he is reported to have said: "Pretty soon, all go back, get saddles and bridles and go to village—I will take all young men, go warpath to Texas."[21]

Yet it was a losing battle. By 1875, tired and starving Comanches were reporting in to the military authorities. There were no more buffalo and the soldiers and many Politicians wanted the Comanche exterminated. Quanah learned English and turned from warrior to statesman. As a direct result of his efforts most of the Comanches settled on the reservation in Oklahoma, where he continued as their leader. Too many warriors had died. They had fought bravely for over 150 years.

They had lived in Kansas, Colorado, Oklahoma, Texas and New Mexico. Around 1700, there were between twenty and thirty thousand Comanches roaming this territory. By 1910, there were only 1,171 reported in the census, mostly on their reservation. The reservation tribal rolls in 2001 counted 9,500 Comanches living under the red and blue flag that commemorates their heritage as "Lords of the Southern Plains."

12

"Shrinking Leather Thongs" — The Apache

In the Zuni language, the word "Apache" means "enemy."

According to one perspective, "It matters not by what process or method of schooling, the Apache has become the most treacherous, blood-thirsty, villainous and unmitigated rascal upon earth; it is quite sufficient that he is so, and that he is incapable of improvement. Kindness and generosity provoke his contempt, and he regards them as weaknesses. Chastisement does not procure his vengeance with any more certainty than want of caution."[1]

A mid-nineteenth-century authority on the Apache, John C. Cremony, wrote these words to awaken the bureaucrats of the Bureau of Indian Affairs in Washington, D.C. to the problems the United States government faced in dealing with the tribe. It was no secret that Cremony hated all Apaches.

The sixty bands of Apaches who roamed the plains, mountains, and deserts of the West at the time were true nomadic raiders who defied, for over three hundred years, efforts to pacify them by the government of Mexico and later, the United States. They lived by cunning, theft and clever deception. When they captured travelers, they kept the women and children, and tortured to death those men not killed in the raid.

Cremony, who fought the Apache, learned their language, and lived among them as the Indian Agent at the Fort Sumner Reservation, claimed that to the Apache "every expression of pain or agony is hailed with delight, and the one whose inventive genius can devise the most excruciating kind of death is deemed worthy of honor."[2] As Cremony wrote, their torture was in-

160

ventive, not ritual. When an Apache band captured eight Mexican families on their way to California, they took their weapons and all of their other posses- sions, including the women and children, but left the men and the wagons. They tied the men upside-down to the wagon wheels. Then they placed wood and brush under the captives' heads, which were about eighteen inches from the ground. When the brush was lit, the Apaches and their captives watched and listened as the flames evoked death screams from boiling brains.[3]

The burning hate the Apache felt for the Spaniards and Mexicans had blazed for two hundred years before the boiling-brains incident. It began around 1650,[4] and accelerated when land granted to New-World grandees required labor. The Spanish were religiously compelled to "save" the heathen Apache, so the Indians were captured, enslaved, and compelled to labor for their conquerors. One historian put it this way: "The conquerors looked on the wild tribes as their legitimate prey, to be seized and sent to do hard labor whenever a slave was needed . . . some of the Spanish governors . . . were completely unscrupulous in their attempts to secure this sort of raw material and make money from it."

Starting with the Spanish and continuing to the Anglo-American period, hunting and killing Apaches was sport. And the Apache retaliated in every way they could.

The Apache tale is a story of shameful subjugation, and a conflict of cul- tures with few parallels in North American history.

Unlike most other tribes, the Apaches were widely scattered over the West, from the plains of southern Colorado through Oklahoma, Texas, Ari- zona, New Mexico, southern California and northern Mexico. They were di- vided into six groups, each with its own name: Western Apache (Coyotero), Chiricahua (also called Eastern or Mimbres), Mescalero, Jicarilla, Lipan and Kiowa, and they were not always friendly with each other. For that reason, generalizations about the culture of a people called loosely "Apache" are al- most always false. Though individual bands and regional groups joined to fight the Mexicans and the Americans, they did so because of the one thing they all had in common: enemies.

Anyone interested in the history of the Apaches and their conflicts even- tually turns to one or more books by Dan L. Thrapp, who wrote or edited seven authoritative studies on the Apache, their battles and their leaders. In the preface to his book *Victorio and the Mimbres Apaches,* Thrapp wrote:

Brutality then was a part of life; ruthlessness even more so. Neither was exceptional, nor long remembered. Yet there were whites who shunned them both, and, although this is less well-known, there were Apaches, too, who had no stomach for cruelty or torture and who withdrew when it was practiced, avoiding it when possible. The Apaches, like the whites, were a complex people, with both good and bad among them, and it would be in error to over generalize, although, being of a tightly integrated society, they adhered to common customs, as do we all.[5]

After Mexico became an independent republic in 1823, and as the new government attempted to stabilize itself, the Apaches made a concerted attempt to reclaim their lands in what was then northern Sonora.[6] Mexican authorities claimed that the Indians killed five thousand settlers and that an additional four thousand fled from the terror of the warpath. Eventually, remnants of the Mexican military and civilians holed up in Tubac and Tucson, awaiting their fate.

A defining moment in Mexican-Apache relations came in 1835 when—in desperation—the new government of Sonora declared a bounty on Apache scalps, and in 1873, when Chihuahua followed Sonora's lead. The offerings were one hundred pesos for each warrior's scalp, fifty pesos for a woman's scalp, and twenty-five pesos for the scalp of a child. In those days, a peso was equal in value to one U.S. dollar. It was government-sponsored genocide, and it did not work.

Long, straight black hair is long, straight black hair. Apache hair was no different than that of Native Americans of any tribe or from many Mexicans and Anglo-Americans. Unsuccessful traders, settlers wiped out by drought, the desperate castoffs of the cities, and a group of "professional" scalp hunters on either side of the U.S.-Mexican border shot or clubbed to death any weaker black-haired indigents they could find. Some of the victims doubtless were Apache, but there is no record of the count and the origins of the dead. We do know that most Apaches wisely stayed in their mountain retreats.[7] But even mountain retreats were not always safe, as the Mimbres Apache discovered when James Johnson visited in 1837.

Chief Juan José Compa of the Mimbres Apaches, knew and apparently trusted the American adventurer-trader Johnson, who invited José and any member of the tribe who wished to attend to an outdoor banquet with plenty to eat and drink—a real feast. When the food had been consumed in good fellowship, and the Indians were enjoying the strong drink, Johnson got all of the guests together to view a huge pile of trade goods. Hidden behind the goods and out of sight of the Indians, a cannon loaded with shot and scrap metal boomed and tore the Apaches apart. José, who was not in the line of cannon fire, was shot by Johnson. Johnson and his crew scalped each Indian and collected the bounty in Mexico. An Apache not in the slaughtered group—who, distrusting, stood away from the festivities and watched the massacre instead of dying in it—ran away, carrying the infant son of José.[8] An alternate version of this story has it occurring at José's camp, with the Indians helping themselves to a bag of "pinole," (cornmeal) before they were killed. Keep this mysterious survivor in mind; he returns later in a different context.

Many times in the history of the Apaches the true savages were white. There were military men among them.

Early in the Civil War, in July 1861, a lieutenant colonel of the Confederacy captured seven Union companies and occupied Fort Fillmore, near present day Las Cruces, New Mexico. This officer, John R. Baylor, appointed himself the new governor of a huge territory that he named, and the Confederate congress confirmed, the "Territory of Arizona." This was the home of the Mimbres. Baylor wanted them dead.[9]

Two groups of volunteers were dispatched to an area near Tucson to open the roads that had become hazardous because of Indian attacks on travelers. To a captain of one of the volunteer companies, Thomas Helm, Baylor sent these instructions:

> I learn from Lieut. J. J. Jackson that the Indians have been in to your post for the purpose of making a treaty. The Congress of the Confederate States has passed a law declaring extermination of all hostile Indians. You will therefore use all means to persuade the Apaches or any tribe to come in for the purpose of making peace, and when you get them together kill all the grown Indians and take the children prisoners and sell them [into slavery] to defray the expense of killing the Indians. Buy whiskey and such other goods as may be necessary for the Indians . . . . Leave nothing un-

done to insure success, and have a sufficient number of men around to allow no Indian to escape.

. . . I look to you for success against these cursed pests who have already murdered over 100 men in this territory.[10]

Baylor erred (or lied) when he claimed there was a law declaring extermination of all hostile Indians. Union leaders somehow obtained a copy of the letter or gained knowledge of its intent, and used the information to win Apaches to their side and accelerate Indian attacks on the Confederates. Confederate president Jefferson Davis removed Baylor from office as governor of the territory. The infamous Baylor did, however, verify one of John Cremony's claims, when he wrote:

> . . . the mails were robbed; in one or two instances the messengers were found hanging up by the heels, their heads within a few inches of a slow fire, and they thus horribly roasted to death. Others were found tied to the wheels of the coach, which had been burned.[11]

When the Confederates retreated down the Rio Grande to El Paso and the security of Confederate Texas later that year (1862), a Union general by the name of James Henry Carleton took over. Carleton had been commander of the California Volunteers, an 1800-man force, which had been charged with the task of chasing the rebels away. When his force arrived, most of the rebels were gone, because of the help of the Colorado Volunteers. Carleton was no better than Baylor when it came to handling the Indians in the territory. Like Baylor, he instructed his troops to kill all Indian males. He wrote to Colonel Christopher Carson (better known as the frontiersman Kit Carson):

> All Indian men of that tribe [Mescaleros] are to be killed whenever and wherever you can find them. The women and children will not be harmed, but you will take them prisoners, and feed them at Fort Stanton until you receive other instructions about them. If the Indians send in a flag and desire to treat for peace, say to the bearer that when the people of New Mexico were attacked by the Texans [in the Civil War], the Mescaleros broke their treaty of peace and murdered innocent people, and ran off their stock; that now

our hands are untied, and you have been sent to punish them for their treachery and their crimes; that you have no power to make peace; that you are there to kill them wherever you can find them; that if they beg for peace, their chiefs and twenty of their principal men must come to Santa Fe to have a talk here; but tell them fairly and frankly that you will keep after their people and slay them until you receive orders to desist from these headquarters; that this making of treaties for them to break whenever they have an interest in breaking them will not be done any more.[12]

Carleton, like most military and civilian government officials, did not understand the lack of authority of the chiefs, and the right and ability of the individual warriors to do much as they pleased. He shared the belief of many of his peers that over time, the Indians would disappear, simply die out. When a joint special committee of the United States Senate and House of Representatives, appointed to determine the condition of the Indians, wrote the generals in the field for their opinions, Carleton was ready with a reason for decreasing Indian populations:

The causes which the Almighty originates, when in their appointed time He wills that one race of men—as in races of lower animals—shall disappear off the face of the earth and give place to another race, and so on, in the great cycle traced out by Himself, which may be seen, but has reasons too deep to be fathomed by us. The races of the mammoths and mastodons, and the great sloths came and passed away: the Red Man in America is passing away![13]

From the period of the Johnson massacre and the Mexican scalp bounty to the beginning of the Civil War, a period of more than twenty years, the chief of an Eastern Chiricahua-Mimbres band[14] called Mangas Coloradas by the Mexicans, was the arm of vengeance for his people. He was a giant for an Apache, standing six feet-four, an imposing, muscular individual with great charismatic presence. Those unfortunates who faced him in battle, especially one-on-one, knew at least for their few last moments that he was an exceptional warrior. He was born in the early 1790s, and ascended to the leader-

Apache Chief Mangas Coloradas

ship of his band in his mid-forties, in 1838. Apache legend says it was Mangas who watched the massacre by Johnson at a distance and rescued the son of the chief.

A trapper who saw Mangas said he was

> . . . a large athletic man considerably over six feet in height, with a large broad head covered with a tremendously heavy growth of long hair that reached to his waist. His shoulders were broad and his chest full, and muscular. He stood erect and his step was proud and altogether he presented quite a model of physical manhood.[15]

Another American called him "As noble a specimen of the Indian Race as I have ever seen . . . the poetic ideal of a chieftain."

For the March 1872 issue of *The Overland Monthly*, John Cremony wrote an article entitled "Some Savages." Cremony did not like Mangas nor any Apache, but he had personal experience with this chief. Cremony wrote that Mangas was called "Red Sleeves," because he smeared his arms up to his sleeves with blood when he was on the warpath.

Neither King Phillip, nor Logan, Uncas nor Keokuk, Black Hawk nor White Cloud ever possessed the genius and ability of Mangas Coloradas. None had his broad mental grasp, his wonderful craftiness, his unbounded ambition, his subtle and comprehensive knowledge of the elements he collected and managed; and none ever equaled him in blood-thirsty ferocity.[16]

At first, Mangas seems to have been on good terms with the *Nortamericanos,* but he became a menace to all Mexicans when he succeeded Juan José Compa as chief of a Mimbres Apache band, after Compa was murdered in the Johnson cannon attack.

Mangas turned on the Americans or "pindahs," as the Apaches called them, for a number of reasons. First, there was a serious dispute with the military and the American-Mexican Boundary Commission over two Mexican boys held by the Indians. There was the death of an Apache, shot by a Mexican employee of the commission who was never punished. After trying to be friendly, Mangas soon felt betrayed. And because he felt betrayed, the commission began losing livestock to Apache raiders. When the commission left the area of the Mimbres (near what is now Silver City in New Mexico), the military went with them. The Santa Rita copper mines in the vacated area, mines that always had been an insult to the Mimbres, were left unguarded. There were repeated incidents of miners and Mexicans killing Apaches. A new gold rush began in Pinos Altos, not too far from the Santa Rita mines, and ever more gold-hungry pindahs invaded the Mimbres' land.[17]

Mangas knew that more mines meant more trouble was brewing for his people, so several times in the autumn of 1851, he rode into the miners' camp at Pinos Altos in an attempt to convince them to move further south to Sonora, where, he told them, there was a better cache of gold and the weather was warmer. He offered to show the miners personally where the gold was. Whether the prospectors expected a trick, a ruse to get them out where they could be attacked, or whether they were so frustrated at the meager results of their work that they exploded in frustrated anger at the great chief, the results were the same. They tied Mangas to a post and brutally lashed him close to death with a bullwhip. As one writer summed it up: "It would have been far, far better for the miners, and hundreds of others, if they had finished him there."[18]

When he recovered, his anger was so great that no white man, woman or child was safe. The military reported in February 1852 that the territory was out of control. Mangas was attacking soldiers, robbing the mail, sacking government wagon trains, and burning wagons and throwing men on the fires to burn with them. He killed or chased away almost everyone in what is now southern Arizona. And he continued to raid in Mexico as well.

It was during the 1851 time of terror that the Oatman family—mother, father and seven children—were traveling through Apache territory, heading for California. The Oatmans found themselves as the last wagon of a train that began in Independence, Missouri, but split up on its way west. Shortly after a difficult crossing of the Gila River, about seventy miles from Yuma, they were attacked by Apaches. Six of the family members were killed. A son, Lorenzo, was left for dead, but later recovered and miraculously made it to Yuma. Two girls, Olive and Mary Ann, were taken captive. Mary Ann, only seven, would die of starvation.[19]

Five years later, Olive was ransomed from the Mohave Indian[20] who had purchased her from her captors. Survivors Olive and Lorenzo, brother and sister, told their story to a writer-lecturer in California, R. B. Stratton, who wrote a book about the Oatman family. The first printing of five thousand copies sold quickly, and the book became one of the bestsellers of the late 1850s.

Compared to the hundreds of other stories of massacres, attacks, murders, and raids published in the newspapers, magazines, and books of the nineteenth century, the experiences of Olive and Lorenzo Oatman transcend the genre in sheer reality and believability. The narration in the book abruptly switches back and forth from Olive to Lorenzo, so the excerpt below has been edited.

> LORENZO: I saw several Indians slowly and leisurely approaching us in the road. I was greatly alarmed and for a moment dared not to speak. At the time, my father's back was turned. I spoke to him, at the same time pointing to the Indians.
>
> After the Indians approached, he became collected, and kindly motioned them to sit down; spoke to them in Spanish, to which they replied. They immediately sat down upon the stones about us, and still conversing with father in Spanish made the most vehement professions of friendship. They asked for tobacco and a pipe, that they might smoke in

token of their sincerity and of their friendly feelings toward us. This my father immediately prepared, took a whiff himself, then passed it around, even to the last. . . .

Suddenly, as a clap of thunder from a clear sky, a deafening yell broke upon us, the Indians jumping into the air, and uttering the most frightful shrieks, and at the same time springing toward us flourishing their war clubs which had hitherto been concealed under their wolf-skins. I was struck upon the top and back of my head, came to my knees when with another blow, I was struck blind and senseless. One of their number seized and jerked Olive to one side, where they had dealt the first blow.

OLIVE: As soon as they had taken me to one side, and while one of the Indians was leading me off, I saw them strike Lorenzo, and almost at the same instant my father also. I was so bewildered and taken by surprise by the suddenness of their movements and their deafening yells, that it was some little time before I could realize the horrors of my situation. . . . I looked around and saw my poor mother, with her youngest child clasped in her arms and both of them still as if the work of death had already been completed; a little distance on the opposite side of the wagon, stood little Mary Ann, with her face covered with her hands, sobbing aloud, and a huge looking Indian standing over her; the rest were motionless, save a younger brother and my father, all upon the ground dead or dying. . . .

After these cruel brutes had consummated their work of slaughter, which they did in a few moments, they then commenced to plunder our wagon, and the persons of the family whom they had killed. They broke open the boxes with stones and clubs, plundering them of such of their contents as they could make serviceable to themselves. They took off the wagon wheels, or a part of them, tore the wagon covering off from its frame, unyoked the teams and detached them from the wagons, and commenced to pack the little food, with many articles of their plunder, as if preparatory to start on a long journey. . . .

LORENZO: I soon must have recovered my consciousness after I had been struck down, for I heard distinctly the repeated yells of those fiendish Apaches. And these I heard mingling in the most terrible confusion with the shrieks and cries of my dear parents, bothers, and sisters, calling, in the most pitiful, heart-rendering tones, for "Help, help! In the name of God, cannot any one help us?"

. . . I heard their preparations for leaving, and distinctly remember to have thought, at the time, that my heart had ceased to beat, and that I was about giving my last breath. I heard the signs and moans of my sisters, heard them speak, knew the voice of Olive, but could not tell whether one or more was preserved with her.[21]

The Apache rampage under Mangas lasted until July 1852, when a few en-lightened military officers talked peace to Mangas. Mangas pledged to halt his war against the pindahs, but stolidly refused to stop his campaign against the Mexicans.

When he signed the treaty with the Americans, he told Major John Greiner why he still would fight the Mexicans:

I will tell you. Some time ago my people were invited to a feast; aguardiente, or whiskey, was there; my people drank and became intoxicated, and were lying asleep, when a party of Mexicans came in and beat out their brains with clubs. At another time a trader was sent among us from Chihuahua. While innocently engaged in trading . . . a cannon con-cealed behind the goods was fired upon my people and quite a number were killed. How can we make peace with such people?[22]

And he never did.

In the long progression of American political hacks and inept military commanders who ruled over the Apache lands, there was one man who seemed to understand and respect the Indians, while acknowledging that real peace could not be established as long as the Apache continued raiding, steal-ing horses, mules and cattle wherever they found them. Dr. Michael Steck came to the Southwest from Pennsylvania to provide his ailing wife a warmer, more favorable climate. He was the government agent to the Mescaleros, but his ability was quickly recognized, and President Buchanan promoted him to

Superintendent of Indian Affairs for the New Mexico Territory. He was unusually popular with the Apaches. It was Steck who worked with Mangas when the Mimbres expressed an interest in farming. In the four years after 1855, the Tci-he-nde Mimbres farmed a three-mile field along the Santa Lucia River and confined their raids to Mexico.

It is estimated that Mangas' group on the Santa Lucia began with around four hundred men and their families. In only four years the group had shrunk to about 150 men, as the Indians fell to diseases, alcohol, and probably some desertions from the new, different farming existence. That Mangas was willing to work with Steck to bring some peace and stability to the region and that his people went along with the plan under very difficult circumstances, proves the foresight and pragmatism of this great leader. The plan, however, was doomed from the beginning. The Mimbres needed more space and desperately—in Dr. Steck's opinion—needed to be at distance from the white settlers and the miners. Progress on a large scale was impossible, because the government was preoccupied with the divisions in the country that lead to the Civil War.

Meanwhile, more and more miners went to Pino Altos, around four hundred by 1860. Unable to support themselves digging, they took to stealing Apache livestock. So, the cycle began all over again, this time with the murder of a chief of the Chiricahuas named Elias.[23]

Mangas had tried to unite the disparate Apaches. He had married his three daughters to young and promising chiefs. He was the father-in-law of a young man the whites knew as Cochise, and in the ensuing years it was Cochise who inspired and led the fighting Apaches with the aging Mangas at his side. Mangas was wounded at the famous battle with the U.S. Army at Apache Pass, but survived once again.[24]

In January 1863, Mangas was camped not far from Pinos Altos, where he had been whipped almost to death twelve years earlier. This was now a war zone, and there were no longer any miners around. Mangas, Cochise, and a young Bedonkohe Apache named Geronimo made travel through their territory very difficult for the unwary.

A colorful, tough old adventurer and prospector, Joseph Walker, wandered down the continental divide with a party of around forty gold seekers. They had several skirmishes with the Apaches and they could often see them in the distance, watching them. One of the prospectors suggested that if they could capture an important chief and hold him hostage, they might get out of the area alive. Under a flag of truce, they finally got Mangas to come visit them by telling him that they would give the Indians blankets and food if they were allowed to proceed in peace.

The chief was betrayed and taken captive. Carleton's California Volunteers were camped nearby. The troops relieved the prospectors of their prisoner and took him to Fort McLane.[25] General Joseph West questioned Mangas, then turned him over to guards with a sly suggestion to "make sure he doesn't escape under any circumstances."[26]

As Mangas lay wrapped in a small, inadequate blanket on the cold January ground near a campfire on his first night in captivity, his guards heated their bayonets in the fire and began touching them to the chief's feet and legs. He rose in protest, and they shot him. The next day a soldier scalped him, and they threw him in a shallow grave in a gully. The official report by General West stated that he was shot while trying to escape.

Two days later a doctor at the fort had the body dug up and cut off Mangas' head. The head was boiled until the flesh separated from the skull, and the skull was sent to phrenologist O. S. Fowler in New York. Phrenology, now a discredited non-science, sought to determine and analyze character by skull shape. It was all the rage in the 1800s. The location of the skull today is a mystery.

In later years, Geronimo would say that what happened that night was one of the greatest wrongs ever done to the Indians. Mangas was in his seventies when he was murdered, and had become an idol to his people. More than any other leader, he had tried to find a way to exist with the pindahs. Had the doctor at Fort McLane known that Apaches believed that you lived in the afterlife in the body shape in which you died, he may not have cared. But when word of the decapitation eventually got to the Indians, they pictured their great chief aimlessly walking in the next world, looking for his head.

Modern Apaches admit their ancestors tortured and mutilated their victims, and they say that the practice began when they learned of the decapitation of Mangas.

That may not be the whole truth, but there is little doubt that the practice accelerated after January 1863. And within ten years after the death of Mangas the U.S. Army and the Apache scouts who worked for them managed some beheadings of their own.

By 1873, Geronimo had surrendered, and the Apaches began wandering

Geronimo, the last of the warring Apache Chiefs.

into the San Carlos Reservation. That same year, an army lieutenant at the reservation was shot by Tonto Apaches, when unarmed, he walked up to a group of troublemakers. Fearing the consequences of what had happened, three chiefs—Cochinay, Chan-Deisi, and Chunz—and their followers bolted the reservation. Many settlers and travelers died, some horribly, at the hands of the fugitive Tontos. Troops and scouts scoured the mountains.

In May, Cochinay was killed and beheaded. The next month, the same fate befell Chan-Deisi. The heads were pole-mounted on the reservation at San Carlos. Chunz, probably the worst of the lot, was cornered in July. When the troops attacked, all of his followers fled except six of his captains. The heads of Chunz and his captains arrived at San Carlos on July 25. The nine rotting heads remained on poles until the middle of August.[27] Mangas is not the only chief who wanders in the Apache afterworld without a head.

In the 1930s, the Federal Writers Project interviewed thousands of older citizens across the country and assembled a massive collection of oral history. Many of those interviews were in the Southwest, and in them we find stories like this:

Pedro M. Rodriguez, Carrizozo, New Mexico:

> They took up the Indians' trail and followed them back though the Agua Azule Flat where they found Marcial's body. The Indians had cut off his right arm and scalped him before leaving him . . . Someone in the posse noticed two squaws up on the side of the mountain and started after them. The Apodaca woman (a captive) was with them and when the two squaws saw the white men coming they split the Apodaca woman's head open with an axe and made their getaway.

Louie Taren, Silver City, New Mexico:

> I stood and watched them butcher small children unable to give them any aid whatever. I soon saw [that] while the Indians were so interested in their spoils and mutilating the families that I could escape and let the people of Silver City come to the scene. I rode to town as fast as possible, where the people formed a rescue party, but all too late we arrived back at the scene . . . as all the people were dead, some were scalped while others were badly burned over the fire while some of the children were hung on meat hooks. This part of the work was always left for the squaws to do, which it seemed they took great delight [and] tried to see who could be the most cruel. We followed the Indians over into the country, but were unable to ever overtake them, but as long as we followed them we found a trail of blood. Over on the river we found where they had gone into a small hut, and killed an entire family and placed one member of the family that wasn't killed in the attack on the stove to burn. They

had held him by some means on the stove until he died, and then left him there.

Mrs. O. S. Warren, Silver City, New Mexico:

> About nine o'clock I was called to the door and there stood a nine year old boy with a red scarf tied around his neck and waist. He had his baby sister under the shawl. The youngster had been in the cornfield when the Indians attacked. He knew his little sister was up in a shed asleep. He crawled back to the cornfield then after the fight with his baby sister, and later walked into town carrying his little sister. (They were) the survivors of two large families. One small baby was found hung up by a meat hook. The Indians were very cruel to the people they captured, especially women and girls. They liked to take white boys to raise.

Around the time these and hundreds of other real-life experiences were collected from the settlers and old-timers in the Southwest, an ethnologist living on the San Carlos Reservation, Grenville Goodwin, was gathering field notes that he planned to use in published studies of the Apache.

Goodwin's extensive notes include the following:

> One time they captured two Mexicans and brought them back here. One of them was a Mexican captain, and these two men were made to dance with two women. Then as they danced, the chief under whom the dance was given rode up to them and said to the captain: "You know that these two women you are dancing with here will be the ones to kill you in a little while?" "No, there is never a woman who will kill me at all. I am not a woman, I am a man," the captain said.
>
> But pretty soon they took these two men and bound their hands behind their backs and led them over to the foot of a hill. Some of the women went with rifles, and it was these who shot and killed them. Pretty soon they came back bearing the arms and legs of the two men. They danced with these.
>
> It was when the captive was killed that they scalped

him and danced with his scalp as I told you. They sometimes scalped on the warpath, but they did not dance over
it—just threw it away and never brought it home.[28]

The Apaches did not record their history. The memories of some of the reser-
vation- confined warriors did make their way into studies by whites and oc-
casionally into a book or magazine article, but these Indians rarely trusted
their new keepers enough to relate real war stories. The most notable exception comes from a "white Apache," a boy who was captured when he was
eleven years old and who became a warrior and sub-chief.

His name was Herman Lehmann, the son of German immigrants who
had a small farm near Fredericksburg, Texas. This is the same Herman
Lehmann who provided stories of the Comanches in the previous chapter.

When he was twenty, Lehmann was placed on an Indian reservation. He
had forgotten how to speak English and German, and hated the palefaces as
much as any Indian warrior. He had been both an Apache and a Comanche—
leaving the Apache band when he killed a revered Medicine Man, and living
for a year in the wilderness as a wandering, often starving hermit before joining the Comanches. Years after being reunited with his mother and family, he
told his story to a family friend, Judge Jonathan H. Jones, who published it in
1899. A slightly different edited version was published in 1927 under the
title *Nine Years Among The Indians, 1870–1879.*

So cruel are the events in which he participated, Lehmann often expressed hesitation in reciting "these revolting crimes," but explained that he
had no choice. He was an Apache warrior. He recalled being a member of a
raiding party, which stumbled upon a wagon with a man, wife, infant, and
two small children—a boy about six and a girl around eight. The man,
woman and infant were immediately killed and scalped. The Indians took the
two youngsters but they would not eat and constantly cried. Their noise put
the raiders in jeopardy. After several days, two of the Indians took the little
girl, and holding arms and legs, swung her high in the air. She turned several
times before falling to the ground and breaking her neck. They did the same
with the boy, then trampled the dead children with the hooves of their horses
before hanging their mangled corpses on a tree for the vultures to eat.[29]

The inventiveness and creative cruelty of the Apache on the warpath is so
thoroughly documented that even the most sympathetic scholars and historians admit to it, as do the Apache of today. Captives were tied behind horses

and dragged over rocky deserts until they died; they were tied to cacti with wet, shrinking leather thongs. Some were buried near ant hills with their mouths propped open with sticks. The list goes on and on. Apache boys, warriors-to-be, were given animals to torture to death and were rewarded for originality, so it should be no surprise that they became the masters of long and painful death.

The Apache, it can be safely said, gave as good as he got. It stopped on September 3, 1886, with the surrender of the last warring chief, Geronimo, to Brigadier General Nelson A. Miles. Geronimo received many promises from the general and other U.S. officials. Of course, they were never delivered.[30]

Many of the native peoples whose practices are chronicled in other chapters have been wiped out by disease or by their enemies. Not the Apache. In 1860, it was reliably estimated that their population was six thousand. Today more than fifty eight thousand reside on reservations in Arizona, New Mexico, and Oklahoma.

13

"It's the Hand of God" — White Scalp Hunters

The Apaches were battered from all sides. In the early 1700s, they were pushed farther into Mexico by the Comanches. The Mexicans, when they could capture Apaches, made them slaves. In the early 1800s, it was the unstoppable Euro-American drive for land, settlement, and mineral wealth that took their lands from them. The Apache story is the American story, a story where bloodletting begat bloodletting. Cruelty and bestiality are matched. In the previous chapter, there is a claim that "Many times in the history of the Apaches, the true savages were white." The worst of these were professional scalp hunters.

Marauding in Northern Mexico between the towns of Chihuahua and Galeana in the 1840s, an American named John Joel Glanton led about thirty of the meanest, most unmerciful men ever to roam the border country. They were looking for Apaches, especially the Mescaleros. The municipal government of Chihuahua had promised Glanton $200 for each warrior scalp he could bring back.

Other scalp hunters had scoured the countryside earlier, and all Glanton and his men found was dirt, dust, rocks and rattlers—that is, until they came upon an emaciated, wrinkled old squaw, deserted by her people because she couldn't keep up. Glanton asked the ancient Indian woman a few questions, then told one of his men, José María Díaz, to kill her. Bullets were expensive; Díaz used his knife. As the squaw lay bleeding on the hot desert sand, the knife cut a circle around her crown, and with his knees on her shoulders, another Glanton man, Felix López, jerked loose her hair and a bloody patch of pale skin. The scalp was rushed to Chihuahua, and though the current deal with the scalp hunters excluded females, Glanton received $100.[1]

Various scalping bounty laws had been on the books in northern Mexico for fourteen years on that day when an Indian grandmother was knifed and scalped in the desert. The scalp-bounty laws were not repealed in Chihuahua until 1886.

Scalp hunters were mercenaries who were paid per killing or per captive. Their sole purpose was the extermination of a people. The Mexican authorities had concluded that the only way to stop Indian raiding was to kill all of the Indians, including infants and children. The individual farmers and ranchers were not properly armed nor sufficiently numerous to oppose the mounted bands of Apaches and Comanches that burned their homes, killed or captured their families, and stole their livestock. Except for the campaigns of the American General George Crook, both the Mexican and American Armies were unsuccessful in stopping or even slowing down the pillage.[2] The Mexican state of Sonora instituted scalp bounties in 1835. At that time Sonora comprised much of what would later become the American states of California, Arizona and New Mexico.

In Washington, President Andrew Jackson's opposition to the national banking system flared into the second great financial panic of the young country, just as Martin Van Buren took office in 1837. Jackson had taken federal funds out of the Second Bank of the United States and put them in state banks, so the latter were printing currency as fast as they could buy paper, and the entire U.S. economy almost collapsed. Banks closed, savings were wiped out, and "real" silver or gold money was hard to come by. Miners, ranchers, farmers and trappers in the American west searched for ways to earn money. They heard about James Johnson's sudden wealth, or the successes of James Kirker, and besides, dislike and fear of Indians was pandemic in the western territories. There were no brakes on hostility to Indians. Even President Jackson had said:

> They [the Indians] have neither the intelligence, the industry, the moral habits, nor the desire of improvement which are essential to any favorable change in their condition. Established in the midst of another and a superior race, and

without appreciating the causes of their inferiority or seeking to control them, they must necessarily yield to the force
of circumstances and ere long disappear.[3]

For over fifty years Americans could be paid in Mexico for killing any Indian
in the United States or Mexico. At first, the Mexicans specified Apache and
Comanche Indians, but later added Seri Indians (a tribe living on the eastern
coast of the Gulf of Mexico in Sonora), but the Mexican scalp inspectors
could not distinguish between Indian and non-Indian scalps, and certainly
could not determine tribal allegiances from a scrap of hair. Eventually, the
scalp commissioners and inspectors became suspicious of the death receipts
they received. It was easy to cut a large scalp into pieces and submit the sec-
tions as representing several Indian victims. The Commissioners then altered
the rules, specifying that each scalp had to include an ear.

It is difficult to determine how many gangs participated in the kill-for-
hire program. A single scalp was worth more than most men could earn in a
year of honest work, and there were obviously hundreds of men attracted to
the get-rich-quick appeal of scalp hunting. In 1850, it was reported that Chihuahua paid out $17,000[4] in half a year for the deaths of approximately two
hundred men, women and children. By 1850, Chihuahua was only one of
three Mexican states paying scalp bounties.[5] There is no count of the total
number of Indians killed and desecrated during the fifty-one years of planned
genocide. There are only stories of particular massacres and narratives of the
lives of the most infamous of the killers.

Sadly, Indian killing attracted other Indians. A Seminole chief, Coa-
coochee, hammered out a deal for himself and his cohorts with Coahuila to
trade land for scalps. John Horse, a runaway black slave, did the same thing
for his renegade companions. A group of Kickapoo Indians, migrants to Mexico from Indiana and Illinois, joined a Mexican scalp gang, got into a dispute
with their partners, and found themselves relieved of their own hair. The
most infamous scalp gang leader, James Kirker, always had his Shawnee and
Delaware Indians with him.[6]

In Chihuahua, the government even tried to pay Apaches to scalp Comanches, hoping against hope that they would both go away. They did, west
to Sonora—where the scalping payments had the effect of compensating the
Apache for raiding a neighboring Mexican state.

In one raid in 1841, the Indians killed three hundred Mexicans and stole

*Professional Indian killer and scalp hunter,
James Kirker*

18,000 head of livestock and kidnapped well over a hundred women and children

Any man who could kill with impunity—a mustered-out soldier, ex-Texas Ranger, trapper, miner, Indian, escaped slave, adventurer—anybody, regardless of nationality, could get into the lucrative game. Among the worst killers-for-hire were Michael Chevallié, James Kirker, John Dusenberry, and John Glanton, all Americans. These pages will trace the careers of two: James Kirker and John Glanton.

The first mention of James Kirker between the covers of a book came in 1851, shortly after the infamous scalp hunter retired his bowie knife. Captain Mayne Reid wrote a book called *The Scalp Hunters,* one of the first western novels to become a bestseller. Reid had been a trapper, a journalist, and a captain in the American army in the Mexican War. He knew the territory. His book told the story of a young adventurer from the East who after numerous misadventures, found himself the member of a scalp-hunting troop. The book had the appeal of Indian fighting, conflict among the scalp hunters, and romance. On six occasions, Reid refers to one of his fictitious scalp hunters as James Kirker. There is indeed some similarity between Kirker and one of the principal characters of the book, Segin, the head of the scalp hunters. With only a little stretching of the imagination, the real Kirker's Indian second-in-command, Spybuck, can be detected in the novel.

Reid idealized an altogether merciless and unforgivable campaign in *The Scalp Hunters,* and launched a new genre of American literature, the western novel. His clumsy attempt to replicate a mountain man's speech makes the following excerpt demanding reading today, but Reid's clear understanding of what scalp hunting was about is apparent in every line. The fictional scalp hunters are stalking a small herd of buffalo when

> I heard the click of a rifle along with this abrupt exclamation. I turned suddenly. Rube was in the act of leveling his piece. My eye involuntarily followed the direction of the barrel. There was an object moving in the long grass. "A buffalo that still kicks," thought I, as I saw the mass of dar-brown hair.
>
> I had scarcely made the observation when the animal reared up on its hind legs, uttering a wild human scream; the shaggy hide was flung off; and a naked savage appeared, holding out his arms in an attitude of supplication. I could not have saved him. The rifle had cracked, the ball had sped. I saw it piercing his brown breast, as a drop of sleet strikes upon the pane of glass; the red spout gushed forth, and the victim fell forward upon the body of one of the animals. . . .
>
> The old trapper rode up to the corpse, and leisurely dismounted from his mare. "Fifty dollar a plew," he muttered, unsheathing his knife and stooping over the body. "It's more'n I got for my own. It beats beaver all hollow. Cuss beaver, say this child. Plew a plug—ain't worth trappin' if the varmint wur as thick as grass-jumpers in calf-time. Ee-up, niggur," he continued, grasping the long hair of the savage, and holding the face upward: "let's get a squint at yur phisog. . . . Hooraw! Coyote Pash! [Coyotero Apache] Hooraw!"
>
> . . . So saying, he gathered the long crown locks in his left hand; and with two slashes of his knife, held quarte and

tierce, he cut a circle around the top of the head, as perfect as if it had been traced by compasses. He then took a turn of the hair over his wrist, giving it a quick jerk outward. At the same instant, the keen blade passed under the skin, and the scalp was taken!

"Counts six," he continued, muttering to himself while placing the scalp in his belt; "six at fifty-three hunder shiners for Pash har: cuss beaver trappin'! says I."

Having secured the bleeding trophy, he wiped his knife upon the hair of one of the buffaloes, and proceeded to cut a small notch in the woodwork of his gun, alongside five others that had been carved there already. These six notches stood for Apaches only; for as my eye wandered along the outlines of the piece, I saw that there were many other columns in that terrible register.[7]

The attitude toward the Apaches expressed by Rube, and in fact, throughout the book was thoroughly accepted by Americans in the mid-1800s.

From 1837 until 1845 Jim Kirker killed or supervised the killing of 487 Apaches[8] and handed over hundreds of Apache women and children to Mexican authorities, in whose hands they lived their short lives in the worst kind of slavery.

Kirker was sixteen when he immigrated to New York in 1810 to escape conscription into the British army, then at war against Napoleon. His family had been prosperous grocers in a small village near Belfast, and Kirker followed the family profession in New York, working as a clerk. Within two years after his arrival, war broke out with the British, and young Jim signed on with a privateer, the *Black Joke*, a raider of British shipping. This was Kirker's first experience with the slaughter of innocents. The *Black Joke* crew boarded and massacred sailors and passengers of unarmed freighters in the Caribbean. Oddly, in newspaper interviews Kirker gave in later life, he never mentioned these experiences on the *Black Joke*, saying only that he had served on the ship.

At the conclusion of the War of 1812, Kirker returned to New York and the grocery to find that his employer had died and left a young widow with a small child. He married the widow and eventually had a son, James Kirker, Jr. The store prospered, and Jim became a respected, well-to-do young businessman. When five cousins arrived on a ship from Belfast in 1817, they moved in with Jim for a while and beseeched him to help them get to St. Louis, a haven for Scotch-Irish immigrants. Kirker took them overland to Pittsburgh and by river to St. Louis.

Kirker never returned to New York, and never saw his wife or son after that summer day when he departed with his cousins in 1817. He was twenty-three when he left.

For the next eleven years, he was a St. Louis grocer, a trapper, fur trader, and an active participant in the St. Louis to Santa Fe trade. In his trapping business in Mexico, he often stowed his furs at the old Santa Rita mines to hide them from the authorities, for he did not always have the required trapping permit from the authorities in Chihuahua. When the mines went back into operation in 1828, Kirker made an arrangement to trap in the winter and work for the mining company during the summer as a guard for the mule trains that shipped out with ore and returned with supplies.

The route went from waterhole to waterhole, straight through Apache territory. Kirker probably got the job because he understood the necessity of cultivating friendly relations with Apache chiefs. He practiced this friendship to the extent that he was allowed to sell mules and horses stolen by the Apaches to customers as far away as Louisiana. It is known that Kirker and the Apache chief Juan José Compa were friends; Kirker also knew and had some dealings with Cochise. By this time, Kirker was known as Don Santiago Querque, the Spanish translation and spelling of his Irish name.

Around 1831, trapper, guard and broker James Kirker married the prettiest girl in Juarez,[9] Rita Garcia. Of course, he still had a wife in New York.

In 1835 to 36, Kirker and the eighteen trappers who worked with him had their most successful season ever, returning from what is now northern Arizona with 1050 beaver pelts on 176 mules. Kirker had become a Mexican citizen, so this time he had a real license from the governor of Chihuahua, Albino Perez. On his way back to his new home and wife, a group of Zuni and Navajo Indians relieved the trapper group of eighteen months' work. When he reported the theft to a friendly Mexican calvary officer, Jim Kirker found that Perez had put a price on his head for trading with the Apaches.

The furs and mules were recovered by the Mexican military, and supposedly ended up as the personal property of Perez, but Kirker had no options—he fled Mexico for Bent's Fort, Colorado. There was an $800 bounty for him, dead or alive.

At Bent's Fort, Kirker met the man who was to have an immense effect on his career, the Shawnee Spybuck, a tall, handsome and fearless Indian chief who became a legend in the Southwest. Missourian James Hobbs, who as a young man, hunted and trapped with Spybuck, said he was the best shot, the best rider and the most courageous fighter in the West. Taught by missionaries near Cape Girardeau, Missouri, he spoke and wrote English perfectly. At the time when the fugitive Kirker trapped for furs in Colorado, Spybuck may have been with him.[10] The Shawnee did go with him back to New Mexico when a series of bloody events allowed Kirker to return to his adopted home.

A mob had jerked the governor, Perez, out into the dusty streets of Santa Fe and cut off his head on August 9, 1837. Opponents of Perez had spread the rumor that the governor was planning a tax on sexual intercourse. So, of course, he had to die. This rumor, which played into general discontent at Perez's authoritarian ways was spread by his political enemies, especially Manuel Armijo, and perhaps Kirker, as well. Armijo became the new governor, and Kirker was invited back home to Chihuahua (now New Mexico). Four months earlier there had been a more ghastly murder when John James Johnson fired his cannon at a peaceful gathering of Mimbre Apaches and killed a friend of Kirker's, Chief John José Compa.

As indicated in Chapter 12, there are different versions of the Johnson massacre of the Mimbres, but there was a single effect: all-out war by the Apaches. The vengeance that had been mostly directed at the Mexicans, now included all of the invaders of Apache lands. The Santa Rita mines closed after the warring Apaches closed the Copper Trail, and the owners pleaded with their former guard, James Kirker, to come back to his old job.

He did so with a vengeance. Gathering a bunch of Delaware and Shawnee Indians, including Spybuck, and a rough group of unemployed outcasts, Kirker surrounded an Apache village in New Mexico Territory and attacked without warning. Of approximately 250 warriors present that day, Kirker's crew killed fifty-five and stole all of their stock. They took one captive, told him that this battle was a small sample of what would happen unless the Indians left the mines alone, and released him so he could spread the word among his people. Kirker and his fighters were treated as heroes when they entered Socorro, New Mexico. The Santa Rita mines reopened. James Kirker embarked on a new and bloody career.

Governor followed governor in the state of Chihuahua, but none of them seemed able to do anything to protect the people. The ranchers and farmers could hardly protect themselves, because the Mexican dictatorship in Mexico City, fearing more revolutions, made it difficult for the populace to get guns.[11] The unfettered Apaches came on raids right into Chihuahua City, or virtually any place they wanted to go. With the support of a new governor, José Maria de Irigoyen, a citizens' committee began raising money to hire Kirker and his band of mercenaries, since all confidence in the ability of the Mexican army to protect the people had disappeared.

By September, 1839, the committee had collected $100,000 to finance the conflict, and Kirker got $5,000 for initiating hostilities. With Spybuck as second in command, fifty men, including Shawnee and Delaware Indians, rode out into the wasteland near Taos and made camp, staking out a remuda of horses and mules to entice the Apaches. During the night, when the Apache raiders thought the troop was asleep, they coaxed out a small herd of horses and fled, doing exactly what Kirker had expected them to do.

Quickly mounting up, the mercenaries took a shortcut to where they believed the Apaches would travel to get into the mountains. The ambush almost worked, but the Indian force numbered about 150 and those who survived the first volley fled down the gorges into the little village of Rancho de Taos and tried to get into the church. It didn't work. Forty Apaches were killed, and those that survived were stripped of their horses and ran for their lives on foot. The pay for Kirker's killers was $1 a day plus one-half of what was taken from the Indians, so the horses were important.[12]

By December, the ragtag band of mercenaries was back in Chihuahua, where Kirker asked for and received another $5,000. As his campaign continued, and as they stripped more and more horses and cattle from dead Apaches, arguments began as to who really owned the recaptured livestock. Ranchers who saw their own brands in Kirker's corals began questioning the policy of allowing the Indian fighters to possess all that they captured. They accused Kirker and his troop of stealing cattle from them and saying it came from the Apaches.

At the same time, the Mexican military authorities, until then happy to see others put their lives on the line to fight the Apaches, began to resent the successes of the band of killers. The minister of war in Mexico City said that "it was disgraceful to the Mexican government and 'unpatriotic' to employ foreigners to protect its citizens."[13] In July 1840, this same minister of war became both governor and military commander of the state of Chihuahua.

He fired Kirker and his gang, accused Kirker of stealing mules belonging to the government, and put a $9,000 reward on his head.

The disgruntled mercenaries disbanded, and James Kirker went home, reportedly complaining: "The hell with it! Mexico will never learn that she has to use force with the Apaches—they cannot be bargained with."

What Kirker did during the next two years remains a mystery. A historian of the scalp trade, Ralph A. Smith, contends that he changed sides and worked for the Apaches, that he became an Apache war chief.[14] A biographer—William Cochran McGaw—points to Kirker's brokering of horses and mules for the Apaches, yet this activity seems to have occurred earlier, before he became a scalp hunter.

Arizona historian Ray Brandes is quite specific:

> Don Santiago [Kirker] could take no more threats; he moved to western Chihuahua and changed sides to play his cards on the other side of the table. As a partner of the Chihuahua Apaches and their chieftain Cochise, he raided haciendas, and attacked Mexican trading parties for the loot which could be sold in the northern trading centers. In this interim as a chief of the Apache Nation, Kirker bartered plunder with the unscrupulous American traders on a very large scale.[15]

In 1845, Governor Angel Trías reinstituted the scalps-for-pesos program. If in truth, he had been leading the Apaches, James Kirker now changed sides again, and the $9,000 bounty was withdrawn. Once again, there was more money to be made killing Apaches than working with them.

The payment schedule was $100 for the scalp of a warrior, $50 for the scalp of a squaw, and $25 for the death-hair of a child. With these incentives, Kirker put together a force of over 150 men.

He quickly received an assignment. A long mule train loaded with food and merchandise belonging to a rich local merchant was on its way to Chihuahua City, and almost made it before the Apaches struck. All of the eighty or so mule drivers were killed, except one, and the mules and their loads were captured by the raiders. When the sole survivor made it to town, the merchant sought out Kirker and his new "army" and offered him half of whatever he could recover. Within four days, the scalp hunters found the Indians celebrating their victory by drinking the spoils.

Kirker and Spybuck waited until they passed out from the alcohol or exhaustion, or both. Not one shot was fired. Kirker's killers calmly walked into the Indian camp and slit the throats of all forty-three Apache raiders. Shawnees and the Delawares did the scalping, delivering the bloody hair to Spybuck, who sprinkled the scalps with salt to preserve them.

With the red blood turning black as it soaked the ground around them, Kirker's army went on a two-day binge, drinking the whisky the dead Indians couldn't finish.

Kirker knew that an important Apache village lay to the west in the general direction of Sonora, about three days from where they were. He asked his men if they wanted to tackle it, and they said yes.[16]

Kirker sent out scouts ahead of his main troop. They reported seeing warriors entering the village with kegs of whiskey. So Kirker decided to employ the same tactic as before. They would let the Apaches drink and dance until they decided to sleep it off, and then attack in the morning before the Indians realized what was happening. This was a large village of around a thousand inhabitants—men, women, and children unknowingly waiting for the scalper's knife.

There was a miscue at attack time when one of the scalpers fired a musket before the mercenaries were ready, and the Apaches evidently had not suffered the anticipated hangovers. They fought back, and many warriors successfully fled to a nearby mountain slope, but it was the end for most of the women and children, who were stabbed or clubbed to death. It was a short battle, and a complete victory for Kirker. As it drew to a close, the Apache chief Cochise saw Kirker and shouted an accusation of betrayal. If Kirker knew that this was Cochise's band of Apaches, he did not tell any of his men before the attack. Cochise escaped, and reportedly swore never to trust another white man.[17]

In addition to the horses and livestock Kirker captured, he found that he had accidentally liberated a large number of Mexican women and children who were being held captive by the Indians. When the party returned to Chihuahua with the products of their two encounters—repatriated Mexicans, a large herd of livestock including sheep and goats, and most of the merchandise stolen from the mule train—the killers were feted as heroes.

They had 182 scalps and eighteen women captives, but they were not paid what they had been promised. The governor sadly informed the mercenaries that he had only $2,000 in the treasury. At the same time, ranchers and farmers were again going through the coral of captured livestock and culling out what they believed was theirs. It was too much for Spybuck and his Shawnees. They cut out the number of horses and mules they felt was their share, faced down the governor and his troops and left, regretting, Spybuck is reported to have said, that they did not have the governor's scalp to go with them.[18]

Kirker retired again, but within months, the Apaches almost succeeded in repossessing Chihuahua and Sonora. Kirker got his army back together, and this time the troop came back with 160 scalps. There was another celebration—with a gruesome, sacrilegious twist. The portals of the Chihuahua church were decorated with the hair of the dead Apaches.

A traveler in northern Mexico, British adventurer-journalist George Frederick Ruxton, happened into Chihuahua City just as the celebration was at full blast. He later wrote of the scene:

> Opposite the principal entrance, over the portals which from one side of the square, were dangling the grim scalps of one hundred and seventy Apaches, who had been most treacherously and inhumanly butchered by the Indian hunter in pay of the state. The scalps of men, women and children were brought into town on procession, and hung as trophies in the conspicuous situation, of Mexican valor and humanity![19]

The Mexicans and the Americans were about to go to war, and James Kirker was offered a colonel's commission in the Mexican army. He never told them yes or no, but with his small group of Delawares and Shawnees, leaving his wife and children, he slipped out one night to offer his services to the American army.

He never rejoined either of his families in Mexico or in New York.

Records show that he did make a quick trip to Ireland, probably at the death of a relative, that for a while he owned a hotel, that he was the guide for a large wagon caravan to California, and that he was in California around the time of the gold rush in 1849. He settled in Contra Costa County, California, near Mount Diablo, in 1852. There, he and the Indians who came with him hunted game for the meat-hungry residents of San Francisco. There are a few reports that suggest he also raised cattle.[20]

When he died, early in 1853, his Shawnee and Delaware Indian companions mounted up and rode away. His cabin was taken over by his doctor, probably for the payment of medical bills. The doctor, Samuel Adams, was a cancer specialist who believed skunk oil was a good treatment for the affliction.

The doctor used the Kirker cabin as a home for the skunks he raised. Appropriately.

The pastoral history of the United States expansion into placid virgin land taught in schools includes stories of Davy Crockett, Sam Houston and the valiant defenders of the Alamo and "the American way of life." Stories of a few battles between Indians and the U.S. cavalry may find their way into textbooks after they are sanitized of the horrific realities of these conflicts. Nowhere, however, will the gore-besotted lives of scalp hunters of the Southwest appear.

If James Kirker was cold and heartless, John Joel Glanton was subhuman. Glanton claimed to be a South Carolinian who came to Texas when his parents moved to a settlement started by Stephen Austin at Gonzales. He professed to be a deeply religious man who had been engaged to a beautiful seventeen-year-old orphan girl whose parents had been killed by Lipian Apaches. At some point after he had built a log cabin for his young wife-to-be, the Lipians attacked again and took her and other women and children as captives. On the following day, when Glanton and a large group of Texans from Austin's settlement caught up with the Indians, the girls were tomahawked and scalped by the Lipians during the battle. Glanton told this story to all who would listen, in explanation of his hatred for Indians and his entrance into the scalping business.

It was a good story, but Stephen Austin did not have a settlement at Gonzales, and the Texas Historical Society can find no *early* records of any Glantons in the territory at the time he professed to be there. He also claimed that the blonde scalp he carried was all that was left of his murdered love.

Glanton was in Texas, but far later than he claimed. He apparently fought in the Mexican War, and was involved in the earlier war for Texas independence. He was a morose and heavy drinker, always looking for a fight.[21]

He is known to have been part of a scalping company in Chihuahua headed by Major Michael H. Chevallié in May 1849. Chevallié got into the scalping business while on his way to California, but he had enough of it by June, and continued his trip west. This man who had financed his travels with the lives of Apaches and Comanches accidentally shot himself during the first few miles of his journey and died on the trail. Glanton took over the Cheval-lié operation and for a year was the terror of the Southwest.

During his first killing expedition in June, he took four adult male scalps and the scalp of a small child. He also captured three warriors, a young girl, and two teenage Apaches. The scalps were hung up for the public to see in Chihuahua City, and the new hero received $1350. There is no record of what happened to the captives.

Glanton next decided to cash in on the special $1000 reward offered by Chihuahua for the scalp of the Mescalero chief Gomez, who in turn offered a $1000 reward for the scalp of any Mexican or American. After playing tag through the wilderness, sometimes with Gomez and 150 warriors behind them, Glanton's gang of only eighteen scalp hunters surprised the Mescalero Apaches near Presidio, Texas, in early August 1849, killed at least eleven, and captured several more. Gomez escaped.[22] The Indians had a herd of mules that one observer estimated at two thousand head. Glanton sold the captured animals for $22 each to gold-seekers on their way to California.

Only weeks later, hunting on both sides of the Rio Grande, he sliced off the hair of seven warriors and two teenagers. Then, near El Paso, he engaged the Apaches in a raging battle and again came away with scalps and livestock. Few details are available, but it was reported[23] that early in 1850, he attacked an Apache winter camp in Texas and collected another 250 scalps.

Though feted and praised by many Mexican administrators for spreading fear among the dreaded Apaches and sending them North, Glanton was nevertheless feared and hated by the Mexican populace. The often drunk, garrulous, ill-tempered killer went too far when he dressed his scalpers as Indians, encircled small Mexican settlements, killed and scalped all of the inhabitants, then left after his band shot arrows into the livestock they didn't take the trouble to steal. When there were no warring Indians to fight, Glanton attacked peaceful, agricultural tribes and turned them into warring Indians. His bestiality became too much even for the bloodthirsty administrators in Chihuahua. The scalp hunter was declared a fugitive, and an $8,000 reward for his capture, dead or alive, was posted by the governor. Glanton switched allegiance from Chihuahua to Sonora, where, though the scalp bounties were smaller, he at least was not a wanted man.

In one of his many misadventures, Glanton wandered northwest into Navajo country, lost thirteen men, and collected no scalps. Yet success seemed always around the next canyon, and it wasn't long before he had thirty-seven bloody cashable warrants, some coming from the heads of innocent Mexicans. Glanton and ten of his men decided to take the scalps to the capital of Sonora and collect.

Heading south, they saw a small group of wagons—Mexicans from Sonora going to California. The scalp hunters donned Indian garb and rushed the caravan, shooting arrows, whooping and hollering. The Mexican men, who were on horseback, fled, except three who were caught, killed, and scalped; five women were left in the wagons. Three of the women were old, so they were clubbed to death and scalped. The two young women were stripped and repeatedly raped by Glanton and the ten men he had with him.

The fleeing Mexicans, confident that they had been attacked by Apaches, sought help nearby, and at night, began firing on the scalp hunters. Glanton and his men finished off the two young women, scalped them, and fled. Three scalp hunters were killed in the fusillade.

After selling $6,000 worth of scalps to the Mexicans, the Glanton gang, then thirty-eight strong, rode through the desolate lands around the Little Colorado River southeast of present-day Holbrook, Arizona, seeking anyone with straight, long black hair. They didn't see Indians, but they saw columns of smoke on the high mesas and knew the Indians were there, and the Apaches probably knew who they were watching.

Suddenly the scalp hunters were surrounded, and a storm of arrows and gunshots killed fourteen of the Glanton gang. Seeking some cover in a small grove, Glanton assessed their situation. They were far from water and the nearest town—their only chance for survival was to break out and run for it. But seven of the men were wounded. The pseudo-doctor of the gang, Doc Irving, told Glanton that three of the wounded could travel, but four could never make it. They marked the points of four arrows and put them in a quiver with sixteen others. Each of the able-bodied men drew out an arrow. The men who got the marked arrows were thereby elected to kill their wounded comrades.

During the night, they butchered several mules and prepared the meat for emergency food during the breakout that was scheduled for sunrise. They took good care of the doomed companions overnight, but as the sun rose, dispatched them with Apache war clubs and fled north toward Yuma.[24] Two other wounded scalp hunters died on the trip. Over the objections of Glanton, the remaining scalp hunters visited a peaceful Pima village where, for once they did no harm to the occupants.

When they arrived in Yuma, the Yuma Indians also greeted them peacefully and shared food with them, obviously not knowing who they were. Glanton thought the makeshift ferries over the Colorado River operated by the Yumas could be his El Dorado, an easy way to gather gold from the caravans moving west to California. Surprising their hosts, and capturing nine young women, the scalp hunters took over the ferries and quickly erected a stone barricade to protect them from an anticipated retaliatory attack by the Indians. They operated the ferries, charged outrageous fees, and often robbed or murdered their passengers.

"Sick and disgusted with the hellish orgies," the robberies and bloodshed, four of the gang deserted for California on April 23, 1850. Just as they were leaving, the Yumas attacked. One of the deserters, called "Crying Tom" Hitchcock, supposedly said, "Glanton rubbed out." And his companion, "Father" Ben Tobin, who had once trained for the priesthood, took off his hat and remarked, "It's the hand of God."[25]

John Joel Glanton died as he lived, under a scalping knife. A savage killed a savage.

Kirker and Glanton were small time players in North America's long sad story of violence inevitably tied to conflicting cultures. Conflict perpetuated savagery. Indian fought Indian for vengeance, food, or territory, and white invaders fought Indians to reaffirm the myth of a civilized natural order.

14

The Past in the Present

One or two million years ago, starving bipedal creatures screamed and waved sticks as they raced after larger but less intelligent animals, who, fleeing in extreme panic, plunged to their death as they ran over a cliff. This small band, ancestors to modern man, had discovered the power of terror, and the benefits of cooperative action to attain it. From that day to this, man has used the threat or act of terror, and the intense fear it instills, as a primary tool of governance. It is used to force change or prevent it. In some degree, it is in everyday life.

History books tell of conflicts where invaders have torched a village and mercilessly killed all of the men, raped the women, and speared the children, then discovered that the next village in the valley welcomed them as saviors. Terror works. A more modern analogy is found in the destruction of Nagasaki and Hiroshima in World War II, when the terror of atomic warfare resulted in the immediate surrender of Japan.

Terrorists cause change. The September 11, 2001, attack on the World Trade Center in New York City killed 2823 innocents. It also caused the loss of billions of dollars in the stock markets of the world, started a war, helped turn a government surplus into a deficit, and aroused fear to a degree that even crippled grandmothers were searched and forced to take off their shoes in airports and the U.S. government urged citizens to spy on one another.

Terror as a tool of last resort for stressed, underprivileged, and oppressed peoples to achieve specific goals that improve their own well-being, is less successful. It is a tool of reaction, an attempt to answer a real or imagined wrong by peoples who have no other weapons. When used, as it often was,

194

by Native Americans, it did not work. Jeffery Hart has written, "The Indians lost the long war because their overall culture and Stone Age tribal organization were inferior and could not prevail."[1] Hart discounts technology differences, and overlooks two other significant Euro-American advantages: a larger population and some immunity to common diseases.

The terror described in the preceding pages: cannibalism, headhunting, torture, and genocide—was terror with a purpose—however good or bad that purpose is judged to be today. This book samples the terror of North American history, and has purposely omitted well-reported massacres such as Sand Creek, Wounded Knee, Jamestown and dozens of others easily found in libraries and bookstores. Many of the chapters conclude with population estimates, census, or reservation data, in an effort to examine the growth or lack of growth of the subject tribes. Counting the survivors is a tricky business.

It is not difficult to find the argument that the history of contact and conflict between the American Indian and the European-American resulted in the "most horrendous holocaust in history."[2] Statistics are used to prove it.

If there were, say, fifteen million American Indians in 1492, and there are less than three million today, then the epidemics, and the merciless killing inflicted on Native Americans by European invaders was a "horrendous holocaust."

It is not that simple.

Even though the pre-Columbian population estimates include the United States and Canada (i.e., "all of the lands north of the Rio Grande River"), present population numbers are often quoted for the U.S. alone and for Americans who consider themselves "full blooded" Indians. This distorts any analysis of current Indian population.

An equally significant part of the problem is the questionable methodology used in computing pre-Columbian populations. Using American-Indian census data gathered in the 1800s (or in some cases even earlier) and "working backwards," scholars decide on disease and warfare mortality estimates for each tribe, and add to this historical population estimates of extinct tribes like the Calusa and Timucua. To again oversimplify: if there were one thousand members of a tribal unit in 1834, earlier in their history, this group suffered a disease epidemic from viruses carried by whites or Indians who had white contact. During the epidemic, it is estimated that half of the population perished, therefore, prior to the white incursion, there must have been not one thousand tribal members, but *two* thousand.

Sufficient oral and written history exists to estimate the number of plagues suffered by Indian population groups. Recent research indicates that groups with high mortality from disease epidemics experience higher birth rates after the epidemic and grow to previous population levels within about fifty years. Taking the 1834 one-thousand-member tribal group example above, if they had suffered a 50 percent mortality rate in an epidemic in 1784—fifty years before they were counted in 1834—chances are the tribe would have replaced those who died because of the higher birth rate that follows high mortality events. Using this logic, the tribal size would be the same—one thousand members.[3]

Yet there are further complications. If plague follows plague, if warfare exists during or soon after plague, if plague and loss of workers results in famine, any of these events can halt the rebuilding of a devastated population and possibly lead to extinction. Opportunistic enemy tribes or European-Americans often took advantage of epidemic weakened opponents.

Other factors influence pre-Columbian population estimates when they are derived from hypothecated mortality rates prior to the headcounts in the 1800s. One neglected factor is the unknown percentage of a population that became immune to certain viruses because of prior non-lethal exposures.

Another approach to pre-historic population counts relies upon definitions of subsistence methods (farming, hunting and gathering), and relating this to how many people the land can support. The system infers that if a square mile of fertile land can support two people, two people will be on it.

The problems encountered in the development of formulae to establish the pre-Columbian American Indian population have not been solved. More plainly put: no one knows what the Native American Indian population was before Columbus.

It is almost as difficult to determine the native American Indian populations in the United States and Canada in the 2000s as it is in the 1400s. The 2000 U.S. census reports that 4.1 million Americans claim to be Indian or part Indian. The Canadian government reports 885,499 of its citizens are Indian or Métis. The numbers combine to five million Native North Americans who consider themselves Indian or part Indian.

The unanswered question is how many citizens of the U.S. and Canada can claim one or more ancestors who were North American Indians? How can the racial/ethnic dilution of two hundred generations be factored into the North American Indian population count? If, as stated in an earlier chapter, three million Americans can claim they are descendants of the 102 *Mayflower* Pilgrims, how many more can claim they are descendants of native North American Indians?

If there were five or six million native North American Indians in 1492, then a strong, courageous, and durable people have fought their way back after centuries of oppression and genocide. If the 1492 population proves to be closer to contemporary estimates—fourteen or fifteen million—it will take longer.

The obsession with population statistics accomplishes very little in the continuing search for real equality between native and non-native Americans. Had each and every European who stepped on the shores of North America done so in friendship and respect, the results would have been *almost* the same. For the Americas were a true paradise, a land bereft of disease where death came from accidents, starvation, old age or warfare. Perhaps the journeys of the first Americans across the frozen Bering Strait "served to freeze to death most human disease carriers" and left the first Americans disease-free in a land that did not suffer from the pathogens of Europe, Africa and Asia.[4] Before the Europeans, the native American Indian did not know measles, diphtheria, chorea, influenza, and smallpox, or any of a long list of diseases that periodically and grimly swept across the Old World.

What happened in the Americas had already occurred in Europe with the Black Death and the accompanying famine, and was continuing while Columbus slaughtered the Indians of the Indies. (In Finland alone, one third of the population starved to death.) Four years after Columbus made landfall, Savonarola was proclaiming that in Florence, Italy, "There will not be enough men left to bury the dead; nor means to dig enough graves." Seventy-five per cent of the population of Florence perished. In Europe, the plague lasted three hundred years and killed thirty-five million people.

The plague in Europe brought more wars, more persecution, and more torture, as a stressed population turned upon itself. "Death was so daily, brutality so commonplace, destruction of the animate and inanimate so customary—that it is shocking even in our own age of mass destruction."[5]

The plague of the Black Death turned peaceful citizens into raging mobs. The medieval prejudice against Jews rapidly surfaced. Inquisitions cruelly tortured Jewish merchants, and then publicly announced that the merchants had confessed. The Jews, the inquisition said, had poisoned the public wells and that was why people were dying everywhere. On February 14, 1349—

Valentine's Day—two thousand Jewish men, women, and children were herded to a wooden platform and burned to death in Strasbourg, Germany. Similar atrocities occurred through out Europe for over a hundred years.

The misery and dejection of sudden, unexplainable death in a population where disease had been relatively unknown must be counted as one of the forces that pushed Native Americans into periods of aberrant behavior, just as it did the Europeans.

The paradise of the Americas was fated to end. Man moves. Had it not been Columbus or any of the adventurers of the fifteenth or sixteenth century, eventually other virus-laden Europeans would have walked on the land of no diseases, and millions would have died—as they did. If disease and epidemic were unavoidable, the organized genocide and brutality that accompanied it were not. The inevitability of disease does not absolve the invader of responsibility. M. Annette Jaimes has written: "the mass starvation at issue was largely induced through the deliberate dislocation of indigenous nations from their traditional homelands, the impounding of their resources, and destruction of their economies through military or paramilitary action."[6] Only those acts the Europeans suffered upon themselves during the Black Death surpass what happened in the Americas.[7]

Endnotes

Introduction

1. Peter Hume, "Introduction: the Cannibal Scene" from *Cannibalism in the Colonial World,* (Cambridge: Cambridge University Press, 1998) 7. This book also includes a chapter by William Arens titled "Rethinking anthropophagy."

Chapter One—Temples of the Sun

1. John Upton Terrell, La Salle, *The Life and Times of an Explorer* (New York Weybright and Talley, 1968) 186–187.
2. Pierre Margry, *Decouvertes et etablissements des Francais dans l'Amerique Septentrionale 1614–1754* (Paris: Maisonneuve, 1876–1886) 2:211. Quoting Membre.
3. Ibid. 211.
4. John R. Swanton, *The Indian Tribes of Lower Mississippi Valley*, Bulletin 43. (Washington D. C.: Bureau of American Ethnology, Smithsonian Press, 1911), 44.
5. Margry, *Decouvertes*, (1880) 412. Quoting Iberville.
6. John R. Swanton, *The Indian Tribes of North America,* Bulletin 145. (Washington D.C.: Bureau of American Ethnology, Smithsonian Press, 1952), 209
7. Dumont de Montigny, *Memoires historiques sur La Louisiane* (Paris C. J. B. Bauche, 1753) 1:175.
8. Margry, *Decouvertes* 5:452. Quoting Penicaut.
9. Ibid., 452–455.
10. Le Page Du Pratz, *Historie de La Louisiane* (Paris: De Bure, l'aine, 1758) 1:189–194.
11. Ibid. 2:341
12. Ibid. 2:341
13. Ibid. It should be noted that the guardian of the temple's recitation of the Sun's five commandments happened after at least fifty years of exposure to French Catholicism, and that Indians were very successful in telling their conquers what they wanted to hear.

14. Swanton, *Mississippi Valley*, 173.
15. The tablet was a carved wooden plank with an image of the sun. In effect, the Natchez left their calling card.
16. Du Pratz, *Historie*, 413–437 (complete text) .
17. Dumont, *Memoires*, 1:170.
18. Swanton, *Mississippi Valley* , 93.
19. Dumont, *Memoires*, 1:155.
20. Margry, *Decouvertes*,5:447–448. Quoting Penicaut.
21. Du Pratz, *Historie*, 1:88.

Chapter Two—"I Shall Receive You with Love and Charity,"

1. Phillip M. Pollock, "Calusa, Kingdom in the Sun," *Florida Heritage Magazine*, Fall 1997.
2. For historians and anthropologists, the amazing ability of the Calusa to mobilize a force of eighty war canoes in one day to fight the Spanish means they had a highly structured, organized society—extremely unusual for a hunter-gatherer, non-agricultural tribe.
3. The exact location is unknown even though most authorities agree it was somewhere in Charlotte Harbor.
4. His Indian name was "Escampaba."
5. *Memoir of Do. D'Escalente Fontaneda respecting Florida,* written in Spain around 1575, translated by Buckingham Smith in 1854, edited with notes. (Miami:Glade House, 1944), 20.
6. Jerald T. Milanich, in *Florida Indians and the Invasion from Europe* (Gainesville: University Press of Florida, 1995), 39. gives ten years as the age of Fontaneda when captured. In his *Memoir*, Fontaneda said he was thirteen years old, and thirty-one when released (*Fontaneda,*17). Based on the probable year of his shipwreck (1545) and when he was freed (1566) and accepting his age at thirty-one when freed, Milanich is probably right.
7. Fontaneda, *Memoir*, 21.
8. A detailed list of faunal food sources utilized by the Calusa and how food allocation led to a central power structure appears in Randolph J. Widmer, *The Evolution of the Calusa* (Tuscaloosa: University of Alabama Press, 1988), 261–276.
9. Robin C. Brown, *Florida's First People* (Sarasota: Pineapple Press, 1994), 9.

10. Gonzalo Solís de Meras, *Pedro Menéndez de Avilés,* trans. Jeannette Thurber Conner (Deland: Florida Historical Society, 1923), 149–151.

11. Gonzalo, *Pedro,* 221.

12. John H. Hann, *Missions to the Calusa,* (Gainesville: University Press of Florida, 1991) 223, quoting Felix Zubillaga, S. J., *Monumenta Antiquae Floridae,* Jesuit Historical Institute, Rome, Italy.

13. Ibid., 245.

14. Ibid. 316.

15. Ibid. 309. In a report in the Colonial Records, Marqués gives a deposition that states he beheaded the cacique Carlos (Felipe?) and twenty other Indians because of an attack on a supply ship going to the soldiers.

16. *Colonial Records of Spanish Florida,* Jeanette Thurber, ed., trans., (Deland: Florida State Historical Society, 1925.) vol.1. 105.

17. Hann, *Missions,* 8.

18. John U.Terrell, *American Indian Almanac* (New York: Barnes and Noble Books,1971), 8.

19. Hann, *Missions,* 199.

20. Milanich, *Florida Indians,* 51–52.

21. Hann, *Missions,* 427. Quoting Joseph Javier Alaña, S.J., Letter of 1760, "Report on the Indians of Southern Florida and It's Keys."

22. The Spanish eventually eliminated all of the Arawaks of the Caribbean through massacre, slavery and disease. They described these Indians as ugly with low brows, protruding eyes and black teeth.

23. While many historians now doubt the Ponce de Leon "fountain of youth" story, it was reported as early as 1575 in the *Memoir* of Fontaneda, 14–15 (See note 5).

24. Terrell, *Indian Almanac,* 91.

25. Harold E. Driver, *Indians of North America* (Chicago: University of Chicago Press, 1961), 324.

26. Mallory McCane O'Connor, *Lost Cities of the Southeast* (Gainesville: University Press of Florida, 1995)

27. Terrell, *Indian Almanac,* 93.

28. In 1736, two hundred years after De Soto, there were only seventeen Timucuans. They are now extinct.

29. Contrary to what most schoolbooks say, De Soto did not discover the Mississippi River. At least two other explorers saw it before he did.

30. The most thorough examination and comparison of the texts of these

authors appears in John R. Swanton, *Final Report of the United States De Soto Expedition Commission* (Washington, D. C.: Smithsonian Press, 1985), a reprint of the 1939 report.

31. This Garcilaso is not to be confused with the famous Spanish poet of the same name who was born in Toledo in 1503. Our Garcilaso was born in Cusco, Peru, in 1539.

32. Garcilaso de la Vega, *The Florida of the Inca*, trans. John and Jeannette Varner (Austin: University of Texas Press, 1988) 60.

33. It is not unusual for different historic narratives to vary the spelling of Indian place names and individuals; the writers were attempting to write phonetically in the writer's language. In this work, the names and place names used in the various documents are printed as the particular author spelled them. Words like "Hirrihigua" are spelled three different ways in the text.

34. Garcilaso, *Florida of the Inca*, 61.

35. Ibid.

36. Ibid. 95.

37. John Lee Williams *The Territory of Florida*, 1837. Facsimile edition, intro Herbert J. Doherty, Jr. (Gainesville: University of Florida Press), 156–157.

38. The *requirimento* appears in many historical publications. This abbreviated quote is from *500 Nations*, Alvin M Josephy, Jr. (New York: Alfred A. Knopf, 1994), 140. A more comprehensive *requirimento* appears in Milanich, *Florida*, 100–101. (See note 6)

39. Garcilaso, *Florida of the Inca*, 118.

40. Ibid. 118.

Chapter Three—Sons of The Morning Star

1. King was commissioned to paint portraits of all of the members of the five-tribe delegation that was visiting Washington when Pitalesharo received his medal. They took sixteen years to paint and were the basis of the National Indian Portrait Gallery. A fire destroyed the originals, but there were lithographic copies that were saved.

2. There is another spelling of his Pawnee name used by some historians— Ritsirisaru. To avoid confusion, this text uses his English name, Knife Chief.

3. Gene Weltfish, *The Last Universe* (Lincoln: University of Nebraska Press, 1965), 115.

4. The Ietans, also called the Aes, may have been a group of Apaches or Comanches, although Swanton (*Indian Tribes of North America*) says the word was used to designate members of various Shoshonean groups—Utes and others.

5. George E. Hyde, *The Pawnee Indians* (Norman: University of Oklahoma Press, 1951), 160.

6. Ibid. 162.

7. Matthew W. Stirling, "Indians of Our Western Plains," *National Geographic Magazine,* July, 1944, 73–108. Stirling's claim that morning star sacrifices ended with Pitalesharo's rescue of the girl appears on page 108.

8. Hyde, *Pawnee*, 8.

9. Fray Isidro Felis de Espinosa, "Descriptions of the Tejas or Asinai Indians, 1691–1722," translated by Mattie Austin Hatcher. *Southwestern History Quarterly*, 31:174, 1927.

10. "Diary of a visit of inspection of the Texas missions made by Fray Gaspar Jose de Solis in the year 1767–1768," *Southwestern History Quarterly,* 35:42–43, 1931. The Caddoan practice of cutting off slivers of flesh of their captives and victims may have been the inspiration for an unusually vicious act of revenge that occurred in Nebraska in 1852. A wagon train on its way to California had as a passenger a silversmith from Geneva, Wisconsin, by the name of Rhines. Rhines boastfully had pledged to kill the first Indian the wagon train encountered. After stopping for the night near a stream on the Military Road about five miles from Elkhorn, the travelers arose the next morning and spotted a small group of young Pawnees peacefully riding their ponies up to the wagons. These were the first Indians the party had seen. Someone, perhaps jokingly, reminded Rhines of his boast. The silversmith got his rifle, and shot and killed a young Indian girl. The Pawnees fled to their village, returning with a large group of warriors who surrounded the wagon train and demanded that the killer be turned over to them. Rhines obviously was not much admired by his fellow travelers, because they turned him over to the Indians almost immediately. He was stripped of his clothing and tied, spread-eagle, to a wagon wheel. The Pawnees began skinning the killer alive. He pleaded to the Indians and the travelers to shoot him to put

him out of his misery, but the Indians would not allow it. All of the travelers were forced to watch. He died as the skinning process was almost completed, then he was dismembered by Indian women with hoes and hatchets. The small stream nearby where it happened got its name from the event: Rawhide.

11. Hyde, *Pawnee*, 15.

12. Luis Hernandez Biedma, *Narratives of the career of Hernando De Soto*, ed Edward G. Borne. (New York:Trail Makers Series, 1904), 2:32–33.

13. For hundreds of years after Coronado, scholars speculated over the exact location of Quivira. There seemed little doubt from the documents of the Coronado expedition that the villages were somewhere in Kansas. At one time there was a monument near Junction City in Kansas, put up by the Quivera Historical Society, claiming the place was the location of the lost villages. The major problem with the site is that there was no evidence any Indians had ever lived there. However, there were Caddoan ruins in the Little Arkansas and Cow Creek drainages, considerably west of the Quivira monument. The situation became a heated political issue in Kansas in the 1920s, and wasn't settled decisively until scraps of Spanish chain armor were found in the ruins on the Little Arkansas. The first examination of the sites by trained field archaeologists began in 1937 under the direction of Waldo R. Wedel of the Smithsonian. In the many small villages excavated by Wedel and his crews, huge temple remains were found, circular structures averaging 100 feet in diameter. Wedel's report of the excavation published by the Smithsonian details the find:

> "On at least four village sites in Rice and McPherson Counties there are large ditched circles with mounded centers. The circles average about 90 to 120 feet in diameter, and are sometimes discontinuous. They have been locally termed 'council-circles;' no village site has more than one. Excavations by the National Museum within such a circle at the Tobias site disclosed curving dug basins with post molds, hearths, successive floor levels, and quantities of burned wattle-impressed clay. From one basin came disarticulated human bones."

The human disarticulated bones that were found on the floor of the temple is evidence of Caddoan cannibalism. George E. Hyde has written that this wasn't unusual, and that it happened in Nebraska and Iowa in the Missouri Valley, and that there is one cannibalism site on the Elkhorn River.

Hyde wrote:

> "It is useless to make phrases about the mere eating of a tiny sliver of human flesh in a purely ceremonial manner. These Indians cut up entire bodies, cooked and ate them, roasting and cracking the bones to obtain the marrow. The Iroquois, supposed to be kindred to the Caddoan Indians, were seen by the early French, indulging in similar cannibal feasts."

Wedel also reported on the discovery of glass beads, chain mail fragments and an iron ax head, evidence of early European visits. Dating of artifacts from the location indicate it was occupied in 1541, and Wedel believed that this was the Quivira of Coronado, and that the explorer entered the area from the north in Rice County.

14. He is often referred to as Lamothe Cadillac or Antoine Cadillac. He is best known as the founder of Detroit, Michigan.

15. Pierre Margry, *Decouvertes et etablissements des Francais dans l'Amerique Septentrionale* (Paris: Maisonneuve, 1876–1886), 5:502–504.

16. James R Murie., *Ceremonies of the Pawnee, Part 1: The Skiri.* Smithsonian Contributions to Anthropology, Number 27 (Smithsonian Institution Press, Washington, D. C., 1981), 115.

17. Margry, *Decouvertes,* 117.

18. White feather down used in a ceremony, or as decoration, primarily in the hair, occurs in many tribes in both North and South America. Both the Nootka and Kwakiutl of British Columbia sprinkled white feather down on their hair, the more northern Sitka did the same. Early travelers in California reported in their journals that they too saw Indians with white down in "their long disordered hair." The famous missionary explorer Father Hennepin (while a prisoner) saw a ceremony, possibly Sioux, celebrating the killing of a bear in which white feather down was used. Knox's Voyages (J. Knox. *A New Collection of Voyages, Discoveries and Travels.* London, 1767) reported that the Iroquois painted part of their shaved heads red and added white feather down. The practice was not uncommon in South America, or in Australia. There is a Chinese legend that says that feathers can be cursed to fly away and bring destruction and bad luck wherever they fall, while in Russia early in the last century,

sprinkling white feather down on the heads of newlywed peasants was said to insure good luck. No one seems to know where the North American Indian's feather down fixation began or why. There has been some speculation that the custom endured with peoples who at an early time in their history depended upon birds for an important part of their diets.

19. Murie, *Ceremonies,* 123.

20. Ibid. 134.

21. Hyde, *Pawnee,* 161. The story, and the quotation, probably came from Edwin James, who wintered in Nebraska as part of an expedition and spent his time interviewing traders like Pappan.

22. George Bird Grinnell, *Pawnee Hero Stories and Folk-Tales* (New York: Forest and Stream Publishing Company, 1889). Reprinted (University of Nebraska Press, Bison Books, 1961), 363.

23. Grinnell, *Hero,* 367.

24. This event is reported in both Hyde, *Pawnee,* 184, and Weltfish, *Last Universe,* 116.

25. Hyde, *Pawnee,* 184.

26. 1838 wasn't that long ago. How did a religious ritual sacrifice of a young person occur on the plains when none of the other Pawnee tribes engaged in human sacrifice, nor did any of the hunter-agriculturist groups that depended on the buffalo and corn for subsistence? In many respects, the only significant difference between the Skidi Pawnee and the other tribes in the plains were their religious beliefs and ceremonies.

Chapter Four—"Curses on You, White Men"

1. One diary of the day says the first corn was taken from an uninhabited dwelling near the shore, and does not mention graves.

2. John S. C. Abbott in his 1857 book *The History of King Philip* states that there were 101 Pilgrims.

3. Frank James Speech, Council on Interracial Books for Children, Bulletin 10:6, 1979 as quoted in James W. Loewen, *Lies My Teacher Told Me* (New York: Simon & Schuster, 1995), 96.

4. Robert M. Utley and Wilcomb E. Washburn, *Indian Wars* (Boston: Howard Mifflin Company, 1977), 43.

5. The English attempted to distribute the Pequots to other tribes, but were not successful. Today, the Pequots are the richest, and most influential tribe in the East.

6. Douglas Edward Leach, *The Northern Colonial Frontier* (New York: Holt, 1996), preface, 12.

7. There is some conflict in historical records as to whether the Indian was injured or killed.

8. *The Present State of New-England with Respect to the Indian War,* London, 1675. (It is assumed that the author was a Boston merchant named Nathaniel Saltonstall and that the narrative was sent to his friend in London, Dorman Newman, who had it printed.) The original book did not have numbered pages. Counting the title page as "one," the quote appears on page "four." It is copied in Charles H. Lincoln, ed, "Original Narratives of Early American History," *Narratives of the Indian Wars 1675–1699* (New York: American Historical Association and Scribner's Sons, 1913), 31.

9. John Tebbel & Keith Jennison, *The American Indian Wars* (New York: Harper & Row 1960) 43–44.

10. Cotton Mather, *Decennium Luctuosum: or, The Remarkables of a Long War with Indian Savages,1699* (Boston: B. Green and F. Allen, 1699) Mather opens the book with a letter to the people of New England in which he explains that he wishes to remain anonymous. The quotation appears on the first page of the introduction. An original copy of this work is at the Boston Public Library.

11. Reports also exist that Metacomet's wife and son were exiled or fled to the Sokoki tribe.

12. *The Present State of New England,* as reprinted in Lincoln, *Narratives of the Indian Wars,* 34. (see note 8)

13. The Pocasset were a band of the Wampanoag, more accurately called "the band of Weetamoo." Pocasset was the name the band gave to their territory. Some historians list them as a separate tribe.

14. Douglas E. Leach, ed., *The Second William Harris Letter of August, 1676* (Providence: The Rhode Island Historical Society)

15. Alvin M. Josephy, Jr., *The Patriot Chiefs* (New York: Viking Press, 1961) Also published by Penquin Books, 1993. (The chapter titled "The Betrayal of King Philip" from which the quotation was taken, is recommended reading for anyone interested in Indian and colonial history.) A detailed account of Canonchet's death is also found in Lincoln, *The Present State of New England,* 91. (See note 7)

16. Lincoln, *The Present State of New England,* 150.

17. These were Abnaki, members of a tribe who first resisted an attempt by the Plymouth Company to settle on their lands in Maine in 1607–1608.
18. Alderman's Indian name is unknown, if he ever had one. Many Indians who worked for or lived among the colonists were given English names.
19. Benjamin Church, *Diary of King Philip's War,* intro. Alan and Mary Simpson (Chester, CT: The Pequot Press,1975). This book was first printed in 1716. The quotation is from the Introduction.
20. This is dramatic license, at best. The historic record is jumbled as to whether they were killed by the militia or enslaved. The play was written by John A. Stone and was the first of thirty-five different plays on Metacomet's life during the next twenty years.
21. Eugene R. Page, ed., *Metamora and Other Plays* (Princeton: Princeton University Press, 1941), 40. as quoted in Roy Harvey Pearce, *Savagism and Civilization* (Berkeley: University of California Press, 1988), 177.

Chapter Five—Promises to the Sun God

1. Terri Hardin, ed., *Legends & Lore of the American Indians* (New York: Barnes and Noble, 1993), 71.
2. Ibid. 72.
3. There are many versions of the story of Deganawidah and Hiawatha's first meeting. This one is from Alvin M. Josephy, Jr., *The Patriot Chiefs* (New York, Penguin Books, 1976), 20. Also see Snow (note 6) 58.
4. The Tuscaroras joined the original five tribes about 1715, increasing their number to six.
5. This quote is included in Bruce Johnson and Roberto Maestas, *Wasichu: The Continuing Indian Wars* (New York: Monthly Review Press, 1979), 35.
6. Dean R. Snow, *The Iroquois* (Cambridge, MA.:Blackwell Publishers, 1994), 38.
7. Ibid. 54.
8. Ruben Gold Thwaites, *Jesuit Relations 1632.* "Brief Relation of the Journey to New France, made in the Month of April last, by Father Paul Le Jeune of the Society of Jesus." (Cleveland: Burrows Brothers, 1886–1901), 5:23. This was also published in S. R. Mealing, *The Jesuit Relations and Allied Documents* (Ottawa: Carleton University Press, 1990) as part of the Carleton Library Series. The 73–volume Thwaites translation is difficult to find,

(only 750 were printed) and when and if you do a special pass or permission is required to browse these volumes which are normally in a library's rare book or special collections' section. Since Mealing and other texts are more readily available, page numbers will also be given for books that have reprinted the Thwaites text. Mealing, *Relations*, 17.

9. Snow, *Iroquois*, 93.
10. *Jesuit Relations*, 1632. 5:29–31 (Mealing, 19)
11. "Brébeuf" is the spelling used in the *Catholic Encyclopedia*, but the name is also commonly spelled "Brebeuf" without the "é " in the United States. In the *Relations* the name is spelled "Breboeuf." Lallemant is sometimes spelled "Lalemant," and is spelled "L'Alemant" in the *Relations*. Spelling in quotations has not been changed, and *Catholic Encyclopedia* spellings are used elsewhere.
12. *Jesuit Relations*, 1678, 34:27–35. (Mealing, *Relations*, 67.)
13. *Jesuit Relations*, 1637, 13:77–79. This quotation also appears in John Upton Terrell, *American Indian Almanac* (New York: Barnes & Noble, 1994), 190.
14. Anka Muhlstein *La Salle, Explorer of the North American Frontier*, trans. Williard Wood (New York: Archade Publishing, 1994), 127.
15. Pierre Margy, *Decouvertes et etablissements des Francais dans l'Amerique Septentrionale Paris*, 1614 and 1754, as quoted in Muhlstein, *La Salle,*129 .
16. John Upton Terrell, *La Salle, The Life and Times of an Explorer* (New York: Weybright and Talley, 1968), 168.
17. *Jesuit Relations*, 1632, 5:33.

Chapter Six—A Chief for Dinner
1. This is generally acknowledged, although the Chippewa did side with the British in the War of 1812.
2. John R. Swanton, *Indian Tribes of North American* (Washington D. C. Bureau of American Ethnology, 1952), lists twenty-four names for the tribe.
3. Joseph Campbell, *Primitive Mythology* (New York: Viking Penguin,1959) Campbell remarks on the universality of the virgin birth theme in religion. (Adonis, certain Pharaohs, Confucius, Quetzalcoatl, and, of course, Jesus) He claims it is a confirmation of the unity of the race of man. ". . . for we find that such themes as the fire-theft, deluge, land of the dead, virgin birth, and resurrected hero have a world wide distribution . . . "
4. This was the common spelling for the Iroquois used by the French.

5. Saulteurs, Nepissins and Amikouets were Chippewas, described by the author by their village names. The Outaouas were the Ottawa Indians.
6. Algonquin is the language spoken by the Chippewa and the Ottawa.
7. Nicolas Perrot, *Memoir on the Manners, Customs, and Religion of the Savages of NorthAmerica,* edited by he Reverend Jules Tailhan, S. J., Paris, 1864. (Lincoln: Bison Books, University of Nebraska Press, 1196), 178–181. The parenthesis in the text are those of the editor of the original edition. The first English edition of Perrot's *Memoirs* was printed by Arthur H. Clark Company, Cleveland Ohio in 1911. The *Jesuit Relations of 1663* also reported on the event, but gives the victory only to the Chippewa, omitting any mention of the Ottawa tribe. The report also asserts that the invading Iroquois war party was made up of Iroquois from the Mohawk and Onieda tribes.
8. Piqua, Ohio—northwest of Dayton in Miami Country. The State of Ohio has a museum at the site.
9. An early settlement near present day Pittsburgh.
10. *Journal of Captain William Trent,* (1752) Alfred T. Goodman, editor, (Cincinnati: Albert Clark Co.,1871), 86–87. Some of the punctuation in this quotation has been changed to make it more understandable.
11. *Handbook of American Indians North of Mexico,* Bulletin 30 (Washington, D. C.: The Smithsonian Institution Bureau of American Ethnology, 1910).
12. It is assumed that the author references the work of William W. Warren, a Chippewa descendent who wrote *History of the Ojibaway Nation* in 1853. Jones was an ethnologist. The wrote *Ethnology of the Fox Indians,* and edited *Ojibaway Texts.*
13. This reservation is in north central Minnesota, and today features a large casino among beautiful lakes.
14. Johann Georg Kohl, *Kitchi-Gami* (London: Chapman and Hall, 1860), Reprinted, (St. Paul: Minnesota Historical Press, 1985), 27. Robert E. Bieder's introduction to the 1985 edition of this book states that Kohl had met Longfellow and read "Hiawatha" before publication and speculates that Longfellow may have encouraged him to visit the Chippewa.
15. Ibid., 345–364
16. Ibid. 355
17. Ibid. 358
18. Ibid. 371–372

Chapter Seven—"Arms and Legs for Sale,"

1. J. C. Beaglehole, *The Life of Captain James Cook* (Stanford: Stanford University Press, 1974), 585.

2. James C Cook, *A Voyage to the Pacific Ocean 1784* (London: G. Nicol and T. Cadell, 1776–80), 2:4:270.

3. The editor was Dr. John Douglas, Bishop of Salisbury.

4. De Fuca was actually a Greek named Apostolos Valerianos who had changed his name.

5. "Maquinna" is variously spelled "Mokwina, Muquinna and Moquinna." The present line of chiefs of the tribe spell it "Maquinna," which is the spelling used in this text. It is possible that the chief that met Cook was the father of the Maquinna that ruled during the fur-trading boom.

6. Nootka Sound.

7. Cook, *Voyage to the Pacific,* second edition, vol 2, 1785.

8. Alexander Walker, *An Account of a Voyage to the North West Coast of America in 1785 & 1786,* Robin Fisher and J. M. Bumsted, eds. (Seattle: University of Washington Press, 1982), 82–83. (Reproduced from the unpublished manuscript in the National Library of Scotland, MS 13780)

9. Extract from Caamano's diary as quoted in *British Columbia Historical Quarterly,* as cited by Jim McDowell, *Hamatsa* (Vancouver, B. C., Ronsdale Press, 1997), 77–78.

10. See Sérgio Luis Prado Bellei, "Brazilian anthropophagy revisited" in *Cannibalism and The Colonial World,* Cambridge: Cambridge University Press, 1998. p. 96.

11. John Rogers Jewitt, *Adventures and Sufferings of John Rogers Jewitt,.* The reprint of the 1815 edition is titled *White Slaves of the Nootka* (Surrey, B. C., Heritage House Publishing Co. Ltd, 1987), 26. There is an edited version of the work appearing in Frederick Dimmer, ed. *Captured by the Indians* (New York: Dover, 1961) titled "The Headhunters of Nootka." 216–255.

12. Jewitt, *White Slaves,* 31.

13. This is the district of the Mowachaht and Chief Maquinna.

14. A Mowachahtn tribe north of the Mowachaht.

15. Phillip Drucker, *The Northern and Central Mowachatn Tribes,* Bulletin 144 (Washington, D. C.: Smithsonian Institution, Bureau of American Ethnology, 1951), 341–342.

16. Jewitt, *White Slaves,* 60. The quotation is from Dimmer, *Captured,* 233.

17. Ibid. 92.

18. These numbers are the author's estimates. War canoes held from ten to fifteen warriors and the village contained sixteen houses. Most houses had twenty-five or more occupants.

19. Walker, *Voyage*, 114. Fisher and Bumsted, eds., suggest that Walker may have been confused about the daggers. The weapon was probably a whale bone club, a weapon that was often used in a stabbing, thrusting motion, much like a dagger. Bone tipped spears are not mentioned by others , nor are they in the large collections of Mowachaht weapons in museums around the world. Their spears or pikes were fire hardened pointed long staffs of yew wood seven or eight feet long. (See Drucker, *Nootkan*, 335)

20. Jewitt, *White Slaves*, 99–100.

21. Drucker, *Nootkan*, 361.

22. Ibid. 364

Chapter Eight—Life for Life

1. Boas' students at Columbia read like a Who's Who of American anthropology—Alfred L. Kroeber, Robert Lowie, Edward Sapir, Margaret Mead, Ruth Benedict, and Ashley Montagu.

2. Franz Boas, *The Social Organization and the Secret Societies of the Kwakiutl Indians* (Washington, D.C.: U. S. Printing Office, 1879) It appears that Boas spoke and understood conversational kwak'wala, the Kwakiutl language, but felt inadequate in translating some of the songs. ". . . my knowledge of the language is not sufficient to overcome the difficulties of an adequate translation," 317.

3. Hunt provided a great deal of the information included in the report. Hunt later wrote *The Ethnology of the Kwakiutl* first in Kwakiutl phonetic, then later in English, edited by Boas and published in the Smithsonian Annual Report of 1914.

4. Non-Indians consider the Kwakiutl those tribal groups who speak the kwak'wala language, its many dialects, and who share similar cultural and social structures, whereas the native peoples of the area are specific in designating the Kwakiutl as the tribal group that lived near Fort Rupert.

5. Robert Gray, Dionosio Alcala Galiano, Cayetano Valdes.

6. See Philip Drucker and Robert Heizer, *To Make My Name Good* (Berkeley, University of California Press, 1967), 22.

7. The "potlatch" process is widely misunderstood. The gifts, which a recipient can not refuse, are actually loans which must be paid back at interest rates up to 100%. See Boas, 342–343, and Drucker and Hiezer, *To Make My Name Good*, a study of the potlatch custom.

8. The speaker, Quoalxala, is quoted by Boas, 571.

9. This is an abbreviated version—the full text of the story appears in Boas, 372–374.

10. The Kwakiutl considered the ocean a river that ran north.

11. Boas, 394–395.

12. Peggy Reeves Sanday, *Divine Hunger, Cannibalism as a Cultural System* (New York: Cambridge University Press, 1986), 121. This book contains many interpretations of Kwakiutl ritual. See also Eli Sagan, *Cannibalism: Human Aggression and Cultural Form* (New York: Harper & Row, 1947)

13. Boas, 425.

14. Boas, 427. There is some archaeological evidence that the first attack by the Bilxula did result in canoes full of heads and dismembered bodies on the shore. Human bones have been found near the village on Gilford Island where Kwakiutl oral history places the massacre.

15. Boas, plate 23 facing 400.

16. Boas, 439–440

17. Edward S.Curtis, *The Kwakiutl* (New York: Johnson Reprint Company, 1978) This book is volume 10 of The North American Indian Series, 1915.

18. Boas, 441–442. Boas describes the dancing, thusly: " . . . The hamatsa has two ways of dancing—one representing him in a stage of greatest excitement, the other when he is becoming pacified. The first dance represents him as looking for human flesh to eat. He dances in a squatting position, his arms extended sideways and trembling violently. He first extends them to the right, then to the left, changing at the same time the position of the feet so that when extending his arms to the left he rests on his left foot and the right foot is extended backward; when extending his arms to the right, he rests on his right foot and the left foot is extended backward. Thus he moves on slowly with long steps. His head is lifted up, as though he was looking for a body that was being held high up in front of him. His eyes are wide open, his lips pushed forward and from time to time he utters his terrible cry, hap.

"His attendants surround him, and two of them hold him at his neck ring that he may not attack the people. When in the rear of the house, he suddenly changes his position, putting his hands on his hips and jumping in long leaps with both legs at the same time, his face still bearing the same expression. In this position he turns in the rear of the fire. Thus he continues his four circuits, changing from time to time from the slow trembling movement to the long leaps. During this time his kinqalalala—if he is a novice—dances backward in front of him. She stands erect and holds her hands and forearms extended forward as though she was carrying a body for the hamatsa to eat. Then his eyes are directed to her hands, which she keeps moving up and down a little with each step. Her open palms are turned upward.

In his second dance the hamatsa dances standing erect. While in his first dance he is naked, he is now clothed in a blanket. "The painting of the face of the hamatsa . . . depends upon the legend from which he derives his origin. Most of them have their faces painted black all over, while others have two curved red lines on each cheek fanning from the corner of the mouth to the ear in a wide curve concave on the upper side. This, it is said, is where Baxbakualanuxsiwae rubbed off the hamatsa's skin, or to indicate that they are living on blood."

19. Boas, 462.
20. The number "4" was also a mystic number to the Crow, Kiowa and Comanche. A world away, it was considered magic in ancient Greece and by some near eastern cultures.
21. R. P. Roner and E. C. Bettauer, *The Kwakiutl, Indians of British Columbia* (Prospect Heights, IL: Waveland Press, 1970), 38.

Chapter Nine—Anomalous Californians
1. Alfred L. Kroeber, *Handbook of Indians of California*, Bulletin 78 (Washington, D. C.: Smithsonian Bureau of American Ethnology, U. S. Government Printing Office, 1925). Reprinted (New York: Dover Publications, 1976) Page numbers listed are from reprinted edition: 159 and 169.
2. See Chapter 11 for facts about the beheading of Apache chiefs by the U. S. Army.
3. Walter Goldschmidt, "Nomlaki Ethnography," *University of California*

Publications in American Archaeology and Ethnology, 42:4 (Berkeley: University of California Press, 1951) 378 and 401. See also Powers, *Tribes* (n.4), 153.

4. Stephen Powers, " Tribes of California," in *Contributions to North American Ethnology* (Washington, D. C.:, U. S. Government Printing Office, 1877) Reprinted (Berkerly: University of California, 1976.) Page numbers listed are from the reprinted edition: 71.

5. Kroeber, *Handbook*, 526.

6. Powers, *Tribes*, 181. Powers got this story from Joseph Fitch, an early settler in Gallinomero country in 1871. Powers does not give the year in which the incident occurred.

7. Kroeber, *Handbook,* 468–469.

8. Powers, *Tribes*, 126.

9. Walter Goldschmidt, George Foster and Frank Essene, "War Stories from two Enemy Tribes," *The Journal of American Folklore* 52:204 (April-June 1939), 149–150.

10. Kroeber, *Handbook*, 400.

11. Ibid. 752 and 647.

12. Ibid., 157–158. This excerpt has been edited; some Indian place names and sub-tribal names and locations have been omitted.

13. Powers, *Tribes*, 125.

14. Goldschmidt, *War Stories*, 149–150.

15. All of these stories appear in *War Stories.*

16. Goldschmidt, *War Stories*, 141–143.

17. George Foster, *A Summary of Yuki Culture,* Anthropological Records (5:3) (Berkeley: University of California Press, 1944.), 189.

18. These atrocities and many others are detailed in Lynwood Carranco and Estle Beard, *Genocide and Vendetta* (Norman: University of Oklahoma, 1981). For an excellent study of prejudice and discrimination in California, see Robert F. Heizer and Alan F. Almquist, *The Other Californians* (Berkeley: University of California Press, 1971) See also Robert F. Heiser, *The Destruction of California Indians* (Lincoln: University of Nebraska Press, 1974)

19. Heizer's quotation is included in the editor's preface to "Ethnographic Interpretations: 12–13," No.23, Contributions of the University of California Archaeological Research Facility (Berkeley: University of California, Department of Anthropology, 1975)

Chapter 10—"But, if not Starvation, What?"

1. Under the rules of the Native American Graves Protection and Repatriation Act of 1990, Peabody must retain these relics because they cannot be identified as affiliated with any present tribal group. The time given for the painting of the head-skin is speculative. The specimen could have been created as early as 500 B.C. or as late as A.D. 400. The sex of the mummy is now classified as "unknown" by the museum.

2. The Basketmakers were preceded by the Paleo-Indians (unknown to 6500 B.C.) and Indians of the Archaic period (6500–1500 B.C.). The Basketmaker culture in the Four Corners area dates from 1500 B.C. to A.D. 750. Their culture differed from the Archaic hunter-gatherers—the Basketmakers had limited farming and built more permanent houses. They also made elaborate coiled and twined basketry.

3. These trapezoidal or triangular figures may represent breast plates or, in some cases, women wearing diaper-like menstrual aprons.

4. This canyon is located in the Canyon de Chelly National Monument in the Navajo Indian Reservation.

5. Grand Gulch is within a Bureau of Land Management primitive area and is located approximately twenty-five miles northwest of the town of Mexican Hat.

6. Sally J. Cole, "Analysis of a San Juan (Basketmaker) Style Painted Mask in Grand Gulch, Utah," *Southwestern Lore* 50(1) March, 1984, 1–6.

7. Samuel J. Guernsey and Alfred V. Kidder, *Archaeological Explorations in Northeastern Arizona*, Bulletin 65 (Washington, D. C.: Bureau of American Ethnology, 1919) 190–191.

8. For years interested students and visitors to the Four Corners were told that "Anasazi" was the Navajo word meaning "ancient ones," instead of "enemy ancestors." Modern Pueblo peoples do not like "enemy ancestors," and it is embarrassing to the Navajo because it is not true—the Anasazi left the area long before the Navajo arrived, so they could not be enemies, nor are they Navajo ancestors. (See Gary Matlock, *Enemy Ancestors*, Flagstaff: Northland Publishing, 1988.) The new acceptable term "ancestral pueblo peoples" emerged in the mid-1990s. Since practically all-recognizable Indian tribal names originated outside the tribe itself, (for instance, "Apache" is a derivative of a Zuni word meaning "enemy") this text uses the traditional "Anasazi" name.

9. Atlatls were used throughout the contiguous forty-eight states, and by

the Aztecs in Mexico. The earliest known atlatl comes from Europe and is dated to 20,000 B. C. The atlatl is still used by natives in Papua, New Guinea, and by some Australian aborigines.

10. Ann Axtell Morris, *Digging in the Southwest* (Chicago: Cadmus Books, E. M. Hale and Company, 1933), 217.

11. Fred M. Blackburn and Victoria M. Atkins, "Handwriting on the Wall: Applying Inscriptions to Reconstruct Historical Archaeological Expeditions," Anasazi Basketmaker, Papers from the 1990 Wetherill-Grand Gulch Symposium, Cultural Resource Series #24 (Salt Lake City: Bureau of Land Management, 1993.) 72.

12. Winston B. Hurst and Christy G. Turner II "Rediscovering the 'Great Discovery:' Wetherill's First Cave 7 and its Record of Basketmaker Violence," *Anasazi Basketmaker*, 146. This quotation originally was published in *The Archaeologist Magazine* anonymously, but probably was written by Richard Wetherill.

13. Ibid.

14. Hurst and Turner, *Anasazi Basketmaker*, 179.

15. Ibid.

16. See Kristin A. Kuckelman, et. al. "Changing Patterns of Violence in the Northern San Juan Region," *KIVA, The Journal of Southwestern Anthropology and History,* 66:1 Fall, 200, 147–168 (Tucson: Arizona Archaeological and Historical Society, 2000).

17. Hurst and Turner, *Anasazi Basketmaker*, 148.

18. Richard A. Marlar, et. al. "Biochemical evidence of cannibalism at a prehistoric Puebloan site in southwestern Colorado." *Nature*, 407: 74–78, September 7, 2000 (London: McMillian Publishers, Ltd.).

19. A room-cluster in this instance consists of several small pit houses grouped together. Pit houses are dwellings dug into the earth and roofed with timbers, small branches, and mud.

20. Steven A LeBlanc, *Prehistoric Warfare in the American Southwest* (Salt Lake City: University of Utah Press, 1999), 174–176.

21. Drought periods in the Four Corners area have been determined by dendroclimatic reconstruction, i.e., examination of the structure of tree rings of douglas fir and piñon pine.

22. LeBlanc, 183.

23. Christy G. Turner II and Jacqueline A. Turner, *Man Corn, Cannibalism and*

Violence in the Prehistoric American Southwest (Salt Lake City: University of Utah Press, 1999), 413.

24. Ibid. 484.

Chapter Eleven—"Go Warpath to Texas,"

1. One hundred is the smallest number used in the various histories of this event. Other reports say five hundred, and one sets the number of Indians at eight hundred. A raiding party of even one hundred was unusually large.

2. Bill Neeley, *The Last Comanche Chief* (New York: John Wiley & Sons, Inc., 1995), 72. "The custom among the Comanches and Kiowas had long been to share captive women with each member of the raiding party. When they reached camp, the warrior who had captured a woman would be her master, and he could use her as he saw fit."

3. T. R. Fehrenback, *Comanches: the destruction of a people* (New York: Knopf, 1974), 290.

4. G. P. Winship, "The Coronado Expedition" *Bureau American Ethnology Fourteenth Annual Report* (Washington, D. C.: Government Printing Office, 1891), Part 1, 523–524.

5. John Swanton, in the classic *The Indian Tribes of North America* puts the tribe in Kansas in 1719, and historians Ernest Wallace and E. Adamson Hoebel (see note 7), write that "the evidence is thin" that the Comanche were visited by Coronado. Frank McNitt, *Navajo Wars* (Albuquerque: University of New Mexico Press, 1990) writes that the Indians seen by Coronado "almost certainly were Plains Apaches."

6. The Mexicans named the Comanche homeland the Comancherìa, which included the western half of Oklahoma, north-central Texas almost to San Antonio, the eastern third of New Mexico, the south-east corner of Colorado, and the west and west central part of southern Kansas. On a map the Comancherìa has a shape like a human heart.

7. Ernest Wallace and E. Adamson Hoebel, *The Comanches, Lords of the South Plains,* (Norman: University of Oklahoma Press, 1986), 245.

8. Fort Davis is located in the Big Bend area near the Mexican Border in the Davis Mountains. It is one of the few surviving examples of a southwestern frontier military post. It is now a National Historic Site.

9. Jesse Edward Thompson, "Overland Staging in the Fifties," *Overland*

Monthly and Out West Magazine, 12:69 (San Francisco: September, 1888) 291.

10. Wallace, *Comanches,* 261–262. This quote differs from the original in that an attempt has been made to spell the proper Comanche names phonetically, whereas in the original text the sign "]" is used for the "aw" sound.

11. Ibid. 174.

12. See Kavanagh, Thomas W., *The Comanches,* Lincoln: University of Nebraska Press, 1999, pages 28–62 for a thorough examination of Comanche political culture.

13. Ten Bears, Comanche chief, "Speech," October 20, 1867, "Record Copy of the Proceedings of the Indian Peace Commission Appointed under the Act of Congress Approved July 20, 1867" (MS, National Archives Office of Indian Affairs, Washington), 1, 104.

14. This was a sure route to extinction; their descendant or associated tribe, the Tonkawa dwindled down to about 300. In 1862 on a reservation, Delaware, Shawnee, and Caddo Indians massacred 137 of their number as a pay back for old grievances. The Muruam band may have been the Indians encountered by Francisco Casañas de Jesus Maria in 1691.

15. This is a extrapolation by the author based upon the assumption that five female children would have been born in a population of two hundred within eighteen months and adding this number to the twelve boys known killed.

16. John Upton Terrell, *American Indian Almanac* (New York: Barnes and Noble Books, 1994), 107–108. Terrel has condensed information from the Cabeza de Vaca journals, both of which are available on the internet: *Cabeza de Vaca, Adventures in the Unknown Interior of America,* Chapter 30: "The Life of the Mariames and Yguaces" from *http://eldred.ne.mediaone.net/cdv/rel.htm* and Fanny Bandelier, trans., *The Journey of Alvar Nuñez Cabeza De Vaca,* from *http://www.pbs.org/weta/thewest/resources/archives/one/cabeza.htm*

17. Herman Lehmann, *9 Years Among the Indians,* 1870–1879 ed. J Marvin Hunter (Albuquerque: University of New Mexico Press, 1998), 153–156. This is an edited and revised edition of Jonathan H. Jones. *A Condensed History of the Apache and Comanche Indian Tribes as told by the general conversation of Herman Lehmann* (San Antonio: Johnson Brothers Printing Company, 1899) The only material difference between the texts describing this episode in the two books is the mention of "cutting out

the tongues" that only appears in the Hunter version. This episode is also mentioned in Wallace, *Comanches*, 260.

18. John R. Cook, *The Border and the Buffalo* (Topeka KS: Crane and Company, 1907), 113.
19. Jones, *History*, 158–161. (See note 16)
20. Zoe A. Tilghman, *Quanah, The Eagle of the Comaches* (Oklahoma City: Harlow Publishing, 1938), 68–69. Tilghman's text has been edited and condensed.
21. From an interview of Quanah by Captain Hugh Scott at Fort Sill (Hugh Scott Collection, Fort Sill Archives, Lawton, Oklahoma 1897). As quoted in Neeley, *Last Comanche*, 101.

Chapter Twelve—Shrinking Leather Thongs,

1. John C. Cremony, *Life among the Apaches*, reprinted from the 1868 edition (Lincoln: University of Nebraska, 1983), 320.
2. Idid. 266
3. Ibid. 266–267.
4. A priest, Father Lázaro Ximénez, complained in a letter that "los yndios apaches" constantly raided horse herds in 1608, but the Indians were probably Navajos. Spanish cleric Fray Alonso de Posada wrote that during the period 1650–1660 "the Apachas" were constantly at war with the Spanish, and they stole horses, killed men "atrociously," and took women and children as hostages. He may have been describing Western Apaches. There is a report that Gaspar Castaño de Sosa, an explorer, was attacked by Apaches in New Mexico in 1590. See Frank McNitt, *Navajo Wars* (Albuquerque: University of New Mexico Press, 1990), 3–12, and Herbert Howe Bancroft, *History of Arizona and New Mexico*, reprint of 1889 edition (New York: Arno Press, 1967), 171. The de Sosa incident is also reported in C. L Sonnichsen, *The Mescalero Apaches*, (Norman, University of Oklahoma Press, 1958), 37–38.
5. Dan L. Thrapp, *Victorio and the Membres Apaches* (Norman, University of Oklahoma Press, 1984) xvii.
6. This territory became part of Arizona after the Gadsden purchase in 1853.
7. Dan L. Trapp, *The Conquest of Apacheria* (Norman, University of Oklahoma Press, 1967) 6–8.
8. There are three versions of this story where the details differ, but all

conclude that the Indians were tricked, killed by a large weapon and scalped. The version used in the text is from Cremony and appears to be verified by Mangas' remarks to Greiner.·

9. The area that Baylor declared as "Arizona" became New Mexico again after the Civil War. Fort Fillmore is no more. It was located south of Las Cruces. The site has been plowed over and lacks a historical marker to commemorate this historically significant military post.

10. George W. Baylor, John Robert Baylor: Confederate Governor of Arizona as quoted in Thrapp, *Victorio*.

11. Thrapp, *Victorio*, 78–79.

12. Correspondence of the Commander of the Department of New Mexico, Brigadier General James H. Carleton, Santa Fe, October 12, 1862, available from the *Making of America* digital collection of the University of Michigan Library at *http://moa.umdl.umich.edu/cgi-bin/moa/vie*

13. Proceedings of the United States Senate, Report of the Joint Special Committee of the Two Houses of Congress appointed under joint resolution of March 3, 1865, directing an inquiry into the condition of the Indian tribes, January 26, 1867. U. S. Government Printing Office.

14· The Apache called the band Tci-he-nde, it was also known as 'The Warm Springs Tribe."

15. Robert M. Utley, and Wilcomb E. Washburn, *Indian Wars* (Boston: Howard Mifflin Company, 1985), 173.

16. John Cremony, "Some Savages" *The Overland Monthly*, 8:3 (San Francisco: March 1872), 201–202.

17. Thrapp, *Victorio*, 26–28.

18. James L. Haley, *Apaches* (Norman: University of Oklahoma Press,1981), 203.

19. The Indians did not starve her. She was unfortunate to be with a group at a bad time when the Indians themselves were starving.

20. A carpenter at Fort Yuma, Henry Grinnell, heard that Olive was with the Mohave. Grinnell raised money for the ransom and hired a Yuma Indian to negotiate with the tribal leaders. In late 1856 Olive was purchased for a horse, four blankets, and some beads. For many years she lectured about her experiences.

21. R. B. Stratton, *Captivity of the Oatman Girls: Being an Interesting Narrative of Life Among the Apache and Mohave Indians,* 3rd Edition (New York: Carlton

& Porter, publication date unknown but probably mid to late 1860s.),
80–91.

22. Thomas Edwin Farish, *History of Arizona, vol. 2.* (San Francisco: Filmer, 1918) as quoted in Thrapp, *Conquest,* 13.

23. Haley, *Apaches,* 221.

24. Thrapp, *Victorio,* 79–81.

25. Fort McLane was located in what is now Grant County in the southwestern corner of New Mexico.

26. The story of General West's deceit and the death of Mangas is included in many studies of the Apache. See Haley, *Apaches,* 238–239, Thrapp, *Conquest,* 21–22, and Thrapp, *Victorio,* 82–83. The story is also in many histories of New Mexico.

27. One chapter in each of two books is devoted to the escape, capture, and decapitation of the Tontos: Haley, *Apaches,* 294–302. and Thrapp, *Conquest,* 156–161.

28. Grenville Goodwin, *Western Apache Raiding & Warfare,* Keith H. Basso, ed. (Tucson: University of Arizona Press, 1998), 285.

29. Herman Lehmann, *Nine Years Among the Indians 1870–1879,* ed. J. Marvin Hunter. Reprint of the 1927 edition (Albuquerque: University of New Mexico Press, 1998), 40–41.

30. Geronimo later wrote his biography, which has been repeatedly reprinted. The latest reprint is *Geronimo: His Own Story,* S. M. Barrett, ed. (New York: Dutton, 1970).

Chapter Thirteen—"It's the Hand of God,"

1. Ralph A. Smith, "John Joel Glanton, Lord of the Scalp Range," *The Smoke Signal,* 6: Fall 1962 (The Westerners, Tucson, Arizona), 10.

2. Crook made two important changes in army strategy for winning battles against the Apache. He eliminated the army wagons (and civilian contractors) for more mobile, agile pack mules and burros, and formed the Apache scouts. Crook was convinced that the Apaches were so adapted to the difficult conditions of the border country that white U. S. soldiers could never win fighting them alone. He was obviously right, for he directed the most successful campaigns against the Apache conducted by the Army. Called "the greatest Indian fighter in the history of the United States," his autobiography has been reprinted by Oklahoma University

Press: *General George Crook, His Autobiography,* ed. and annotated by Martin F. Schmitt (Norman: University of Oklahoma Press, 1986).

3. Jered Diamond, *The Third Chimpanze* (New York: Harper Perennial, 1993), 309.
4. "$" is used in Mexico for the peso. Since the peso and the American dollar were equal in value during the period covered in this chapter, no currency differentiation is specified in the text.
5. Sonora and Durango also subsidized scalp hunting.
6. The early 1800s was a time of turmoil for Native Americans living east of the Mississippi. Stripped of their land, and avoiding reservations or forced removals, many bands and individuals migrated west and southwest seeking new opportunities.
7. Captain Mayne Reid, *The Scalp Hunters.* (London: Collins, 1851), 262–264.
8. William Cochran McGaw, *Savage Scene, The Life and Times of James Kirker* (New York: Hastings House, 1972), 189. The "487" number comes from an interview of Kirker by an old friend, Charles Keemle, published in *The St. Louis Saturday Evening Post and Temperance Recorder*, July 10, 1847. Keemle owned the newspaper.
9. Juarez was then called "El Paso del Norte."
10. McGaw, *Savage Scene,* 107.
11. Revolts and revolutions were endemic in Mexico. They occurred in 1810–11, 1821, and 1823 before the Mexican-American war.
12. The story of this incident appeared in *The New Orleans Picayune,* February 28, 1840.
13. McGaw, *Savage Scene,* 130. This statement was made by Garcia Conde, commandant of Chihauhua.
14. Ralph A. Smith, "The Scalp Hunt in Chihuahua–1849," *New Mexico Historical Review,* April 1965, 117.
15. Ray Brandes, "Don Santiago Kirker, King of the Scalp Hunters," *The Smoke Signal*, 6: Fall 1962 (The Westerners, Tucson, Arizona), 2.
16. Ralph A. Smith, "The Scalp Hunter in the Borderlands, 1835–1850," a paper presented at the Third Annual Arizona Historical Convention, Tucson, March 1962, and later published in *Arizona and The West* (Arizona Historical Society, Spring 1964). The paper suggested that this was the village where Kirker had been an Apache war chief .
17. McCaw, *Savage Scene,* 141–143.

18. Ibid., 149–150.
19. George Frederick Ruxton, *Adventures in Mexico and the Rocky Mountains* (New York: Harper and Brothers, 1848), 158–159.
20. McCaw, *Savage Scene*, 211.
21. Samuel Chamberlain, *My Confession, Recollections of a Rogue* (New York: Harper and Brothers, 1956), 274. This book was written between 1855 and 1861, discovered by a collector in manuscript form in an antique shop and later sold to Time-Life, Inc. A lot of what is known about Glanton comes from this book. Chamberlain was a soldier, a deserter, a gunman of sorts, a primitive painter, a writer, and an imaginative historian, but above all, an adventurer. He worked on his book for years, modifying it right up to his death in 1908. After his adventures in the west, where, he wrote, he was a part of the Glanton gang for a while, he returned East and joined the army shortly before the Civil War. During the war he rose to the rank of general. The book had several versions and has felt the scissors of editors. Some of the material was published in *Life Magazine* in the early 1950s. In 1996 The Texas State Historical Association published an unexpurgated and thoroughly annotated edition that includes reproductions of Chamberlain's actual manuscript and his paintings and drawings. It may look like a coffee-table book, but it is a magnificently researched study of the author, his story, and his times. And while there remains some question as to whether Chamberlain was really with Glanton, there seems to be little question about the authenticity of the Glanton story as told by Chamberlain.
22. The editor of *El Faro,* the Chihuahua newspaper, claimed that Glanton did kill Gomez and received $2,000 for his scalp. It was not true. In 1854 (five years later) Gomez still plagued travelers along the road from El Paso to San Antonio. See C. L. Sonnichsen, *The Mescalero Apaches* (Norman: Oklahoma University Press, 1958), 79.
23. Smith, *Glanton*, 12. (see note 13).
24. Chamberlin, *Confession*, 278–281.
25. Ibid. 288–290.

Chapter Fourteen—The Past in the Present
1. McCuen, Marnie, J. ed. *The Genocide Reader*, (Hudson, Wisconsin: Gem Publications, 2000) p.71.
2. This quotation is borrowed from Winona LaDuke.

3. The problem of "working backwards" to estimate early American Indian population is examined in "American Indian Population Recovery Following Smallpox Epidemics" by Russell Thornton, Tim Miller and Jonathan Warren in *American Anthropologist*, March, 1991, Vol. 3–1.
4. Sale, Kirkpatrick, *The Conquest of Paradise*, (New York: Alfred A. Knopf, 1990) 160.
5. Ibid. p.31.
6. Jaimes, M. Annette, ed. *The State of Native America* (Boston: South End Press, 1992) p 6.

Bibliography

A number of the works listed below are not mentioned elsewhere in this book. They are offered for a deeper insight into the ideas and theories of anthropologists, sociologists, and historians on the brutalities of war and institutionalized savagery. Included are numerous books about cannibalism and head hunting. They range from adventure narratives to philosophical treatises, and may be of interest to the reader who wants to delve even further into these subjects. The balance of the list directly relates to the contents of particular chapters, and these books, journals and publications are cited in the endnotes. Many of the books were written in the eighteenth, nineteenth and early in the twentieth century and now would be rare and difficult to obtain except for the enlightened publishers who have reprinted them. These books are noted in the list below—in a slight deviation from bibliographic standards—with the inclusion of the word "Reprinted" after the title.

Information on Internet sources and U. S. Government documents are listed at the end of the bibliography.

Abbott, John S. C. *The History of King Philip.* New York: Harper and Brothers, 1857.

Amsden, Charles Avery. *Prehistoric Southwesterners From Basketmaker to Pueblo.* Reprinted. Los Angeles: Southwest Museum, 1949.

Anasazi Basketmaker, Papers from the 1990 Wetherill-Grand Gulch Symposium. Cultural Resource Series #24. Salt Lake City: Bureau of Land Management, 1993.

Arens, W. *Anthropology and Anthropophagy: The Man-Eating Myth.* New York: Oxford University Press, 1979.

Basso, Ellen B. *The Last Cannibals.* Austin: University of Texas Press, 1995.

Bancroft, Herbert Howe. *History of Arizona and New Mexico.* New York: Arno Press, 1967.

Barker, Francis, Peter Hulme, Margaret Iverson, eds. *Cannibalism and the Colonial World* Cambridge (UK): Cambridge University Press, 1998

Barrett, S. M. ed. *Geronimo: His Own Story.* New York: Dutton, 1970.

Baylor, George Wythe. *John Robert Baylor: Confederate Governor of Arizona.* ed. and intro. Odie B. Faulk. Tucson: Arizona Pioneers' Historical Society, 1966.

Beaglehole, J. C. *The Life of Captain James Cook.* Stanford: Stanford University Press, 1974.

Blair, Emma Helen, ed., trans. *The Indian Tribes of the Upper Mississippi Valley & Region of the Great Lakes.* vol. 1. Lincoln: Bison Books, 1996.

Boas, Franz. *The Social Organization and the Secret Societies of the Kwakiutl Indians.* Included in the Annual Report of the Smithsonian Institution, Report of the U. S. National Museum. Washington: U. S. Government Printing Office, 1897.

Bolton, Herbert Eugene. *The Hasinais.* Norman: University of Oklahoma Press, 1978.

Bourne, Russell. *The Red King's Rebellion, Radical Politics in New England, 1675–1679.* New York: Oxford University Press, 1990.

Brandes, Ray. "Don Santiago Kirker, King of the Scalp Hunters." *The Smoke Signal* no.6 (Fall 1962).

Brown, Robin C. *Florida's First People.* Sarasota: Pineapple Press, 1994.

Campbell, Joseph. *The Masks of God.* 5 vols. New York: Viking Press, 1962.

Catlin, George. *Letters and Notes on the Manners, Customs, and Conditions of North American Indians.* 2 vols. Reprinted. New York: Dover, 1973.

Chagnon, Napoleon A. *Yanomamo, Case Studies in Cultural Anthropology.* Fifth edition. Orlando: Harcourt Brace, 1997.

Chamberlain, Samuel. *My Confession, recollections of a rogue.* New York: Harper and Brothers, 1956.

Church, Benjamin. *Diary of King Philip's War,* (1716) Reprint with introduction by Alan and Mary Simpson. Chester: The Pequot Press, 1975.

Cole, Sally J. *Legacy on Stone.* Bolder: Johnson Books, 1992

———. "Analysis of a San Juan (Basketmaker) Style Painted Mask in Grand Gulch, Utah." *Southwestern Lore* 50 no.1 (1984).

Cook, Captain James. *Captain Cook's third and last voyage to the Pacific Ocean* (1801 edition) also titled *A Voyage to the Pacific,* (1885 edition). Original edition published by order of the King of England. Dublin: T. M'Donnel, 1801.

Cook, John R. *The Border and the Buffalo.* Topeka KS: Crane and Company, 1907.

Cotlow, Lewis. *In Search of the Primitive.* Boston: Little Brown, 1966.

_____. *Amazon Head-Hunters.* New York: Henry Holt, 1953.

Cremony, John C. *Life Among the Apaches.* San Francisco: A Roman and Company, 1868.

_____. "Some Savages." *The Overland Monthly* 8 (March 1872).

Crook, General George, *General George Crook, His Autobiography.* ed. Martin F. Schmitt. Norman: University of Oklahoma Press, 1946.

Curtis, Edward S. *The Kwakiutl.* vol 10. The North American Indian Series, 1915. Reprinted. New York: Johnson Reprint Corp.,1978.

Danziger, E. J. jr. *The Chippewas of Lake Superior.* Norman: University of Oklahoma Press, 1979.

de Solis, Gaspar Jose. "Diary of a visit of inspection of the Texas missions made by Fray Gaspar Jose de Solis in the year 1767–1768." *Southwestern Historical Quarterly* 35 (1931).

De Smet, Pierre-Jean S. J. *Oregon Missions and Travels Over the Rocky Mountains in 1845–46.* Reprinted. Fairfield: Ye Galleon Press, 1978.

Debo, Angie. *Geronimo, The Man, His Time, His Place.* Norman: University of Oklahoma Press, 1976.

Dennis, Elsie F. "Indian Slavery in the Pacific Northwest." *The Oregon Historical Quarterly* 31, nos.1, 2 and 3. 1930.

Diamond, Jared. *The Third Chimpanzee.* New York: Harper, 1993.

Dickason, Olive Patricia. *Canada's First Nations.* Norman: University of Oklahoma Press, 1992.

Dockstader, Frederick J. *Indian Art in America.* New York: Promontory Press, 1961.

Drimmer, Frederick, ed. *Captured by the Indians, 15 Firsthand Accounts, 1750–1870.* New York: Dover, 1961.

Driver, Harold E. *Indians of North America.* Chicago: University of Chicago Press, 1961.

Drown, Frank and Marie Drown. *Mission to the Head Hunters.* New York: Harper and Brothers, 1961.

Drucker, Philip. *The Northern and Central Mowachahtn Tribes, Bulletin 144.* Smithsonian Institution, Bureau of American Ethnology. Washington: U. S. Government Printing Office, 1951.

_____. and Robert Heizer. *To Make My Name Good.* Berkeley: University of California Press, 1967.

Dumont de Montigny. *Memoires historiques sur La Louisiane,* (1687) 2 vols. Paris: C. J. B. Bauche, 1753.

Durant, Will. *The Story of Civilization.* vol.1. New York: Simon and Schuster, 1935.

Eastman, Edwin. *Seven and Nine Years among the Camaches and Apaches, an Autobiography.* Jersey City: Clark Johnson, 1879.

Farish, Thomas Edwin. *History of Arizona.* vol. 2. San Francisco: Filmer, 1918.

Farmer, James D. "Iconographic Evidence of Basketmaker Warfare and Human Sacrifice: A Contextual Approach to Early Anasazi Art." *Kiva* 62, no.4 (1997).

Fehrenback, R. *Comanches: the Destruction of A People.* New York: Knopf, 1974.

Felis de Espinosa, Fray Isidro. "Descriptions of the Tejas or Asinai Indians, 1691–1722." *Southwestern History Quarterly* 31 (1927).

Ferguson, R. Brian, ed. *Warfare, Culture, and Environment.* Orlando: Academic Press, 1984.

Fontaneda, Do d'Escalente. *Memoir of Do d'Escalente Fontaneda respecting Florida.* Reprinted. Miami: Historical Association of Southern Florida, 1944.

Garcilaso de la Vega. *The Florida of the Inca.* Translated by John and Jeannette Varner. Austin: University of Texas Press, 1988.

Goddard, Pliny Earle. "Kato Texts." *University of California Publications in American Archaeology and Ethnology* 5, no.3. (1909).

Goldschmidt, Walter. "Nomlaki Ethnography." *University of California Publications in American Archaeology and Ethnology.*42, no.4. (1951).

———. George Foster and Frank Essene. "War Stories from Two Enemy Tribes." *The Journal of American Folklore* 52, no.204 (1939).

Good, Kenneth and David Chanoff. *Into the Heart: One Man's Pursuit of Love and Knowledge among the Yanomama.* New York: Simon & Schuster, 1991.

Goodwin, Grenville. *Western Apache Raiding & Warfare.* Tucson: University of Arizona Press, 1998.

Greene, Jerome A. *Battles and Skirmishes of the Great Sioux War, 1876–1877.* Norman: University of Oklahoma Press, 1993.

Grinnel, George Bird. *The Cheyenne Indians, History and Society.* vol.1. Reprinted. Lincoln: University of Nebraska Press, 1972.

———. *Pawnee Hero Stories and Folk-Tales.* Reprinted. Lincoln: University of Nebraska Press, 1961.

Haley, James L. *Apaches, A History and Culture Portrait.* Norman: University of Oklahoma Press, 1997.

Hann, John H. ed., trans. *Missions to the Calusa.* Gainesville: University of Florida Press, 1991.

Hardin, Terri, ed. *Legends and Lore of the American Indians.* New York: Barnes and Noble, 1993.

Harris, Marvin. *Cannibals and Kings: The Origins of Cultures.* New York: Random House, 1977.

Heizer, Robert F. ed. *The Destruction of California Indians.* Lincoln: University of Nebraska Press, 1993.

_____. and Alan F. Almquist. *The Other Californians.* Berkeley: University of California Press, 1971.

Highwater, Jamake. *Native Land.* New York: Barnes and Noble Books, 1995.

Hobbes, Thomas. *Man and Citizen.* ed. Bernard Gert. Cambridge: Hackett Publishing, 1991.

Hudson, Charles. *The Southeastern Indians.* Knoxville: University of Tennessee Press. 1976.

Hume, Ivor Noel. *Martin's Hundred.* Charlottesville: University Press of Virginia, 1979.

Hurst, Winston B. and Joe Pachak. *Spirit Windows.* Blanding: Utah Division of Parks and Recreation, 1992.

Hyde, George E. *The Pawnee Indians.* Norman: University of Oklahoma Press, 1951.

Jaimes, M. Annette, ed. *The State of Native America* Boston: South End Press, 1992.

Jameson, J. Franklin, ed. *Original Narratives of the Indian Wars, 1675–1699.* New York: Charles Scribner's Sons, 1913.

Jewitt, John Rogers. *The Headhunters of Mowachaht.* Philadelphia, 1815. Also called *The Adventures and sufferings of John Rogers Jewitt.* Reprinted. Surrey, B. C., Canada: Heritage House Publishing Co. Ltd, 1994.

Jones, William. *Ojibwa Texts collected by William Jones.* ed. Truman Michelson. 2 vols. New York: G. E. Sterchert & Co, 1917–19.

Jones, Jonathan H. *A Condensed History of the Apache and Comanche Indian Tribes as told by the general conversation of Herman Lehmann.* San Antonio: Johnson Brothers Printing Company, 1899. (See also under Lehmann.)

Josephy, Alvin M. Jr. *500 Nations.* New York: Alfred A. Knopf, 1994.

_____. *The Patriot Chiefs.* New York: Penguin Books, 1993.

Kavanagh, Thomas W. *The Comanche.* Lincoln: University of Nebraska Press, 1999.

Keeley, Lawrence H. *War Before Civilization.* New York: Oxford University Press, 1996.

Kennedy, J. H. *Jesuit and Savage in New France.* New Haven: Yale University Press, 1950.

Kohl, Johann Georg. *Kitchi-Gami.* trans. Lascelles Wraxall. Reprinted. St. Paul: Minnesota Historical Society Press,1985.

Kroeber, A. L. *Handbook of the Indians of California, Bulletin 78.* Bureau of American Ethnology of the Smithsonian. Washington: Government Printing Office, 1925. Reprinted. New York: Dover, 1976.

Kuckelman, Kristin, et. al. "Changing Patterns of Violence in the Northern San Juan Region." *Kiva* 66 no.1 (Fall, 2000).

Kurz, Rudolph Friederich. *Journal of Rudolph Friederich Kurz, Bulletin 115.* trans. Myrtis Jarrell, ed. J. N. B. Hewitt. Smithsonian Institution Bureau of American Ethnology. Washington: U. S. Government Printing Office, 1937.

Leach, Douglas Edward. *The Northern Colonial Frontier.* New York: Holt, 1966
_____. *Flintlock and Tomahawk, New England in King Philip's War.* Hyannis: Parnassus Imprints, 1995.

_____. ed. *A Rhode Islander Reports on King Philip's War: the second William Harris Letter of 1696.* Providence: Rhode Island Historical Society, 1963

LeBlanc, Steven A. *Prehistoric Warfare in the American Southwest.* Salt Lake City: University of Utah Press, 1999.

Lehmann, Herman. *9 Years Among the Indians, 1870–1879.* ed. J. M. Hunter. Reprinted. Albuquerque: University of New Mexico Press, 1998.

Lincoln, Charles H, ed. *Original Narratives of Early American History.* American Historical Association. New York: Scribner's Sons, 1913.

Linklater, Andro. *Wild People - Travels with Borneo's Head-Hunters.* New York: Morgan Entrekin, 1990.

Lockett, H. Clairborne and Lyndon L. Hargrave. "Woodchuck Cave" ed. Harold S Colton and Robert C. Euler. *Museum of Northern Arizona, Bulletin 26.* (1953).

Loewen, James W. *Lies My Teacher Told Me.* New York: Touchstone, 1995.

Lowie, Robert H. *Primitive Society.* Reprinted. New York: Harper, 1961.

Marcy, Randolph B. *The Prairie Traveler.* Reprinted. New York: Perigee Books, 1994.

Margry, Pierre. *Decouvertes et etablissements des Francais dans l'Amerique Septentrionale 1614–1698.* 6 vols. Paris: Maisonneuve, 1876–1886.

Marlar, Richard A., et. al. "Biochemical evidence of cannibalism at a prehistoric Puebloan site in southwestern Colorado." *Nature,* (September 7, 2000).

Mather, Cotton. *Decennium Luctuosum: or, The history of a Long War with Indian Savages.* Boston: B. Green and Samuel Gerrish, 1714.

Matlock, Gary. *Enemy Ancestors.* Flagstaff: Northland Publishers, 1988.

Maybury-Lewis, David. *The Savage and the Innocent.* Boston: Beacon Press, 1965.

McDowell, Jim. *Hamatsa.* Vancouver: Ronsdale Press, 1997.

McGaw, William Cochran. *Savage Scene, the Life and Times of James Kirker.* New York: Hastings House, 1972.

McKenney, Thomas L. and James Hall. *Indian Tribes of North America.* Totowa, NJ: Rowan and Littlefield, 1972.

Frank McNitt. *Navajo Wars.* Albuquerque: University of New Mexico Press, 1990.

Milanich, Jerald T. *Florida Indians and the Invasion from Europe.* Gainesville: University Press of Florida, 1998.

_____. and Susan Milbrath, editors. *First Encounters - Spanish Explorations in the Caribbean and the United States, 1492–1570.* Gainesville: University Press of Florida, 1989.

Milner, G. L., Eve Anderson and Virginia G. Smith. "Warfare in Late Prehistoric West Central Illinois." *American Antiquity* 56, no.4, (1991).

Morris, Ann Axtell. *Digging in the Southwest.* Chicago: Cadmus Books, 1933.

Muhlstein, Anka *LaSalle, Explorer of the North American Frontier.* trans. Williard Wood. New York: Archade Publishing, 1994.

Muller, Jon. *Archaeology of the Lower Ohio River Valley.* New York: Academic Press, 1986.

Murie, James R. *Ceremonies of the Pawnee, Part 1: The Skiri.* Smithsonian Contributions to Anthropology, Number 27. Washington: Smithsonian Press, 1981.

Neeley, Bill. *The Last Comanche Chief.* New York: John Wiley & Sons, Inc., 1995.

Neitzel, Robert S. "Archaeology of the Fatherland Site: The Grand Village of the Natchez." *Anthropological Papers of the American Museum of Natural History.* 51: part 1. (1997).

O'Connor, Mallory McCane. *Lost Cities of the Southeast.* Gainesville: University Press of Florida, 1995.

Parker, Francis, Peter Hulme, and Margaret Iversen, editors. *Cannibalism and the Colonial World.* Cambridge: University of Cambridge, 1998.

Pearce, Roy Harvey. *Savagism and Civilization: A Study of the Indian and the American Mind.* Berkeley: University of California Press, 1988.

Perrot, Nicolas. *Memoir on the Manners, Customs, and Religion of the Savages of North America.* ed. the Reverend Jules Tailhan, S. J., Paris 1864. Reprinted. Lincoln: Bison Books (University of Nebraska Press), 1996.

Plog, Stephen. *Ancient Peoples of the American Southwest.* New York: Thames and Hudson, 1997.

Pollock, Phillip M. "Calusa, Kingdom in the Sun." *Florida Heritage Magazine* (Fall 1997).

Popescu, Petru and Loren McIntyre. *Amazon Beaming.* New York: Penguin Books, 1991.

Powers, Stephen. *Tribes of California.* Contributions to North American Ethnology, vol.2. Washington: Government Printing Office, 1877. Reprinted with intro and annotations by R. F. Heizer. Berkeley: University of California Press, 1976.

Reid, Captain Mayne. *The Scalp Hunters.* London: Collins, 1851.

Rohn, Arthur H. and photographer William Ferguson. *Rock Art of Bandelier National Monument.* Albuquerque: University of New Mexico Press, 1989.

Roner, R. P. and E. C. Bettauer. *The Kwakiutl, Indians of British Columbia.* Prospect Heights: Waveland Press, 1970.

Rosaldo, Renato. *Ilongot Headhunting, 1883–1974.* Stanford: Stanford University Press, 1980.

Ruxton, George Frederick. *Adventures in Mexico and the Rocky Mountains.* New York: Harper and Brothers, 1848.

Sagan, Eli. *Cannibalism: Human Aggression and Cultural Form.* New York: Harper Torchbooks, 1974.

Sale, Kirkpatrick. *The Conquest of Paradise.* New York: Alfred A. Knopf, 1990.

Sanday, Peggy Reeves. *Divine Hunger, Cannibalism as a Cultural System.* Cambridge: Cambridge University Press, 1986.

Schaafsma, Polly. *The Rock Art of Utah.* Salt Lake City: University of Utah Press, 1971.

Simmons, Marc. *Massacre on the Lordsburg Road.* College Station: Texas A&M University Press, 1997.

Smith, Ralph A. "The Scalp Hunt in Chihuahua—1849." *New Mexico Historical Review,* (April 1965).

———. "Apache Ranching below the Gila, 1841–1845." *Arizoniana* 3 no.4, (Winter 1962).

_____. *Borderlander, The Life of James Kirker.* Norman: University of Oklahoma Press, 1999.

Smith, Alice E. *The History of Wisconsin, From Exploration to Statehood.* Madison: State Historical Society of Wisconsin, 1985.

Snow, Dean R. *The Iroquois.* Cambridge: Blackwell Publishers, 1994.

Solís de Meras, Gonzalo. *Pedro Menéndez de Avilés.* trans Jeannette Thurber Conner. Deland: Florida Historical Society, 1923.

Sonnichsen, C. L. *The Mescalero Apaches.* Norman: University of Oklahoma Press, 1958.

Stratton R. B. *Captivity of the Oatman Girls: Being an Interesting Narrative of Life Among the Apache and Mohave Indians.* 3rd edition. New York: Carlton & Porter, publication date unknown but probably 1859 or 1860.

Swanton, John R. *Source Material on the History and Ethnology of the Caddo Indians,* Bulletin 132. Smithsonian Institution, Bureau of Ethnology. Washington: Goverment Printing Office, 1942. Reprinted. Lincoln: University of Nebraska Press, 1996.

_____. *The Indian Tribes of North America*, Bulletin 145. Bureau of American Ethnology. Washington: Smithsonian Press, 1952.

_____. *Indian Tribes of the Lower Mississippi Valley, Bulletin 43.* Bureau of American Ethnology. Washington: Smithsonian Press, 1911.

_____. *Final Report of the United States DeSoto Expedition Commission.* Reprinted. Washington: Smithsonian Institution, 1985

Stirling, Matthew W. "Indians of Our Western Plains." *National Geographic Magazine* (July 1974).

Swezey, Sean and Steven R. James, Suzanne Graziani. *Ethnographic Interpretations: Socio-Religious Aspects of Resource Management, and Practices of Warfare Among California Indians.* Berkeley: University of California Press, 1975.

Tebbel, John and Keith Jennison. *The American Indian Wars.* New York: Harper & Row, 1960.

Terrell, John Upton. *American Indian Almanac.* New York: Barnes & Noble, 1971.

_____. *LaSalle, The Life and Times of an Explorer.* New York: Weybright and Talley, 1968.

Thompson, Jesse Edward. "Overland Staging in the Fifties." *Overland Monthly and Out West Magazine.* September, 1888.

Thornton, Russell, Tim Miller, Jonathan Warren, "American Indian Population

Recovery following Smallpox Epidemics," *American Anthropologist,* March, 1991, vol. 93–1.

Thrapp, Dan L. *Victorio and Membres Apaches.* Norman: University of Oklahoma Press, 1974.

Thwaites, Ruben Gold, ed. *The Jesuit Relations and Allied Documents.* 73 vols. Cleveland: Burrows Brothers, 1896–1901.

Tilghman, Zoe. *Quanah, The Eagle of the Comanches.* Oklahoma City: Harlow Publishing, 1938.

Thurber, Jeanette ed. trans. *Colonial Records of Early Spanish Florida.* Deland: Florida State Historical Society, 1925.

Trent, Captain William. *Journal of Captain William Trent (1752).*ed. Alfred T. Goodman. Cincinnati: Western Reserve Historical Society, 1871.

Turner, Christy G. and Jacqueline A. Turner, *Man Corn, Cannibalism and Violence in the Prehistoric American Southwest.* Salt Lake City: University of Utah Press, 1999.

Utley, Robert M. and Wilcomb E. Washburn. *Indian Wars.* Boston: Howard Mifflin Company, 1985.

Varian, Mark D. et. al. "Archaeology in the Northern San Juan Region, papers from the 1999 Conference of the Society for American Archaeology." *Kiva* 66, no.1 (2000).

Vaughn, Alden T and Edward W. Clark, eds. *Puritans among the Indians, 1676–1724.* Cambridge: Harvard University Press, 1981.

Walker, Alexander. *An Account of a Voyage to the North West Coast of America in 1785 & 1786 by Alexander Walker.* ed. Robin Fisher, and J. M. Bumsted. Seattle: University of Washington Press, 1982.

Wallace, Ernest and E. Adamson Hoebel. *The Comanches, Lords of the South Plains.* Norman: University of Oklahoma Press, 1952.

Warren, William W. *History of the Ojibway Nation.* First published in 1853. Minneapolis: Ross & Haines, 1957.

Wedel, Waldo R. *Prehistoric Man on the Great Plains.* Norman: University of Oklahoma Press, 1961.

Weltfish, Gene. *The Lost Universe.* Lincoln: University of Nebraska Press, 1965.

White, Tim D. *Prehistoric Cannibalism at Mancos.* Princeton: Princeton University Press, 1992.

Widner, Randolph J. *Evolution of the Calusa.* Tuscaloosa: University of Alabama Press, 1988.

Williams, John Lee. *Territory of Florida (1837)*. Facsimile edition. Gainesville: University of Florida Press, 1962.

Winship, G. P. "The Coronado Expedition." *Bureau of American Ethnology Fourteenth Annual Report*. Washington, D. C.: U. S. Government Printing Office, 1891.

U. S. GOVERNMENT DOCUMENTS:

Correspondence of the Commander of the Department of New Mexico, Brigadier General James H. Carleton, Santa Fe, October 12, 1862. Ann Arbor: *Making of America* on-line Collection, University of Michigan Library.

Proceedings of the United States Senate, Report of the Joint Special Committee of the Two Houses of Congress appointed under joint resolution of March 3, 1865, directing an inquiry into the condition of the Indian tribes. January 26, 1867, U. S. Government Printing Office.

Record Copy of the Proceedings of the Indian Peace Commission Appointed under the Act of Congress Approved July 20, 1867 (MS, National Archives Office of Indian Affairs, Washington), 1, 104.

INTERNET PUBLICATIONS:

"The Life of the Miriames and Yguaces" from *Cabenza de Vaca, Adventures in the Unknown Interior of America*. (Chapter 30) Available from *http://eldred.ne. mediaone.net/cdv/rel.htm*

The Journey of Cabenza de Vaca, Fanny Bandelier, trans. Available from *http:// www.pbs.org/weta/thewest/resources/archives/one/cabenza.htm*

Index

Acuera, Chief, 32
   reply to De Soto, 33
Adams, Dr. Samuel, 190
Adobe Walls, battle of, 158
Alabama, 26
Aloño, Joseph Javier, 26–27
Alderman, John, 61
Algic Researches (Schoolcraft), 73
American Folklore Society, xii
American Museum of Natural History,
   135
American-Mexican Boundary
   Commission, 167
Americans, Native
   and Old World diseases, 197
   burial ceremonies of, 5–7
   cannibalism and, xiii, xix–xx, 24,
      37–38, 40, 64, 66, 68–70, 76,
      78–81, 86, 141
      among California tribes, 118–19
      as terror, 195
      Cook's observtion of the Nootka, 85
      links to Chacoan culture, 140
      of the Kwakiutl, 98–102, 108,
         110–11, 113–14
      of the Tonkawa, 150, 152
      Pianguisha incident, 78
      the Anasazi Basketmakers, 135–39
      Windigo legend, 80
   caste system of, 3–5
   clan spirit and, 100
   creation myths of, 8–9, 40–44
   decimation of, 34, 51–54, 57, 61
   diets of, xviii–xix, 15, 17, 19

effects of invasions on, 129
gods of, 17, 22–23
headhunting and, xiii, xix, 28–29,
   37–38, 65, 91, 98, 116, 120–21,
   131–32, 139
   as terror, 195
human remains of, xii, 133–35, 138
human sacrifice and, xiii, xix, 1, 5, 12,
   19–21, 23, 26, 34–35, 37, 40,
   44–45, 95
Indian Removal Act (1830) and, xiv
infanticide and, 3–6, 14, 20, 26,
   59–60, 117–18, 150–52, 174–76
inter-tribal warfare and, xiv–xvii, 66,
   69
King Philip's War and, xii, 56–61
migrations of, xvi–xvii, 46, 48
on reservation, xv, 49, 78–79, 82,
   127, 134, 149, 154, 157–60, 173,
   177
poisonings of, 55, 122, 143
populations of, xvi–xviii, 3, 15, 17,
   48–49, 72, 76, 82, 114–15, 128,
   159, 177
   pre-Columbian, 195–96
post-Columbian images of, xiii–xiv
rituals of, xiii, 5–7, 10–12, 19–20,
   22–23, 25, 40–47, 100, 102–04,
   108–10
   winter ceremonies, 103, 105–06,
      108–14
rock art of, *viii,* xiii, 130–32, 139
sacred fire and, 7–8
scalping and, xv, 9–11, 38, 65,

78,116–17, 126–28, 131–32,
135, 143, 149, 153, 157, 172,
175–76
bounties for, 162–63, 165, 178–83,
187–88, 190–93
self-sacrifice and, 5–6
slavery and, 88, 91, 93
supernatural powers and, 100–03
survival methods of. xvi–xvii
torture and, 10–12, 37, 40, 58,
66–71, 119–20, 157–58, 160,
172
as terror, 195
trading practices of, 86
in human parts, 85
in sea otter skins, 87, 97
treatment of elderly by, 118
treatment of young girls among,
12–13, 119, 151
weapons of, 17, 67–68, 76, 81,
89–90, 94, 133
witchcraft and, 62, 136
Apache Pass, Battle of, 171
Arens, William, xix
Arizona, 131, 136, 161, 163, 168,
177, 179
Arkansas, 39, 48
Arkansas River, 144, 149
Armijo, Gov. Manuel, 185
Austin, Stephen, 190
Awashonks. squaw sachem, 58, 61
Aztec Springs CO, 139–40

Barbarism, European, xiii–xiv, xx–xxi
Battle Cave, 134
Baxbakualanuxsiwae (cannibal spirit),
100–01
legendary death of, 102
Baylor, John R., 163–64

bear doctors, 118, 122, 125–26
Beaver Wars, 76
beheadings, 20, 22, 33, 52, 54, 56–57,
60–62, 70–71, 76, 91, 96, 98,
110–11, 116–17, 121, 173–74
See also under headhunting
Bent's Fort, CO, 184
Biedma, Luis Hernando de, 30, 39
Bienville, Jean. *See* Le Moyne, Jean
Babtiste
Big Axe, Chief, 47
Black Chief, 47
Black Death, 197–98
Black, Dr. Glenn, xi
Bluff, UT, 130
Boas, Franz, 45–46, 97–99, 103, 105,
108–10, 114
Boston (ship), 89
Boston, MA, 57
bounties, scalp, 162
bounty hunters, xx
Bradford, Gov. William, 52
Bradley, Bruce, 138
Brandes, Ray, 187
Brébeuf, Saint Jean de, 66–69
Bristol, RI, 56
British Columbia, 97–98
Buchanan, Pres. James, 170–71
buffalo, 149, 154–56
Bureau of American Ethnology, xi, 9,
37, 78, 131
Bureau of Indian Affairs, 48, 160
Bureau of Land Management, 131
Burnt Mesa, NM, 136

Caamaño, Jacinto, 87–88
Cabrillo, Juan Rodriguez, 85
caciques. 19–25
areas ruled by, 15, 21–22

Handbook of Indians of California (Kroeber), 120

headhunting, xiii, xix, 28–29, 37–38, 65, 91, 98, 116, 120–21, 131–32, 139
  as terror, 195

heads, severed, on display, 52, 61–62, 70, 91, 173–74

heads, trophy, 130–32, *137*, 139
  See also under masks, trophy

Heizer, Robert F., 129

heligas, 109

Helm, Thomas, 163

Hiawatha, legend of, 63–64, 72–73

Hickock, Wild Bill, 155

Hill, Capt. Samuel, 95

Hitchcock, "Crying Tom," 193

Hobbs, James, 185

Hoebel, E. A., 146–47

Holbrook, AZ, 192

House of Mahoma (temple), 17

Houston, Sam, 190

Hudson Bay, 73

Hudson Bay Company, 97, 106, 115

Hunt, George, 97, 104–08

Hurst, Winston B., 136

Hyde brothers, C. Fred and P.T.B., 135

Hyde, George E., 39, 45

Iberville. *See* d'Iberville, Pierre Le Moyne

Illinois State Museum. *See* excavations, archaeological

Indian Removal Act, 1830, xiv

Indian Tribes of North America, The (Swanton), xi

Indians. *See under* Americans, Native; Tribes, Native American

infanticide, 3–6, 14, 20, 26, 59–60, 117–18, 150–52, 174–76

Irigoyen, Gov. José Maria de, 186

Iroquois Confederacy, 63–64

Iroquois Point, 76

Jackson, Lt. J. J., 163

Jackson, Pres. Andrew
  quoted on Indian character, 179

Jaimes, M. Annette, 198

James, Frank, quoted on Wampanoag history, 51

Jamestown, VA, 195

Jefferson, President Thomas, 48

Jesuit Relations, xii, 65–66, 69

Jesuits, 65–70, 81
  engagés with, 73–76
  mission of, 73

Jewitt, John, 90–91, 96
  diary of, 92–93, 95
  offer of slavery or death, 91
  rescued by *Lydia*, 95

Johnson, James, 162–63, 165–66, 179, 185

Jones, Judge Jonathan H., 176

Journal of American Folklore 52:204, 1939, xii

Kansas, 148, 159

Kant, Immanuel, xxi

Keeley, Lawrence H., xii, xxi

Kellogg, Elizabeth, 143

Key of Bones, 25

Key West. *See* Key of Bones

Kinboko Canyon, AZ, 130–31

King Phillip's War, xii, 56–61

King Phillip. *See* Metacomet, Chief

King, Charles Bird, 35–36

kinqalalalas, 109–111

Kirker, James, 180–*81*, 182–90, 193